GEORGE W. KNIGHT

MW00439328

HOLY LAND HANDBOOK

History, Geography, Culture, Holy Sites

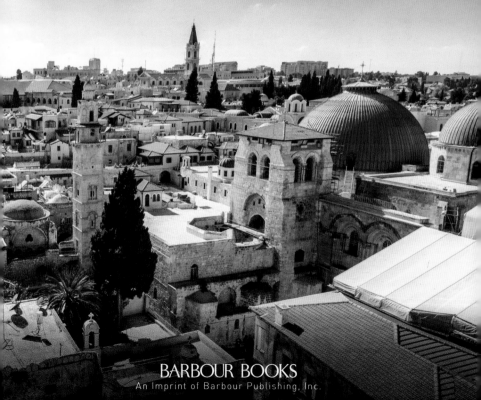

BARBOUR BOOKS
An Imprint of Barbour Publishing, Inc.

ABOUT THE AUTHOR

George W. Knight developed the original *Layman's Bible Dictionary* for Barbour Publishing, spawning a series of Bible reference titles that has sold more than one million books. A former editor with a major Christian publisher, he lives in Hartselle, Alabama.

© 2011 by George W. Knight

ISBN 978-1-64352-400-9

Published by Barbour Books, an imprint of Barbour Publishing, Inc., 1810 Barbour Drive, Uhrichsville, Ohio 44683, www.barbourbooks.com

Our mission is to inspire the world with the life-changing message of the Bible.

 Member of the
Evangelical Christian
Publishers Association

Printed in China.

CONTENTS

CHAPTER 8 175

NORTH OF JERUSALEM UP TO SHECHEM

CHAPTER 9 215

SOUTH OF THE SEA OF GALILEE DOWN TO SAMARIA

INTRODUCTION

This book is for anyone who has ever wanted to know more about the Holy Land—its geography, culture, history, and especially its holy sites. Travelers who want to get the most out of their visit to this unique land should find it a useful guide. But it is also meant for armchair travelers, Bible students, and the downright curious who wonder about the ancient land God promised to Abraham and his descendants.

After an introductory chapter, *The Holy Land Handbook* organizes the land of Israel into nine chapters that cover its territory from south to north. These divisions range from the dry wilderness in the extreme southern part of the nation to the well-watered northernmost region above the Sea of Galilee (see contents pages). A map section, beginning on page 280, will help you realize how the various biblical sites of the land of Israel are related to one another in terms of distance and geography.

But let's assume that you want to find a specific city or town (for example, Nazareth, Jesus' hometown), and you're not sure where it falls in one of these nine geographic zones. In that case, refer to the Index of Sites and Places at the back of the book. This will refer you to the pages in *The Holy Land Handbook* where that site is discussed.

One of the keys to understanding the Bible is having some knowledge of the land—its cities, towns, rivers, mountains, and valleys—where the events of the scriptures took place. This book is dedicated to that goal. My hope is that it will help you realize why this place is called "the Holy Land." It is known by that name because God has sanctified it with His presence and performed mighty acts on behalf of His people in this little corner of the world.

GEORGE W. KNIGHT
HARTSELLE, ALABAMA

A view of the Sea of Galilee, in northern Israel.

CHAPTER 1

THE LAND WITH MANY FACES

The land of Israel—also known as the Holy Land—is a physical dwarf among the nations of the world. Only about two hundred miles long by sixty miles across at its widest point, it would fit within the borders of the state of New Jersey. Yet this tiny land has played a key role in world history. About three thousand years ago, King David of Israel recognized this fact when he prayed to the Lord: "What other nation on earth is like your people Israel? What other nation, O God, have you redeemed from slavery to be your own people?" (1 Chronicles 17:21).

The answer to David's question is a resounding *None*. No other nation on earth has been brought into being by God Himself and designated as His own people. This is why Israel is known as the Holy Land. It is holy or sacred not because of the great righteousness of its people but because the Lord has blessed it with His presence. His blessing also carried a responsibility for the people of Israel to make Him known to the rest of the world (see Genesis 12:1–3).

The Holy Land has been known by many names across its checkered history. To Abraham it was the "land of Canaan" because the Canaanites lived here when he first arrived. But to Abraham and his descendants, it became the "land of promise" because of God's pledge that the land would someday belong to them. The land is also referred to as "Palestine," a name derived from a people known as the Philistines, enemies of God's people who lived in the southern coastal areas along the Mediterranean Sea. Eventually the Holy Land became known as the "land of Israel," named after Abraham's grandson Jacob, whom God renamed Israel. This name was fitting after Joshua's conquest of this territory and its unification in later years under the rule of King David.

Another good name for Israel would be the "land with many faces."

There seems to be no end to the unique characteristics that set this nation apart from all others. Here we will focus on four important facets of its one-of-a-kind personality—location, geography, history, and holy sites.

LOCATION

Many visitors to the Holy Land are surprised at the small size of the country. For example, after visiting Israel in the 1860s, Mark Twain observed: "The word *Palestine* always brought to my mind a vague suggestion of a country as large as the United States. I suppose it was because I could not conceive of a small country having so large a history. I must try to reduce my ideas of Palestine to a more reasonable shape."

Israel is indeed a tiny country—estimated to contain less than 1 percent of the landmass of the entire Middle East. In terms of population, it is home to about more than nine million people—about the same number of residents as the state of Virginia. But don't make the mistake of judging significance by size. Israel's strategic location has always placed it in the middle of the action in that part of the world.

The Holy Land is a "land bridge" that links two great population centers—Egypt in the south and Syria, Iraq, and Turkey in the north. In Bible times, the dominant cultures north and northeast of Israel were Assyria, Babylonia, and Persia, in the region known as Mesopotamia—the land associated with the Tigris and Euphrates Rivers.

This land bridge was hemmed in by the Mediterranean Sea on the west and the vast Arabian Desert on the east (an area now occupied by Saudi Arabia, Jordan, Syria, and Iraq). This meant that caravans of traders carrying goods from Mesopotamia to Egypt—or vice versa—had to pass through Israel. Thus the major world powers of Bible times and beyond struggled to control this tiny sliver of land.

Throughout its long history, Israel has been ruled by the Assyrians, Babylonians, Persians, Romans, Egyptians, and Turks. Not until 1948 did it reclaim its status as a sovereign nation known as the State of Israel. Now it exists as a tiny Jewish state surrounded by Arab and Muslim nations, some of whom would like to see Israel wiped off the map. Its creativity, commitment to progress, and democratic form of government give it a unique status among the nations of the Middle East.

GEOGRAPHY

The Holy Land is also unique because of its geographical diversity. Few places on earth of such small size contain so many contrasting geographic zones. Mount Hermon in the extreme north is capped by snow most of the year. But less than two hundred miles south of this mountain is an area known as the Negev, a hot and dry desert area that receives less than four inches of rainfall per year. In between these two points are several distinctive geographic regions:

SHARON PLAIN

The Sharon Plain is part of the coastal plain that borders the Mediterranean Sea, the large body of water that serves as Israel's western border. This region contains flat land known for its fertility and spectacular scenery. The coastal plain stretches from Gaza in the south to the Phoenician city of Tyre in the north. The Sharon Plain in the south was settled by the Philistines, a hostile people King David of Israel eventually conquered. Biblical cities associated with the Sharon Plain include Joppa, where the apostle Peter received his famous vision about acceptance of Gentiles into the church (see Acts 10:9–29).

Mount Hermon rising above the Hula Valley.

SHEPHELAH

This geographic zone is a strip of foothills about midway between the Mediterranean Sea and the Dead Sea. The word means "lowlands," in contrast to the higher elevation of the adjoining Hill Country. In Israel's early history, the Philistines fought with the Israelites for control of this territory. David defeated the Philistine giant Goliath in the Valley of Elah, located in the Shephelah (see 1 Samuel 17).

NEGEV

The word *Negev* is a Hebrew term meaning "dry" or "parched." This is a perfect description of this large section of Israel, located south and west of the Dead Sea. In Bible times, it was dry and barren because of its lack of rainfall, containing little but scrub brush. But in recent years, the Israeli government has built an irrigation system that channels water to the Negev from Galilee in the north. This public works project has made the Negev an important

The Negev desert.

agricultural region for the entire nation. The patriarchs of Bible times tended their flocks in this region. The city of Beersheba in the Negev is often cited as the southern boundary of Israel ("from Dan even to Beersheba," 2 Samuel 3:10 KJV).

HILL COUNTRY

This section of the Holy Land is also known as the Western Mountains. Located in central Israel, these mountains run south to north across the country all the way up to the Jezreel Valley. The peaks in this range vary in height, from 1,500 to 4,000 feet. Jerusalem, Israel's capital, was built on the southern peaks of these mountains to protect the city from enemy attacks. The virgin Mary lived north of this territory in the region of Galilee. After the angel Gabriel told her she would give birth to the Messiah, she "hurried to the hill country of Judea" (Luke 1:39) to share the good news with her relative Elizabeth.

JUDEAN DESERT

This section of the Holy Land stretches from the Negev along the western side of the Dead Sea up to just north of Jericho. A bone-dry and isolated area noted for its scorching heat, this strip of land is also known as the Wilderness of Judah. This is probably the desolate area to which Jesus withdrew when Satan tempted Him at the beginning of His public ministry (see Mark 1:12–13).

JEZREEL VALLEY

This is perhaps the most famous valley in the Bible. A major north–south highway passed through this valley, giving it an important economic and military role in Bible times. One of its key cities was Megiddo, from which the word *Armageddon* ("mountain of Megiddo") is derived. According to the book of Revelation, this will be the site of the final battle of the end times, when God will destroy His enemies (see Revelation 16:16; 20:1–10).

GALILEE

Most people associate the word *Galilee* with the Sea of Galilee, the lake in northern Israel around which so much of Jesus' earthly ministry took place. But Galilee is also a distinct *region* of the Holy Land. In New Testament times, it was one of three provinces into which the Roman government divided Palestine for administrative purposes (the other two were Judea and Samaria). The region of Galilee ranged from high mountains in the northern section to gently sloping hills and fertile valleys in the southern part of the territory.

The biblical Sea of Galilee being disturbed by a very modern speedboat.

The high concentration of minerals in the water makes it famously difficult to sink in the Dead Sea.

DEAD SEA

Any discussion of the unique geographical features of the Holy Land would be incomplete without giving attention to the Dead Sea. This body of water—actually a mineral-laden lake—receives water from the Jordan River and other smaller streams in the Negev. But it never releases any of this water to continue on its way to the ocean, as a normal lake does. The scorching sun in the surrounding Negev desert evaporates the water as quickly as it runs into the lake. Over the centuries, the salts and minerals left behind have turned this body of water into a stagnant pool in which few living things can survive—thus the name "Dead Sea."

Its location also gives the Dead Sea an additional claim to fame. At 1,300 feet below sea level, it is situated at the lowest point on the surface of the earth. Its waters lie within a geological fault line that passes through Israel on its way from Syria into central Africa. This depression in the earth's crust is called the Arabah.

Modern visitors to the Holy Land sometimes take a "Dead Sea" view of the country. They wonder why anyone would want to settle a land that seems so rocky, drab, and dry. But we must remember that the territory of Israel north of the Negev seemed like a paradise to Moses and the Israelites after they had wandered for more than forty years in the wilderness area south of the Dead Sea. Moses described it as a land "flowing with milk and honey" (Deuteronomy 6:3).

After Joshua succeeded Moses, he led the Israelites into the land of Canaan by crossing the Jordan River at a point near the city of Jericho. After they conquered the land, he divided it among the twelve tribes. Almost every geographic feature of the land discussed above is mentioned in the account of Joshua's division of the land: "Joshua gave this land to the tribes of Israel as their possession, including the hill country, the western foothills, the Jordan Valley, the mountain slopes, the Judean wilderness, and the Negev" (Joshua 12:7–8).

HISTORY

The word *history* puts some people to sleep faster than counting sheep. But history is anything but boring when it comes to the Holy Land's past. Indeed, the history of Israel may be the most amazing thing about this tiny piece of Middle Eastern real estate. Maybe these startling facts will kindle your interest:

* For more than 700 years, Israel existed as nothing but a promise from God.

* Israel finally became a nation and then lived on independently under a succession of Jewish rulers for about 800 years.

* Israel then went into a period of limbo for more than 2,500 years, during which several world powers dominated it.

* Israel was reborn as a sovereign Jewish state in 1948—the only nation in modern times to make such a comeback after it was considered dead.

* Since its resurrection, Israel has built a democratic form of government, defended itself against its enemies, and brought its citizens into the modern age.

Now that your attention is focused, let's expand this general outline into a skeleton of about a dozen points. After all, you can't cover 4,000 years of history in just a few sentences. But the meat will go on the bones in an interesting way if you will stay with this discussion to the end. You will be rewarded with a better understanding of Israel and why it is called the "Holy Land."

GOD'S PROMISE TO ABRAHAM

The history of the Holy Land begins with a man named Abraham. He lived in a culture that worshipped many pagan gods. But somehow Abraham became a follower of Yahweh, the one true God. About 2000 BC, God commanded Abraham to leave his home in Mesopotamia and settle in a territory to the south known as Canaan. God promised to give this land to Abraham and his descendants. But for more than 700 years this promise was not fulfilled because the Canaanites occupied the land.

GOD'S PROMISE FULFILLED

Finally, about 1400 BC, God began to make good on His promise. His people, the Israelites, had been enslaved in Egypt. They must have thought the Lord had forgotten them and His promise. But God raised up a strong leader named Moses to lead His people out of Egypt. Moses guided them for forty years—which must have seemed like an eternity—in the arid wilderness area south of the Dead Sea. This great leader died when they reached the borders of this land of promise. A young man named Joshua finished the task Moses had begun when he led the people into Canaan, which they claimed as their own.

AT HOME IN ISRAEL

The Israelites were now happy and content in their own land. They eventually traded their independent tribal confederacies for a kingship form of government. Beginning with David's reign about 1000 BC, they enjoyed peace and prosperity. But the kingdom divided into two factions after the reign of David's son Solomon. A succession of kings, only a few of them good, ruled over the nations of Judah (the southern kingdom) and Israel (the northern kingdom) for the next four centuries.

In the early 1970s, the first archaeological evidence of a structure built by King Solomon was found at Tel Gezer.

CONQUERED AND EXILED BY THE ASSYRIANS AND THE BABYLONIANS

Remaining faithful to the one true God was always a challenge for the people of Israel. Again and again they slipped into rebellion and worship of false gods. As punishment for their sin, God sent two foreign powers, the Assyrians and the Babylonians, to conquer His people and carry them into exile. Some of the Israelites eventually returned to their homeland, but not as a free and independent people. For the next 2,500 years, with the exception of a few brief periods of self-rule, they remained under the thumb of foreign nations.

REBELLION AND DESTRUCTION

Occasionally during these periods of foreign domination, Jewish nationalists rebelled against their oppressors and were able to gain control of the land of Israel. This happened for a brief time during the struggle of the Maccabees (167–37 BC) against the Greek successors of Alexander the Great. Another uprising against the Roman government took place about thirty years after the death and resurrection of Jesus. As Jesus had predicted, this rebellion resulted in the slaughter of thousands of Jewish nationalists and the destruction of Jerusalem and its holy temple in AD 70.

ISRAEL IN LIMBO

From AD 70 until the early years of the 1900s, Israel was in a state of limbo. Rome, Persia, Egypt, Arab Muslims, and Turkey (then known as the Ottoman Empire) all ruled the Holy Land. During the Middle Ages, the Holy Land was even held for a short time by Christian militants who marched to the Holy Land in a movement known as the Crusades. These "Christian soldiers" succeeded in taking the land from the Muslims, only to have it slip from their grasp after armies under the banner of Islam overpowered them.

The British occupation of Palestine in 1917. Outside the Jaffa Gate (now in Tel Aviv).

WORLD WAR I: THE TURNING POINT

The pendulum began to swing in favor of the rebirth of a Jewish state in the Middle East during World War I. Peace terms finalized in 1919 required Turkey, or the Ottoman Empire, to give up control of Palestine. Jurisdiction in the region was granted to Great Britain, one of the victorious nations in the world conflict.

BRITISH MANDATE OVER PALESTINE

From 1919 until 1948, Great Britain served as caretaker and peacekeeper in Palestine. The British government had declared as early as 1917 that it favored the establishment of an independent Jewish state in the region. In a letter to a representative of the Jewish people, British Foreign Secretary Lord Balfour stated: "His majesty's government views with favor the establishment in Palestine of a national home for the Jewish people, and will use its best endeavors to facilitate the achievement of this objective." This pledge by the British government became known as the Balfour Declaration.

STRUGGLES BETWEEN THE JEWS AND THE PALESTINIANS

Great Britain's pledge that a Jewish state should be reestablished in this region did not win it any friends among the Arabs, who had occupied Palestine for centuries. The years of the British Mandate in Palestine (1919–1948) were marked by riots and outbreaks of violence between these two factions. Finally, the British gave up their role as overseers in Palestine and punted the problem to the United Nations.

ISRAEL REBORN ON MAY 14, 1948

The United Nations decided that the solution to the conflict was a division of the land into two nations—one for the Palestinian Arabs and the other for the Jews. The British Mandate would end on May 15, 1948, and the existence

David Ben-Gurion proclaiming the State of Israel.

of the two separate nations would begin officially on that date. Jewish officials, under the leadership of David Ben-Gurion, accepted the partition plan. They met on May 14, the day before the British Mandate ended, to declare their statehood: "We. . .hereby proclaim the establishment of the Jewish state in Palestine, to be called Israel."

HOSTILITIES BETWEEN ISRAEL AND ITS ARAB NEIGHBORS

The Arabs of Palestine did not accept the partition plan that would have granted them independent statehood alongside Israel. They also refused to accept Israel's status as a sovereign Jewish state. Instead, they attacked the Jews, enlisting the aid of several surrounding Arab nations. Although greatly outnumbered, the Israeli army turned back their enemies and won their right to exist as an independent nation. When hostilities ended, they had actually won more territory than they had been granted in the original United Nations partition plan.

In another outbreak of hostilities in 1967—a conflict known as the Six-Day War—Israel captured from Jordan a chunk of land near Jerusalem that is referred to as the West Bank. You have probably heard this territory discussed on the nightly news in recent years. The Palestinians who live here and the neighboring Jews continue to squabble over the rights to this little piece of property that is no bigger than a medium-size county or two in the United States.

But to put this plot of land in perspective, we must remember that the West Bank is a significant portion of land in relation to Israel's overall size. No wonder it is a sticking point in peace negotiations between these two factions. Palestinians want the entire territory turned over to them. Israel has withdrawn from part of this territory in response to their demands. But it is reluctant to give up the entire West Bank. Israel has built barriers on this property to protect Jerusalem from terrorist attacks, and it continues to develop some of the territory for Jewish settlement—much to the chagrin of the Palestinians.

There are two other disputed or troublesome territories within Israel's borders—the Gaza Strip on the Mediterranean coast and the Golan Heights in northern Israel, a region north and east of the Sea of Galilee.

The Gaza Strip is a small strip of land about twenty-five miles long by six miles wide. It takes its name from its major city, Gaza. In Bible times, Gaza was one of the five major cities of the Philistines. This is the city where the Hebrew champion Samson died when he pushed down the pillars that supported the temple of the pagan god Dagon (see Judges 16:23–31).

During the Jewish-Arab conflict of 1948, thousands of Arab Palestinians fled to this region and settled in refugee camps to escape the ravages of war. Today, more than one million Palestinians, most of them descendants of these early refugees, are crammed into this tiny territory in squalid conditions. Bitter and resentful over their plight, Gaza Strip militants have often retaliated with terrorist attacks against Israel. The Israeli government patrols the area and guards all the crossing points from the Gaza Strip into Jewish territory.

The Golan Heights is a mountainous area in extreme northern Israel. A part of this region was known as Bashan in Bible times. In this territory were the city of Dan, a landmark that designated the northern boundary of Israel ("from Dan even to Beersheba," 2 Samuel 3:10 KJV), and the tallest peak in the Holy Land, known in biblical times as Mount Hermon (see Joshua 12:1).

In the Six-Day War of 1967, Israel captured the Golan Heights from Syria. Israel has governed the territory ever since. But the United Nations and the rest of the international community consider it to be a region *occupied*

Sunset from the Golan Heights.
The Sea of Galilee would be toward the bottom left-hand corner of the picture.

by the Israelis and not actually *owned* by them. Although sparsely populated, the Golan Heights is very important to Israel. Runoff from the snowfalls on Mount Hermon feeds the Jordan River and the Sea of Galilee, the major sources of water for the entire Holy Land.

So there you have it—four thousand years of history condensed to a few pages. Perhaps you learned a few things you didn't know about this amazing country. Anyone who looks objectively at Israel's past has to admit that its very existence is nothing short of a miracle. Moses knew what he was talking about when he tried to convince his father-in-law to go with the Israelites when they left Egypt for the promised land. "Come with us," he told Hobab, "for the LORD has promised wonderful blessings for Israel!" (Numbers 10:29).

HOLY PLACES

Israel's unusual location, geography, and history would be enough to make this country an interesting place to visit. But these things alone don't explain the thousands of tourists drawn to this tiny Middle Eastern nation every year. Most of them come to see the holy places that give Israel its unique reputation as the "Holy Land."

This brings up a question: What makes a place holy? We find the answer in the very first book of the Bible—in the experience of Abraham's grandson Jacob. On his way to visit his relatives in Mesopotamia, Jacob camped at a place in central Canaan not far from Jerusalem. As Jacob lay sleeping that night, God appeared to him in a dream. In this dream, angels went up and down a stairway that stretched into heaven.

God spoke to Jacob through this experience, renewing the promise He had made to Abraham several years before: "I am giving it [this land] to you and your descendants" (Genesis 28:13).

When he woke up, Jacob marveled, "Surely the LORD is in this place, and I wasn't even aware of it!" (Genesis 28:16). He named the place Bethel, meaning "house of God." "What an awesome place this is!" he declared. "It is none other than the house of God, the very gateway to heaven!" (Genesis 28:17).

Jacob was not always perfect in his response to God and in his relationship with others. But in this case, he was right on target. His experience shows clearly that a holy place is anyplace God has touched human lives in a special way. The Holy Land has dozens of such places—from Hebron in the south, where God revealed to Abraham that he would have a son in his old age (see Genesis 18:1–15), to the Sea of Galilee in the north, the lake on which Jesus calmed a storm and scolded His disciples for their lack of faith (see Matthew 8:23–27). In between these two points—and even at a few sites outside the borders of modern Israel—are dozens of other places that will always be known as sacred sites because of their association with the holy God and His claim on our lives.

To visit the Holy Land and these holy sites is a lifelong ambition of many Christians. Most who do so will return home with a better understanding of the Bible and a deeper commitment to His will and purpose in their lives.

But the problem with most such tours is that they typically last from only seven to ten days. It is impossible to take in all the important Holy Land sites in such a limited time. Sometimes even the few places visited leave visitors feeling jaded and overwhelmed because of the "whirlwind" tour schedule.

In the pages ahead, we will cover all the major sites of the Holy Land.

If there are some places that your tour doesn't cover, you can fill in the gaps by reading about them here. If you're just reading this book for your own information and pleasure, you can do so at your own pace without having to be hurried from one place to the next on a tight tour schedule.

Along with each site discussed, you will also find citations of the major Bible passages associated with that place. Many important sites have related passages printed in full for your convenience. This allows you to focus on each site from its scriptural perspective. Be sure to look up all the scripture references cited when you get a break in your study or tour schedule. After all, the Holy Land would not exist unless God had told us about it through His Holy Book.

On the subject of sites, a word about authenticity is in order. All authorities do not agree about the exact location of some of the holy places in the Holy Land. For example, Roman Catholics believe the Church of the Holy Sepulchre (see chapter 5, p. 111) is built over the site in Jerusalem where Jesus was crucified, buried, and resurrected. Evangelicals tend to view Gordon's Calvary and the Garden Tomb (see chapter 6, p. 138) in Jerusalem as the places where these events took place. Muslim tradition also departs from Christian and Jewish tradition about the exact location of some Holy Land sites.

Where these differences exist, they will be noted throughout this book. Try to remember that when it comes to the Holy Land, we are dealing with more than four thousand years of history and three major world religions—Judaism, Christianity, and Islam—as well as numerous branches and denominations of the Christian faith. It would be nothing short of miraculous if all these factions agreed on the exact location of every holy place in the land that produced such important religious personalities as Abraham, Moses, and Jesus.

It's okay for you to have your own opinion about who is right and who is wrong on these matters. But don't let these differences rob you of the experience of drawing closer to God through your study and tour of the Holy Land. The exact location of a holy site is not as important as letting God speak to you through the event that happened here—or at least not far away.

The discussion of some of these holy places in the following pages also includes eyewitness accounts of visits made to these sites by pilgrims from the past. For example, this is what Henry van Dyke, a noted Presbyterian minister and author from the United States, said about Jerusalem and its tumultuous history after he visited Palestine in the early 1900s:

The mystery of the heart of mankind, the spiritual airs that breathe through it, the desires and aspirations that impel men in their journeyings, the common hopes that bind them together in companies, the fears and hatreds that array them in warring hosts—there is no place in the world today where you can feel all this so deeply, so overwhelmingly, as at the gates of Jerusalem.

These personal accounts should inspire you to record your own thoughts and feelings (though perhaps in a little less flowery language than van Dyke's!) about the places in the Holy Land that you visit or read about. Even if you never visit Israel in a physical sense, you can take a spiritual tour through the musings of those who have seen its holy places with their own eyes.

So hang on and get set for your journey to this fascinating land. By the time your study tour is over, you will probably say with the psalmist, "The LORD has chosen Jacob for himself, Israel for his own special treasure" (Psalm 135:4).

The Monastery of the Temptation in the Judean wilderness near Jericho.

The Nahal Zin formed the southern boundary of the Promised Land.

CHAPTER 2

The logical place to begin our tour of the Holy Land is in the wilderness region south of the Dead Sea. Here is where the Lord told His people to halt when the land He had promised them was within their grasp. They had made it all the way from Egypt to this barren place, only to be denied entrance to the land of their dreams.

God had His reasons for His "stop" command. The people had trembled with fear when they learned that Canaan was inhabited by powerful tribes—some of them giants—that lived in walled cities. They had lashed out at their leader, Moses, and the Lord for bringing them to this desolate place. They doubted that God could make good on His promise to give them the land of Canaan. So the Lord sentenced them to forty years of aimless wandering in this wilderness territory (see Numbers 14:26–35).

A few sites from other times in Israel's history are found in this region of the Holy Land. But it will always be known as the place of the Postponed Promise. God eventually gave His people the land of Canaan—but not before He culled out the doubters and raised up a new generation that had the faith to claim His promise.

The significant sites in this section of the Holy Land are scattered from the twin cities of Ezion-geber and Elath in the south to the twin cities of Sodom and Gomorrah in the north. Also included in this discussion are Mount Sinai in Egypt and Mount Nebo in Jordan.

MOUNT SINAI

MEANING Unknown

PRONUNCIATION SIGH-nigh

SITE AND LOCATION A mountain in the Sinai Peninsula of Egypt about 180 miles south of the southern tip of the Dead Sea Map 1, areas D-4 and D-7

Modern-day tourists hike Mount Sinai in the early morning hours.

Mount Sinai is a long way from the "Holy Land" as we define it today. But there is a good reason for including this mountain in this discussion. Before Moses led the Israelites into the wilderness area below the Dead Sea, he had several dramatic encounters with the Lord at Mount Sinai.

At Sinai, also called Horeb (see Exodus 3:1 KJV), God called Moses through a burning bush to lead the Israelites out of slavery in Egypt (see Exodus 3:1–10). On Mount Sinai, during the Exodus, God delivered to Moses the Ten Commandments, the law intended as a moral compass for the lives of His people (see Exodus 20:1–17; see sidebar, "God Reveals His Glory to the Israelites at Sinai," p. 27). Here God also renewed His covenant with the Israelites, promising to guide and protect them if they would follow His commands (see Exodus 34:4–14).

The mountain most widely accepted as Mount Sinai is known today by its Arabic name, Jebel Musa ("mountain of Moses"). This peak rises dramatically above the surrounding plain to an elevation of more than seven thousand feet above sea level.

At the foot of Sinai sits the Monastery of Saint Catherine, home to monks of the Greek Orthodox Church. As you would expect, this monastery memorializes the life and ministry of Moses. It claims to be standing on the site of the burning bush, where Moses talked with the Lord. Built in the AD 500s, St. Catherine's may not be as old as Moses, but it is certainly one of the oldest continually operating monasteries in the world. Nearby is a spring known as Moses' Well, which provides water for the monks.

Most visitors to Mount Sinai come for the spiritual experience of feeling God's presence on top of the mountain. Monks from Saint Catherine's have made this possible by carving steps—more than three thousand of them!—in the solid rock all the way to the summit. It takes two to three hours to make the taxing climb.

Many tourists set out on this trail in the early morning hours so they can take in the spectacular sunrise over the bleak countryside. A fringe benefit of this nocturnal climb is the view of the heavens on a cloudless night. With no city lights within miles to compete with the stars, they shine with a brilliance that few urbanites have ever seen. It's a sight that makes many pilgrims exclaim with the psalmist, "Praise him, all you twinkling stars!" (Psalm 148:3).

God descends on Mount Sinai while the Israelites watch in awe. From a Bible card published by the Providence Lithograph Company.

GOD REVEALS HIS GLORY TO THE ISRAELITES AT SINAI

On the morning of the third day, thunder roared and lightning flashed, and a dense cloud came down on the mountain. There was a long, loud blast from a ram's horn, and all the people trembled. Moses led them out from the camp to meet with God, and they stood at the foot of the mountain. All of Mount Sinai was covered with smoke because the Lord had descended on it in the form of fire. The smoke billowed into the sky like smoke from a brick kiln, and the whole mountain shook violently. . . .

Then the Lord told Moses, "Go back down and warn the people not to break through the boundaries to see the Lord, or they will die. Even the priests who regularly come near to the Lord must purify themselves so that the Lord does not break out and destroy them" (Exodus 19:16–18, 21–22).

WILDERNESS OF PARAN

MEANING   Unknown

PRONUNCIATION   PAY-rahn

SITE AND LOCATION   A dry, desolate region southwest of the southern tip of the Dead Sea   Map 1, area D-3

This wilderness territory is only one of several desolate regions mentioned in connection with the Israelites' travels during the Exodus from Egypt. Others cited in the Bible are the wilderness of Shur (Exodus 15:22), the wilderness of Sin (Exodus 16:1), the wilderness of Sinai (Numbers 9:5), the wilderness of Zin (Numbers 27:14), the wilderness of Etham (Numbers 33:8), and the wilderness of Moab (Deuteronomy 2:8). By the time they reached Canaan, the Israelites must have been experts on the perils of the wilderness.

Years before the Israelites reached the wilderness of Paran during the Exodus, it was a place of wandering for Hagar, the Egyptian wife of Abraham (see Genesis 16:4–12). She lived here with her son Ishmael after they were ejected from Abraham's household. From the Paran wilderness during the time of Moses, he sent spies into Canaan to find out about the land and its people (Numbers 13:1–3).

A quail in the dry, rocky Wilderness of Paran.

WILDERNESS OF ZIN

MEANING Unknown

PRONUNCIATION zihn

SITE AND LOCATION A dry, desolate region around Kadesh southwest of the southern tip of the Dead Sea   Map 1, area E-2

Moses and the Israelites must have rejoiced when they reached the wilderness of Zin. This brought them closer to Canaan than they had ever been. But tragedy struck when Moses' sister Miriam died (see Numbers 20:1).

In this wilderness the people also grumbled and complained that they had no water. God told Moses to command water to gush from a rock. Moses did produce a miraculous supply of water, but he did not follow God's exact instructions. He apparently struck the rock in anger without giving credit to the Lord for producing this miracle. For this rash act, the Lord punished him and his brother Aaron (see sidebar, "God's Punishment in the Wilderness of Zin," below).

The Wilderness of Zin, as seen from the north.

GOD'S PUNISHMENT IN THE WILDERNESS OF ZIN

The Lord said to Moses, "You and Aaron must take the staff and assemble the entire community. As the people watch, speak to the rock over there, and it will pour out its water. You will provide enough water from the rock to satisfy the whole community and their livestock."

So Moses did as he was told. He took the staff from the place where it was kept before the Lord. Then he and Aaron summoned the people to come and gather at the rock. "Listen, you rebels!" he shouted. "Must we bring you water from this rock?" Then Moses raised his hand and struck the rock twice with the staff, and water gushed out. So the entire community and their livestock drank their fill.

But the Lord said to Moses and Aaron, "Because you did not trust me enough to demonstrate my holiness to the people of Israel, you will not lead them into the land I am giving them!" (Numbers 20:7–12).

KADESH

MEANING "sanctuary" or "consecrated"

PRONUNCIATION kuh-DESH

SITE AND LOCATION A wilderness site about sixty miles southwest of the southern tip of the Dead Sea
Map 1, area D-2

This place between the wilderness of Paran and the wilderness of Zin was a site where the Israelites camped during the Exodus. Excavations at the site have uncovered fragments of pottery engraved with Hebrew writing. These link Kadesh with that period of biblical history. In later centuries, cities were built on this site. Kadesh is also referred to in the Bible as Kadesh-barnea (see Joshua 10:41).

Kadesh will always be known as the place from which Moses sent spies into Canaan (see Numbers 13:1–16, 25). Their mission was to gather facts about the land, its crops, and the people who lived there. The spies returned with a good news/bad news report. The land was fertile enough to support the people. But it would have to be taken from powerful tribes who were entrenched behind their walled cities (see Numbers 13:21–29).

Here at Kadesh, the people lost faith in God's promise to give them the land of Canaan. They cried out in despair against the Lord, refusing to

enter the land as He had commanded. God punished them for their lack of faith by forcing them to wander for forty years in the surrounding wilderness until all the doubters were dead (see sidebar, "Bad News at Kadesh," below).

At Kadesh, Moses receives a report from the spies he sent into Canaan (the Promised Land), in an Italian painting from the early seventeenth century.

BAD NEWS AT KADESH

The Lord said, ". . .not one of these people will ever enter that land. They have all seen my glorious presence and the miraculous signs I performed both in Egypt and in the wilderness, but again and again they have tested me by refusing to listen to my voice. They will never even see the land I swore to give their ancestors.". . .

"Because your men explored the land for forty days, you must wander in the wilderness for forty years—a year for each day, suffering the consequences of your sins. . . . They will be destroyed here in this wilderness, and here they will die!" (Numbers 14:20, 22–23, 34–35).

MOUNT HOR

Aaron, Moses' brother, was the first high priest of Israel. He served side by side with Moses in the difficult task of leading the Israelites from Egypt to the land of Canaan. Soon after the death of Miriam, Moses' sister (see Numbers 20:1), Aaron also died (see Numbers 20:28–29). The site of his death was Mount Hor, a mountain peak in the wilderness that has never been identified with certainty.

Some scholars believe Mount Hor was on the eastern side of the Dead Sea near Mount Nebo, the place where Moses later died. But a site southwest of the Dead Sea in the wilderness of Zin is more likely. The Bible tells us that "the whole community of Israel left Kadesh and arrived at Mount Hor" (Numbers 20:22). This verse implies that this mountain was just a short distance from Kadesh.

The mosque on the site where Aaron, brother of Moses, is supposed to have died.

The Muslims accept the tradition that Mount Hor was on the eastern side of the Dead Sea, in the territory of the modern state of Jordan. For centuries they have trekked to a shrine dedicated to Aaron on a mountain that they call Jebel Haroun ("Mountain of Aaron"). Located in modern Jordan, this mountain towers more than six thousand feet above the Dead Sea. At its summit is a little shrine with a white dome said to mark the site of Aaron's tomb.

You don't have to be a Muslim to visit the site. But you do have to be determined. The only way up is by a rough hiking trail. And be prepared to mark out a full day for the strenuous round trip. This is what one Christian pilgrim did in the late 1800s. Fortunately, he left us an interesting record of his visit (see sidebar, "A Visit to Aaron's Tomb on Mount Hor," below).

A VISIT TO AARON'S TOMB ON MOUNT HOR

The mountain was dark red in color, and the higher we climbed the more difficult we found our progress to be. Finally, we came to a dead end. But then we saw an excavation for a well, with masonry around it. Beyond this were steps cut into the rock, going still higher. This encouraged us to push on.

At length we reached the highest peak of the mountain, where there was just enough space for a small Muslim shrine, which they claimed was the site of Aaron's tomb.

It is impossible for me to describe our surroundings. Suffice it to say that massive mountain peaks lay

Inside Jabal Haroun, Aaron's supposed last resting place.

stretched out below us. The entire scene was vast, savage, and abandoned to utter desolation—both the hills and the desert—in every direction. The atmosphere was too thick and hazy for us to see very far. Neither of the two waters—the Red Sea or the Dead Sea—was visible.

Entering the Muslim shrine, we found near the door a common-looking tomb, with an Arabic inscription. Over the tomb was spread a faded pall of silk, striped in red, green, and white. A wooden bowl at one end of the tomb was probably intended to receive alms for the support of the shrine.

Others may doubt that Aaron lies buried on this peak. I choose to believe that here my unworthy footsteps have trod the same soil as the two brothers who led God's people out of Egypt, and that it was here they parted, leaving Moses to carry on the task alone.

—James Finn, *Byeways in Palestine*

SODOM AND GOMORRAH

MEANING	Sodom = "burnt" or "place of lime"; Gomorrah = "submersion" or "a ruined heap"
PRONUNCIATION	SOD-um/guh-MAWR-ruh
SITE AND LOCATION	Twin cities on the western shore of the southern tip of the Dead Sea

Map 2, area C-7

The exact location of these twin cities near the Dead Sea has been debated for centuries. Some scholars argue for a location along the northern section of the Dead Sea, while others think they were located somewhere near its eastern shore.

But the most widely accepted sites for Sodom and Gomorrah are on the western shore of the Dead Sea's southern tip. This area matches the biblical description of how the Lord destroyed the cities—with "fire and burning sulfur from the sky" (Genesis 19:24). Large deposits of sulfur and asphalt, along with salt, still exist in this area today.

Sodom and Gomorrah were two of the five cities known as the "cities of the plain." The others were Admah, Zeboiim, and Zoar (Genesis 14:2, 8). The Lord destroyed all of these except Zoar because of their wickedness. No trace of any of these cities has ever been found. Some people believe God destroyed them with an earthquake that caused the land to sink; then they were flooded by the inrushing waters of the Dead Sea.

This rock formation near the Dead Sea is called "Lot's Wife," after the Bible character who looked back on the destruction of her hometown and "became a pillar of salt" (Genesis 19:26 NIV).

SODOM AND GOMORRAH: A BIBLICAL SNAPSHOT

- Lot moved to Sodom after he and Abraham argued over grazing lands for their livestock (see Genesis 13:5–13).
- Abraham bargained with God to try to prevent the destruction of Sodom (see Genesis 18:23–33).
- God destroyed Sodom and Gomorrah and all their people except Lot and his family (see Genesis 19:24–26).
- Jeremiah compared the sinful Israelites of his time to the wicked people of Sodom and Gomorrah (see Jeremiah 23:13–14).
- Jesus compared the unbelieving people of Capernaum to those of the city of Sodom (see Matthew 11:23–24).

ZOAR

MEANING "little" or "little place"

PRONUNCIATION ZOE-er

SITE AND LOCATION A village just south of the southern tip of the Dead Sea

Map 1, area E-1

Zoar was the only one of the five cities of the plain the Lord did not destroy because of its wickedness (see "Sodom and Gomorrah," p. 33). God apparently spared this city because Lot requested that he and his family be allowed to seek refuge there (see sidebar, "Lot Flees to Zoar," below).

Zoar is also associated with another significant time in the history of Israel. Moses led the Israelites right up to the borders of Canaan. He could almost reach out and touch this territory he had dreamed about for more than forty years. He looked out over it from the top of Mount Nebo (see Map 2, area D-5). It must have been a clear day, because he could see most of the territory of Israel, including the city of Zoar off to the south. But God would not allow him to set foot on this sacred soil.

LOT FLEES TO ZOAR

When they [Lot and his family] were safely out of the city, one of the angels ordered, "Run for your lives! And don't look back or stop anywhere in the valley! Escape to the mountains, or you will be swept away!"

"Oh no, my lord!" Lot begged. "You have been so gracious to me and saved my life, and you have shown such great kindness. But I cannot go to the mountains. Disaster would catch up to me there, and I would soon die. See, there is a small village nearby. Please let me go there instead; don't you see how small it is? Then my life will be saved."

Lot and his daughter flee while his wife looks back at the destruction of Sodom and Gomorrah.

"All right," the angel said, "I will grant your request. I will not destroy the little village. But hurry! Escape to it, for I can do nothing until you arrive there." This explains why that village was known as Zoar, which means "little place" (Genesis 19:17–22).

EZION-GEBER AND ELATH

MEANING Ezion-geber = "backbone of a man"; Elath = "palm grove"

PRONUNCIATION EE-zih-on GHEE-bur/EE-lath

SITE AND LOCATION Twin towns on the Gulf of Aqaba about one hundred miles south of the southern tip of the Dead Sea   Map 1, area E-3

These two towns were only a short distance apart at the northern tip of the Gulf of Aqaba. Today, these sites are as far south as you can travel in Israel before slipping over into the neighboring nations of Egypt and Jordan.

The Bible tells us that Ezion-geber was one of the places where the Israelites camped during the Exodus from Egypt (see Numbers 33:35–36). In later centuries, during Solomon's time, it apparently became the center of a copper mining and smelting industry. Excavations at the site have yielded evidence of smelting furnaces dating back to Solomon's time.

Ezion-geber and Elath were also sites where Solomon stationed a fleet of ships on the Gulf of Aqaba. Here he entered into a trade alliance with King Hiram of Tyre to export and import goods for the economic benefit of his kingdom (see 1 Kings 9:26–28).

Today, this southernmost point in Israel has developed into a modern resort city known as Eilat. With thousands of hotel rooms available, it attracts tourists from Israel and throughout the world. They flock here to enjoy the abundant sunshine, beautiful beaches, and spectacular snorkeling and scuba diving. Other attractions include a marine observatory, a biblical museum, and an amusement park. A popular side trip for many vacationers is a visit by tour bus to Mount Sinai in Egypt about ninety miles away (see "Mount Sinai," p. 26).

The beach at the modern city of Eilat.

MOUNT MOUNT NEBO

PRONUNCIATION KNEE-boe

SITE AND LOCATION A mountain in modern Jordan about ten miles east of the northern tip of the Dead Sea Map 2, area D-5

So close, yet so far away. These words must have reflected Moses' thoughts as he stood on the summit of this mountain in the Pisgah range, looking west across the Dead Sea and the Jordan River into the promised land.

Moses' helper and co-leader, his brother Aaron, had already died (see "Mount Hor," p. 31). Now it was Moses' turn to go "the way of all flesh" and turn over the leadership of God's people to his successor, Joshua. God had promised Moses that he would see Canaan, but he would not live to enter and take possession of the land (see Numbers 20:6–12).

Mount Nebo rises to an elevation of about 2,700 feet in southern Jordan. For more than 1,600 years, Christians and Jews have recognized this as the site where Moses died. Excavations have turned up evidence that a Christian church was built on this mountain as early as AD 394. On the site today is a modern church building known as the Memorial Church of Moses and an active monastery of the Catholic Franciscan order.

From a platform on the summit of Mount Nebo, modern pilgrims can enjoy the same view the Lord granted Moses before he died. On this platform is a modern snake-like sculpture in the form of a cross that represents the pole Moses held up in the wilderness. He used a representation of a snake on a pole to cure the snake bites that God had inflicted on the Israelites because of their disobedience (see Numbers 21:4–9). Underneath the sculpture are the words of Jesus to Nicodemus: "As Moses lifted

The Memorial Church of Moses atop Mount Nebo.

up the bronze snake. . .in the wilderness, so the Son of Man must be lifted up" (John 3:14).

One beautiful spot on Mount Nebo modern tourists seldom visit is a group of springs known as the Springs of Moses. Located about 1,100 feet from the summit, these springs cascade down the mountainside and form a small stream that eventually runs into the Jordan River to the west. J. W. McGarvey, a Bible professor from the United States, camped by these springs during his visit to the Holy Land in the late 1800s. He observed that Moses and the Israelites probably drank from these springs.

"The route that Moses followed when climbing Mount Nebo may have passed by these very springs," McGarvey wrote. "Perhaps it was here that he quenched his thirst for the last time before he closed his eyes in a mysterious death."

The death of this great leader of God's people was puzzling, indeed. The Bible states that Moses was "as strong as ever" when he died (see sidebar, "Moses' View from Mount Nebo and His Final Days," right). If he was still in such good health, why did he die? The only explanation seems to be that his task of leading the Israelites was finished. Since God would not allow him to enter the promised land, it was time for him to step aside and let his successor, Joshua, take over.

And what about the Bible's statement that "the LORD"—not the people of Israel—buried Moses? And the secret location of his grave? You would expect the burial site of such a great leader to be prominently marked so future generations could pay him honor. Perhaps God feared that such homage by the Israelites could slip into idolatry—worship of a weak human being rather than the all-powerful Lord, who holds the life and death of every one of us in His hands.

The view from Mount Nebo.

MOSES' VIEW FROM MOUNT NEBO AND HIS FINAL DAYS

Then Moses went up to Mount Nebo from the plains of Moab and climbed Pisgah Peak, which is across from Jericho. And the LORD showed him the whole land, from Gilead as far as Dan; all the land of Naphtali; the land of Ephraim and Manasseh; all the land of Judah, extending to the Mediterranean Sea; the Negev; the Jordan Valley with Jericho—the city of palms—as far as Zoar.

Then the LORD said to Moses, "This is the land I promised on oath to Abraham, Isaac, and Jacob when I said, 'I will give it to your descendants.' I have now allowed you to see it with your own eyes, but you will not enter the land."

So Moses, the servant of the LORD, died there in the land of Moab, just as the LORD had said. The LORD buried him in a valley near Bethpeor in Moab, but to this day no one knows the exact place. Moses was 120 years old when he died, yet his eyesight was clear, and he was as strong as ever (Deuteronomy 34:1–7).

A camel race in the Negev Desert.

CHAPTER 3

If you have always wanted to see a camel, the section of the Holy Land west of the Dead Sea is for you. Some Arab Bedouins who live in the region near Beersheba still use camels today. In the territory south of this city, you will also see the famous black tents that are part of the traditional Bedouin lifestyle. But don't be surprised to see more modern stone houses mixed in among these movable dwellings.

And you are certain to do a double take when you catch a glimpse of a car, a truck, or an all-terrain vehicle parked next to a flock of camels! This is dramatic proof of the sweeping changes that are bringing all parts of Israel into the modern age.

The section of Israel west of the Dead Sea played an important role in biblical history. The area closest to the coast of the Mediterranean Sea was home to the Philistines. They defeated Saul, Israel's first king, but David eventually conquered them and took over their territory. And even before David became king of Israel, he was painfully familiar with this territory. Here in the wilderness, along the lower part of the Dead Sea, he played a game of cat-and-mouse with King Saul during his fugitive years.

Another famous Bible personality who frequented this territory was Abraham. He wandered from place to place in the lower part of this region, digging wells to provide precious water for his herds of goats and sheep. God had promised this land to Abraham and his descendants. But he never owned any of it, except a small plot on which to bury his family. It was long after Abraham's time when his descendants settled permanently in this land.

Abraham's family burial plot, according to Muslim tradition, is still visible today at the site known as the cave of Machpelah near Hebron. Several other places in this section of Israel are must-see sites for those who visit the Holy Land.

DEAD SEA

A body of water into which the Jordan River empties

Map 2, area D-6

It's hard to miss the Dead Sea when you look at a map of Israel. This body of water is the largest geographical feature of the Holy Land, dominating the southern section of the country. Actually, it's not a sea at all but a large inland lake about forty-five miles long by ten miles wide. Its waters are so salty that only microscopic forms of life can live in it—thus its name, the "Dead" Sea.

The area around the Dead Sea is known for its hot, dry climate. The freshwater that runs into the lake from the Jordan River and other streams evaporates quickly, leaving behind salt and other minerals. Across thousands of years, this process has produced a stagnant lake—the Dead Sea has no outlet—that is more than eight times saltier than most oceans of the world.

This unusual body of water has been known by many names across the centuries. The King James Version of the Bible refers to it as the "salt sea" (Joshua 18:19 KJV), the "sea of the plain" (Joshua 3:16 KJV), and the "east sea" (Joel 2:20 KJV). The Jewish historian Josephus called it the Sea of Sodom, and it is known to Arabs as the Sea of Lot. These last two names are derived from the Dead Sea's association with the wicked cities of Sodom and Gomorrah and Lot's escape from Sodom when the Lord destroyed these cities (see "Sodom and Gomorrah," p. 33).

The Dead Sea and its main feeder river, the Jordan, serve essentially as the modern eastern border of the Holy Land. The nations of Jordan and Syria occupy the territory east of these two border markers. Even before the Israelites occupied the promised land, the Lord cited the Dead Sea as the southeastern boundary of the Holy Land: "The southern portion of your country will extend from the wilderness of Zin, along the edge of Edom. The southern boundary will begin on the east at the Dead Sea" (Numbers 34:3).

Visitors to the Holy Land about 150 years ago reported a ridge of crystallized salt along the southwestern shore of the Dead Sea. This salt formation rose to about two hundred feet above the water and was about seven miles long. Local Arabs called it Jebel Usdum ("Mount of Sodom"). This name and its location were cited as support for the theory that the cities of Sodom and Gomorrah stood somewhere in this area. But no trace of these cities has ever been found; their precise location has remained a mystery to this day.

Salt deposits in the foreground, resort hotels in the background—the modern Dead Sea is an attraction for tourists who enjoy its medicinal waters.

Most maps of the Dead Sea show the lake as one solid body of water from one end to the other. Near its southern tip, where the water is shallow, the lake shrinks from its normal width of ten miles to a channel only about two miles wide. This spot is called El Lisan ("The Tongue"). The width of this channel has varied throughout the centuries, depending on the volume of water in the lake.

In modern times the water level of the Dead Sea has declined so dramatically that a person can walk across the lake on dry land at this point. This is a direct result of the Israeli government's increased draw-down of water from the Jordan River for irrigation purposes. Some estimates place the current water level at seventy feet below what it was less than a century ago.

This situation reflects one of the biggest challenges the nation of Israel faces today—water. This precious commodity has always been in short supply in the Holy Land. Deep wells and cisterns addressed this problem in Bible times. But the industrialization of Israel, along with its growing population, call for more creative and expensive solutions, including the desalination of water from the Mediterranean Sea. Time will tell how this situation impacts the culture and traditions of the Holy Land.

The decreasing water level of the Dead Sea has not affected one of its modern attractions—recreational and medicinal tourism. Visitors from Israel and throughout the world come here to enjoy the abundant sunshine, resort hotels, shops, and restaurants that have sprung up along the Israeli side of the Dead Sea. Also popular are spas and treatment centers for people with breathing difficulties and skin disorders. Some tourists even smear themselves with black mud from the bottom of the lake—a treatment thought to provide nutrients for the skin.

Of course, most people who come to the Holy Land for the spiritual experience don't visit these "touristy" places. But many pilgrims today do nothing but a drive-by of the Dead Sea on their way to visit other places they consider more important. That's unfortunate, because this strange lake is truly a fascinating place. (To read what several other pilgrims from the past have said after their "up-close and personal" tour of this Holy Land site, see sidebar, "Observations on the Dead Sea by Former Travelers," below).

OBSERVATIONS ON THE DEAD SEA BY FORMER TRAVELERS

Swimming in its waters: It is impossible for a person to sink in the Dead Sea. In water that is over your head, you can stand up straight without getting wet from the chest up. But you cannot remain long in this position. The water will soon float your feet to the surface. A horse is so top heavy that he can neither swim nor stand up in the Dead Sea. He turns over on his side at once (Mark Twain, *Innocents Abroad*).

Salt-covered stones by the edge of the Dead Sea.

Its terrible taste: I put a drop or two of water on my palm and touched it to my tongue. I never tasted anything so wretched! I expected it to be salty, but it had a disgusting flavor that was stronger than the salt. Even brandy could not get the taste out of my mouth (Edward Trollope, *A Ride across Palestine*).

Heat and humidity: At 7:15 in the morning the temperature stood at 85 degrees. There is always an oppressive heat in this desolate region that brings on profuse perspiration (James Finn, *Byeways in Palestine*).

A sea of blue in a desolate setting: The country through which we approached the Dead Sea was dismal and desolate enough to satisfy the gloomiest anticipations. But the sea itself came as a pleasant surprise. We had already seen it at a distance from the minaret [Muslim prayer tower] on the Mount of Olives as a dark blue line. But we had imagined that only the enchantment of distance could give it any beauty. Up close, we discovered it to be a beautiful lake of deep blue color. Around it were mountains that had every shade of red and brown. But of green there is none in this desert country (F. R. Oliphant, *Notes of a Pilgrimage to Palestine*).

Bitumen or asphalt: We found a few pieces of bitumen on the shore of the lake. But the peasants of Hebron told us that large blocks of it often break off from the bottom of the lake and float to the surface. We have seen many camel loads of it brought up to Jerusalem for export to Europe (James Finn, *Byeways in Palestine*).

Pillar of salt representing Lot's wife: We looked everywhere, as we passed along, but never saw grain or crystal of Lot's wife. It was a great disappointment. For many years we had known her sad story, and taken that interest in her which misfortune always inspires [see Genesis 19:26]. But she was gone. Her picturesque form no longer looms above the desert of the Dead Sea to remind the tourist of the doom that fell upon the lost cities (Mark Twain, *Innocents Abroad*).

QUMRAN

MEANING "two moons"

PRONUNCIATION KOOM-rahn

SITE AND LOCATION An ancient communal settlement on the north-western shore of the Dead Sea
Map 6, area D-6

Overlooking the Dead Sea at a site not far from Jerusalem is a place almost everyone has heard about. It's called Khirbet Qumran. Here in 1947, in one of the numerous caves dotting the landscape, the first of the Dead Sea Scrolls was discovered. Today, more than sixty years later, this is still considered one of the most important archaeological finds of modern times.

An Arab shepherd boy who was looking for a lost sheep accidentally discovered the first scroll. After his find came to light, archaeologists conducted a search of other caves in the area. They found more than eight hundred ancient manuscripts in eleven different caves. More than two hundred of these writings were copies of Old Testament books or book fragments. Most of these copies were dated to the first or second century BC.

What made these discoveries such a big deal is that they were the oldest copies of biblical manuscripts that had ever been found. They were about one thousand years older than the manuscripts that had been used to translate the Bible from Hebrew into modern languages up to that time.

Qumran's "Cave 4," where several hundred Old Testament scrolls were found in 1947.

It's important when discussing these scrolls to remember that the Bible was written down many centuries ago. This leads to the logical conclusion that the original biblical manuscripts do not exist. Our modern translations of the scriptures are based on handwritten copies of other manuscript copies that have been passed down by scribes, or copyists, from one generation to the next. So the older a manuscript is, the closer it comes to the original writing. Thus, these scrolls discovered at the Dead Sea are more likely to be closer to the original than any other biblical writings in existence.

Careful examination of these scrolls revealed that they are essentially the same as the copies that were made about one thousand years later. The few minor differences between them are attributed to the process of copying and recopying these documents over several centuries. The bottom line is that the text of the Bible we have today is basically the same as the words that were written down many centuries ago. God not only inspired the Bible in the beginning; He worked through a human process to pass it down accurately across the centuries. Most of us have always believed this to be true. But the Dead Sea Scrolls have proved it through scientific observation.

The most famous of the Dead Sea Scrolls is a complete manuscript of the book of Isaiah, written in the Hebrew language. This copy of Isaiah's prophecy is dated to about 100 BC, about five hundred years past the time when Isaiah

Part of an Isaiah scroll found at Qumran.

delivered his message to the southern kingdom of Judah. This famous scroll is on display at the Israel Museum in Jerusalem, where thousands of visitors to the Holy Land view it every year.

How did this version of Isaiah's book and the other manuscript fragments survive in a cave for about 2,100 years? They had been wrapped carefully, then placed in airtight clay jars. The hot, dry atmosphere of the Dead Sea area kept them intact for all those centuries. In addition, it's possible to see the miraculous at work here. After all, the Bible does tell us this about itself: "The grass withers and the flower fades. But the word of the Lord remains forever" (1 Peter 1:24–25).

The Dead Sea Scrolls and the caves in which they were hidden would be reasons enough to visit this Holy Land site. But throw in the people who lived here, and it becomes an even more interesting place to visit.

Qumran was home to a group of people known as the Essenes, meaning "pious ones." They rejected the secularization of Jewish society and withdrew to this wilderness setting about 150 BC. Here they established a communal way of life, copying the scriptures, waiting for the arrival of the Messiah, and living quietly as righteous people apart from a world they considered immoral and corrupt. The Roman army destroyed their settlement in AD 68—but not before they had hidden some of their precious scrolls in nearby caves.

The ruins of the Qumran community have been excavated in recent years. On this site you will find the Qumran National Park, where some of the artifacts the Essenes left behind are on display. Other things to see include an educational film that presents their unique way of life, a room where they copied Bible manuscripts, and ritual baths that were a part of their purification ceremonies. Most pilgrims end their visit to this site with a view of the cave in which most of the Dead Sea Scrolls were found.

For many years, Bible scholars have debated whether John the Baptist, the forerunner of Jesus the Messiah, was associated with the Essene sect. The spot on the Jordan River where John baptized is only about five miles north of Qumran. And it's true that he withdrew into the desert where he dressed like a recluse, preached a message of righteousness, and announced the coming of the Messiah (see sidebar, "John's Life and Message in the Wilderness," below). It could be that this movement influenced John, but there is no proof that he was a card-carrying Essene.

JOHN'S LIFE AND MESSAGE IN THE WILDERNESS

In those days John the Baptist came to the Judean wilderness and began preaching. His message was, "Repent of your sins and turn to God, for the Kingdom of Heaven is near." The prophet Isaiah was speaking about John when he said, "He is a voice shouting in the wilderness, 'Prepare the way for the LORD's coming! Clear the road for him!'"

John's clothes were woven from coarse camel hair, and he wore a leather belt around his waist. For food he ate locusts and wild honey. People from Jerusalem and from all of Judea and all over the Jordan Valley went out to see and hear John. And when they confessed their sins, he baptized them in the Jordan River.

John the Baptist's rough camel hair clothing looks considerably smoother in this stained glass window in Dublin, Ireland.

But when he saw many Pharisees and Sadducees coming to watch him baptize, he denounced them. "You brood of snakes!" he exclaimed. "Who warned you to flee God's coming wrath? Prove by the way you live that you have repented of your sins and turned to God. Don't just say to each other, 'We're safe, for we are descendants of Abraham.' That means nothing, for I tell you, God can create children of Abraham from these very stones. Even now the ax of God's judgment is poised, ready to sever the roots of the trees. Yes, every tree that does not produce good fruit will be chopped down and thrown into the fire.

"I baptize with water those who repent of their sins and turn to God. But someone is coming soon who is greater than I am—so much greater that I'm not worthy even to be his slave and carry his sandals. He will baptize you with the Holy Spirit and with fire. He is ready to separate the chaff from the wheat with his winnowing fork. Then he will clean up the threshing area, gathering the wheat into his barn but burning the chaff with never-ending fire" (Matthew 3:1–12).

ARNON RIVER

MEANING "roaring stream"

PRONUNCIATION ARE-none

SITE AND LOCATION A stream that rises in the nation of Jordan and runs into the Dead Sea on its eastern side   Map 2, area D-6

The Arnon River in the Wadi Mujib canyon.

The Arnon is mentioned several times in the Bible, particularly in connection with Israel's early years before they entered the promised land. This river runs through what was Moabite territory in Bible times.

Under Moses, the Israelites crossed over from the wilderness into the territory of the Moabites around the Arnon River on the eastern side of the Dead Sea (see Numbers 21:10–13). Somewhere near this river, the soothsayer Balaam met Balak, king of Moab (see Numbers 22:36). Balak hired Balaam to utter a curse against the Israelites, but Balaam instead blessed the Israelites three different times (see Numbers 23–24). The Lord prevented Balaam from uttering anything but positive words against Israel.

The modern name of the Arnon River is Wadi el-Mujib. A wadi is a stream bed that dries up during the hot summer months but contains water after a rainstorm or during the wet winter months. The meaning of the Arnon's name—"rushing stream"—refers to its swiftness when filled with water.

The Arnon falls about 3,500 feet along its forty-mile course. Just before emptying into the Dead Sea, it becomes a raging torrent as its waters are forced between a high, narrow ravine—an impressive sight for modern tourists.

HERODIUM

MEANING named for Herod the Great

PRONUNCIATION heh-ROW-dih-um

SITE AND LOCATION A fortress-palace about eight miles west of the Dead Sea

Map 4, area E-5

This site, not far from Jerusalem, has produced one of the most exciting archaeological finds in Israel in recent years. Here in 2007 the tomb of Herod the Great (ruled 37–4 BC) was discovered. Herod was the Roman ruler over Palestine when Jesus was born. He is best known as the cruel king who tried to eliminate the newborn "King of the Jews" by killing all the male babies around Bethlehem (see sidebar, "Herod Tries to Kill the Child Jesus," p. 48).

Herod's infamous death order fits the other things we know about his paranoid personality. He was always looking over his shoulder for anyone who might be a political threat—either real or imagined—to his rule. He ordered one of his wives and their two sons executed when he suspected they were plotting against him.

Tourists inspect an inner court of the Herodium complex.

Herod was also paranoid about his personal safety and security. He built Herodium as a combination fortress-palace as a place to flee to in the event of an attack by his enemies. He also strengthened two other fortresses—Machaerus (see p. 49) and Masada (see p. 51) near the Dead Sea—for the same purpose.

Herodium is not mentioned in the Bible. We know about this palace-fortress through the writings of Josephus, who lived in Herod's time. According to Josephus, the king built this massive structure on this site in 40 BC and named it for himself to commemorate his victory over two enemy armies. The complex sat atop the highest hill in the Judean Desert. This site gave Herod and his army a panoramic view of the southern region of his territory as well as the district of Moab on the eastern side of the Dead Sea.

The Roman ruler spared no expense in building Herodium. His seven-story fortress-palace on top of the hill was surrounded by a massive defensive wall. On the plain below this structure, he built several administrative buildings, a lake, and a Roman garden. Herodium required a lot of water, and this precious liquid was scarce in this dry, desert-like region. Herod's engineers solved the problem by building an aqueduct to bring water from nearby Bethlehem. This was supplemented by cisterns for the collection of rainwater.

The king had another palace-fortress in nearby Jerusalem. But he chose Herodium as the place where he wanted to be buried. Josephus described his royal funeral in great detail (see sidebar, "Herod's Funeral, According to Josephus," p. 49).

Archaeologists labored at Herodium for more than 150 years without finding any trace of a royal tomb. But in 2007, diggers were working about halfway up the hillside on which Herodium sits. They struck a slab of highly ornamented pink limestone, then unearthed an ornate burial chamber—one fit for a king. There is little doubt among Bible scholars today that this is the place where Herod was buried.

Ironically, most of the burial site had been destroyed. The ornate coffin had been shattered into hundreds of tiny pieces and scattered over the area. No bones and none of the treasures with which Herod was buried were found. Archaeologists attribute the destruction at the site

HEROD TRIES TO KILL THE CHILD JESUS

After the wise men were gone, an angel of the Lord appeared to Joseph in a dream. "Get up! Flee to Egypt with the child and his mother," the angel said. "Stay there until I tell you to return, because Herod is going to search for the child to kill him."

That night Joseph left for Egypt with the child and Mary, his mother, and they stayed there until Herod's death. This fulfilled what the Lord had spoken through the prophet: "I called my Son out of Egypt."

Herod was furious when he realized that the wise men had outwitted him. He sent soldiers to kill all the boys in and around Bethlehem who were two years old and under, based on the wise men's report of the star's first appearance (Matthew 2:13–16).

to Jewish nationalists who occupied the site about seventy years after Herod's death. From this location they led a resistance movement against the Roman occupiers of their country. Herod's remains and his burial site would have represented everything these Jewish rebels hated about the Roman Empire.

Even before these Jewish warriors took over the site, grave robbers may have stolen the valuables at Herod's tomb. In death, this ruthless king who wielded such power in his lifetime was defenseless against the greed of common thieves.

HEROD'S FUNERAL, ACCORDING TO JOSEPHUS

After this, they betook themselves to prepare for the king's funeral; and Archelaus [Herod the Great's son] omitted nothing of magnificence therein. He brought all the royal ornaments to augment the pomp of the deceased. There was a bier all of gold, embroidered with precious stones, and a purple bed of various contexture, with the dead body upon it, covered with purple; and a diadem was put upon his head, and a crown of gold above it, and a sceptre in his right hand. . . . And the body was carried two hundred furlongs, to Herodium, where he had given orders to be buried.

—Flavius Josephus, *Antiquities of the Jews*

MACHAERUS

MEANING unknown

PRONUNCIATION muh-KAY-rus

SITE AND LOCATION A fortress near the eastern shore of the Dead Sea

Map 6, area D-6

This fortress, like Herodium (see p. 47), is also associated with Herod the Great. The Roman army destroyed it before Herod's time when they overpowered the Jews and took control of Palestine. Herod rebuilt Machaerus as a military outpost to provide protection for his territories east of the Jordan River. It sat on a high mountain surrounded by deep ravines that extended all the way to the Dead Sea.

When Herod the Great died in 4 BC, his territory was divided among his sons. One of them, Herod Antipas (ruled 4 BC–AD 39), inherited the territory east of the Jordan River in what is now the nation of Jordan. This is the Herod who had John the Baptist executed. The Bible doesn't tell us where this happened. But according to the Jewish historian Josephus, it took place at the fortress of Machaerus (see sidebar, "Why Herod Antipas Had John Put to Death," below).

This Herod reminds us of Pilate, another Roman ruler of Israel in the time of John and Jesus. Herod Antipas didn't want to harm John because of his popularity with the Jewish people. But he caved in to pressure from his wife and agreed to have him executed. Pilate demonstrated the same kind of indecisiveness about Jesus. He knew this prophet from Galilee was innocent, but he let the Jewish authorities persuade him to sentence Him to the death penalty (see Luke 23:13–25).

The Roman army destroyed the fortress of Machaerus in AD 72 during a Jewish revolt, and it was never rebuilt. Excavations have brought to light the ruins of the fortress Herod built, a large courtyard with a ritual bath, and the aqueduct that brought water to the site.

The mound of Machaerus, now in Jordan, with Israel in the background.

WHY HEROD ANTIPAS HAD JOHN PUT TO DEATH

Herod had arrested and imprisoned John as a favor to his wife Herodias (the former wife of Herod's brother Philip). John had been telling Herod, "It is against God's law for you to marry her." Herod wanted to kill John, but he was afraid of a riot, because all the people believed John was a prophet.

But at a birthday party for Herod, Herodias's daughter performed a dance that greatly pleased him, so he promised with a vow to give her anything she wanted. At her mother's urging, the girl said, "I want the head of John the Baptist on a tray!" Then the king regretted what he had said; but because of the vow he had made in front of his guests, he issued the necessary orders. So John was beheaded in the prison, and his head was brought on a tray and given to the girl, who took it to her mother (Matthew 14:3–11).

A very European image of Salome with the head of John the Baptist.

MASADA

MEANING unknown

PRONUNCIATION muh-SAH-duh

SITE AND LOCATION A mountaintop fortress near the western shore of the Dead Sea

Map 4, area E-6

Texas has its Alamo and Israel has its Masada. Both are places where heroic soldiers faced impossible odds but refused to back down and died in the fight for freedom.

Masada is not mentioned in the Bible. But it's a national shrine that's dear to the hearts of all Jewish people. Here is where almost one thousand Jewish rebels, although outnumbered by more than fifteen-to-one, defied the Roman army. The story of this struggle comes down to us through the writings of Flavius Josephus (see sidebar, "Who Was Flavius Josephus?" p. 52).

Masada, like Herodium (see p. 47) and Machaerus (see p. 49), was the site of a fortress-palace developed by Herod the Great. Located in an isolated

Masada and the path leading to the summit.

area near the southern tip of the Dead Sea, Masada was a place of final refuge for Herod in case he ever needed it. It was built on a flat-topped mountain that rose about eight hundred feet above the Dead Sea on its western side.

Around the fortress-palace Herod built a massive defensive wall. Nearby were storage buildings for food and weapons. He also hewed out a huge cistern in the solid rock to store water for Masada's defenders in the event of a prolonged siege.

As it turned out, Herod never had to flee to Masada. But about seventy years after his death, a group of Jewish nationalists did. When Jerusalem fell to the Roman army in AD 70, these rebels succeeded in occupying Masada. They packed in stores of food and water, then proceeded to make life miserable for the Roman army by conducting guerilla raids against them and fleeing to the safety of their Masada stronghold.

Finally, the Roman army, fifteen thousand strong, moved against the entrenched Jews. A direct assault against them was impossible because of its mountaintop location. So the Romans spent several months building an assault ramp up the mountainside with rock and dirt. When they broke through the defensive wall at the top, they were greeted with nothing but smoke and silence. The Jewish defenders had set their buildings and food stores on fire, then committed mass suicide. They preferred death to capture and enslavement by the Romans.

According to Josephus's account, only two Jewish women and five children survived. They provided some of the details that he included in his account of the event (see sidebar, "Masada's Suicide Pact, According to Josephus," p. 53).

The Israeli government has developed Masada into one of the country's top tourist attractions. Known as Masada National Park, the site has been excavated and some of its ruins restored. Visitors get a sense of what its defenders must have felt as the Roman army inched its way up the face of the mountain.

WHO WAS FLAVIUS JOSEPHUS?

- Born in AD 37, about four years after the death and resurrection of Jesus; died about AD 100

- A Jewish writer who wrote two histories of the Jewish people, *Antiquities of the Jews* and *The Jewish War*

- Was an eyewitness to many of the events that he wrote about, particularly the reign of the Herod dynasty in Israel during his lifetime

- Considered an authoritative source for illustrating the people, places, and events reported in the Old and New Testaments; sometimes supplements the Bible by adding details not contained in biblical narratives

Flavius Josephus.

Most visitors are shuttled by cable car to the top. Or, if you prefer, you can walk up by following a serpentine path known as "The Snake." But be warned: this trail is not for the weak. It takes about two hours to climb it to the top.

No matter how you get up the mountain, you will certainly marvel at the view from its summit. Henry Tristram, who visited the site in the mid-1800s, described it as "the most grand in its sternness and desolate magnificence I ever beheld." From this point, you also get a good view of the rock-and-dirt ramp the Romans heaped up from the valley below. Because of the dry conditions of the surrounding area, this structure has been remarkably preserved for almost two thousand years.

In recent years, a first-class museum has been added to the attractions at Masada. Here are displayed some of the artifacts discovered in excavations at the site. In a nearby amphitheater, a light and sound show on the history of Masada is performed for visitors during the height of the tourist season.

MASADA'S SUICIDE PACT, ACCORDING TO JOSEPHUS

- The men of Masada first killed their wives and children.
- Ten men were chosen by lot to kill all the remaining defenders except themselves.
- These ten men chose one man by lot to kill the remaining nine. This lone survivor, when assured that all the others were dead, set fire to the buildings and food stores and committed suicide by falling on his own sword.

EN-GEDI

MEANING	"spring of a kid"
PRONUNCIATION	in-GEH-die
SITE AND LOCATION	An oasis on the western shore of the Dead Sea
	Map 2, area C-6

En is a Hebrew word meaning "spring," while *gedi* means "young goat" or "kid"—thus the meaning of the name of this site, "spring of a kid."

En-gedi is only one of two freshwater springs that bubble up along the western shore of the Dead Sea before running down the steep cliffs to join this salty lake (see "Dead Sea," p. 40). Many springs exist in this area, but most of them send out water tainted with salt or sulphur.

During his fugitive years while on the run from King Saul, David hid in one of the numerous caves among the cliffs that surround this spring (see 1 Samuel 24:1–2). Saul and his troops followed David to this site. By chance, the king went into the very cave in which David was hiding "to relieve himself" (1 Samuel 24:3). David crept up on Saul and cut off a piece of his robe (see 1 Samuel 24:4).

When Saul came out of the cave, David confronted him from the safety of a nearby cliff. He displayed the cloth he had cut from the king's robe to show that he didn't intend to harm him, although Saul was trying to kill him.

William Tristram went into one of these caves near En-gedi while visiting the Holy Land in the mid-1800s. He offered this explanation of how David was able to slip up on Saul undetected and cut off a part of his robe: "These caverns are as dark as midnight, and the keenest eye cannot see five paces inside of one. But a person who has been in a cave a long time and is looking toward the entrance can see everything that happens in that direction. David, therefore, could watch Saul as he came in and notice the exact place where he relieved himself. But Saul could see nothing but impenetrable darkness."

The spring at En-gedi is still visible today. It issues from beneath a rock more than four hundred feet above the Dead Sea and rushes down a cliff into a pool before finally continuing on its way to the salty lake. Today the site is surrounded by the Ein Gedi Nature Reserve. This green oasis is made all the more spectacular by its contrast with the drab desert on its western side and the barren Dead Sea to the east.

The En-gedi waterfall.

CAVE OF ADULLAM

MEANING "refuge"

PRONUNCIATION ah-DULL-um

SITE AND LOCATION An unidentified cave somewhere near Hebron
Map 4, area C-5

The cave of Adullam is mentioned three times in the Bible, each time as a place where David and his men hid from King Saul during David's fugitive years (see 1 Samuel 22:1; 2 Samuel 23:13; 1 Chronicles 11:15). Two other hiding places of David in the area west of the Dead Sea were the oasis of Engedi (see p. 53) and the city of Ziklag (see p. 56).

The cave of Adullam has never been identified with certainty. It could have been in several places west of the Dead Sea, since caves are scattered throughout this region.

At this site, David's forces swelled from a handful of warriors to about four hundred—men who were "in trouble or in debt or were just discontented" (1 Samuel 22:2). This shows that at this early point in his career, David was already attracting a following of loyalists who supported him in opposition to King Saul.

One site identified as the cave of Adullam.

ZIKLAG

MEANING unknown

PRONUNCIATION ZIKK-lag

SITE AND LOCATION An unidentified town in southern Israel

Map 2, area A-6

Ziklag is an important place because of its association with David during his fugitive years when King Saul was trying to kill him. Two other sites in the region west of the Dead Sea that have a similar connection with David are the oasis at En-gedi (see p. 53) and the cave of Adullam (see p. 55).

When Saul went on a rampage, David fled to the territory of the Philistines, where he sought sanctuary in the city of Gath. He probably thought Saul would be afraid to pursue him into the territory of these hostile enemies. Achish, king of Gath, welcomed David and used him and his warriors as mercenaries in his struggle for control of this territory (see 1 Samuel 27:1–4).

Soon David asked Achish for permission to settle his family and his

One suggested location for Ziklag, looking west toward Gerar.

warriors in the town of Ziklag, about twenty-five miles south of Gath (see 1 Samuel 27:5–7). Here David conducted raids against the tribal peoples of the area and shared the spoils of war with Achish in Gath (see 1 Samuel 27:8–12). This strengthened his relationship with Achish and contributed to his growing reputation as a forceful military leader. Soon other warriors who were dissatisfied with Saul's leadership joined David's forces at Ziklag (see 1 Chronicles 12:1–3).

At Ziklag, David also proved he was a person of godly character who could lead the nation of Israel in the right direction. When a party of Amalekites raided Ziklag and carried off all the women and children, he didn't panic when the people blamed him for letting this happen. He sought the Lord's will in the matter and then took decisive action when it became clear how he should proceed.

After he and his men rescued the captives and took spoils from the Amalekites, David insisted that the booty should be shared with everyone—even his warriors who grew exhausted from the march and couldn't finish the campaign (see sidebar, "David's Character Revealed at Ziklag," right). These actions reflected David's sterling character that caused God to describe him as "a man after my own heart" (Acts 13:22).

The ruins of Ziklag have never been identified with certainty. Several sites have been suggested, but the most likely candidate is Tel es-Shariah near Gerar. The problem is that none of the suggested places show any evidence of destruction during David's time. And the Bible says that the raiding Amalekites "crushed Ziklag and burned it to the ground" (1 Samuel 30:1).

DAVID'S CHARACTER REVEALED AT ZIKLAG

His source of strength: When David and his men saw the ruins [of Ziklag] and realized what had happened to their families, they wept until they could weep no more. David's two wives, Ahinoam from Jezreel and Abigail, the widow of Nabal from Carmel, were among those captured. David was now in great danger because all his men were very bitter about losing their sons and daughters, and they began to talk of stoning him. But David found strength in the LORD his God (1 Samuel 30:3–6).

His willingness to share with others: Then David. . .met up with the 200 men who had been left behind because they were too exhausted to go with him. They went out to meet David and his men, and David greeted them joyfully. But some evil troublemakers among David's men said, "They didn't go with us, so they can't have any of the plunder we recovered. Give them their wives and children, and tell them to be gone."

But David said, "No, my brothers! Don't be selfish with what the LORD has given us. He has kept us safe and helped us defeat the band of raiders that attacked us. . . . We share and share alike—those who go to battle and those who guard the equipment." From then on David made this a decree and regulation for Israel, and it is still followed today.

When he arrived at Ziklag, David sent part of the plunder to the elders of Judah, who were his friends. "Here is a present for you, taken from the LORD's enemies," he said (1 Samuel 30:21–26).

CARMEL

MEANING "fruit garden," "orchard," or "a planted field"

PRONUNCIATION KAHR-muhl

SITE AND LOCATION A city about seven miles south of Hebron

Map 4, area C-6

Question: What do a stubborn sheepherder, a beautiful woman, and an angry young man destined to become a king have to do with one another?

Answer: They came together at a city known as Carmel in an area near the southern end of the Dead Sea. The stubborn sheepherder was Nabal, a wealthy man who refused to provide food for David and his hungry warriors. Of course, the angry young man who would be a king someday was David. And the woman in the mix was Abigail, the beautiful wife of the stubborn and rude Nabal (see 1 Samuel 25:2–13).

Nabal's refusal sent David into a rage. He set out with his men to wipe out Nabal and his servants. But Abigail pacified the future king by bringing food for him and his warriors. She told him, in effect, that more reasonable behavior was expected of a person who would someday rule over others as the king. David relented and praised the beautiful Abigail for her wisdom (see 1 Samuel 25:23–35).

But this is not the end of the story. Nabal had a stroke when Abigail told

DAVID'S OTHER WIVES

We know that David had at least seven wives in addition to Abigail, whom he married after Nabal's death. These other wives of David are mentioned in the Bible:

- Ahinoam of Jezreel, the mother of David's first son, Amnon (see 1 Samuel 30:5; 2 Samuel 3:2).
- Bathsheba, the woman with whom David committed adultery. She was the mother of Solomon, who succeeded David as king (see 1 Kings 1:11).
- Michal, the daughter of King Saul (see 1 Samuel 18:27–28).
- Maacah, Haggith, Abital, and Eglah. These wives bore sons to David while he ruled over Israel from the city of Hebron (see 2 Samuel 3:3–5).

Multiple wives were common among the patriarchs and kings of Israel. But David's eight wives were nothing in comparison to his son Solomon's marriage to seven hundred women (see 1 Kings 11:3).

him how close David had come to killing him. He died about ten days later. David knew a good thing when he saw it, so he asked the widow Abigail to become his wife. She became one of several women to whom David was married during his lifetime (see 1 Samuel 25:36–39; see sidebar, "David's Other Wives," p. 58).

The site of ancient Carmel is known today as Khirbet (an Arabic word meaning "ruins") el-Kermel. Here visitors see the ruins of several churches and a huge castle. These were built on the site long after David's time.

VALLEY OF ELAH

MEANING "oak"

PRONUNCIATION EE-luh

SITE AND LOCATION A valley near the city of Gath   Map 4, area C-4

This valley is where a teenage boy named David became one of the greatest heroes in Israel's history. Here, with nothing but a slingshot, he faced a giant—and prevailed with the help of the Lord. His bravery inspired the army of King Saul to win a decisive victory over the Philistines. This event also added to his reputation as a leader and paved the way for his succession to the throne after King Saul's death.

The modern site considered the place where David defeated Goliath is a beautiful valley in the vicinity of the ancient Philistine city of Gath. This area marked the boundary between the territories of the Israelites and the Philistines in David's time. These enemies of Israel were trying to occupy

Like the young David, modern students pick smooth stones from an Elah valley brook.

ONE BOY AND FIVE SMALL STONES AGAINST A GIANT

He [David] picked up five smooth stones from a stream and put them into his shepherd's bag. Then, armed only with his shepherd's staff and sling, he started across the valley to fight the Philistine.

As Goliath moved closer to attack, David quickly ran out to meet him. Reaching into his shepherd's bag and taking out a stone, he hurled it with his sling and hit the Philistine in the forehead. The stone sank in, and Goliath stumbled and fell face down on the ground.

So David triumphed over the Philistine with only a sling and a stone, for he had no sword (1 Samuel 17:48–50).

Caravaggio's vanquished Goliath still has the mark of David's stone on his forehead.

Israelite territory when Saul's army stopped them. Here the two armies faced each other in a stalemate. They were camped on opposite hills with the valley of Elah between them. Neither force moved against the other for several days. But the Israelites had to endure the taunts of the Philistine giant, who challenged Saul to send one of his warriors to meet him in battle (see 1 Samuel 17:1–11).

When the shepherd boy David arrived on the scene, he insisted on answering the giant's challenge. David trusted God to give him the victory, but he was also savvy in his battle tactics. He didn't let Goliath lure him into hand-to-hand combat; instead, he felled him from a distance with a stone from his sling (see sidebar, "One Boy and Five Small Stones against a Giant," left).

Why did David pick up five stones from the brook that ran through the valley of Elah? He needed only one to kill the giant. Some people say he selected five in case he had to face Goliath's four brothers. But perhaps there is another reason. Although he trusted God, he didn't presume on the Lord's providence and protection. He had reserve ammunition in his shepherd's bag, just in case he missed with the first stone.

David knew that if a giant is breathing down your neck, you probably don't have time to reach down and grab another rock! The five he picked up before the battle began must have been chosen with great care—just right for the man-sized task of killing a giant.

The brook that provided David's sling stones still meanders today through the valley of Elah. Its modern name is Wady es Sunt, a streambed that has water during the winter months but dries up during the summertime. Tourists can't resist picking up small stones from this stream to take home as souvenirs.

ASHKELON

MEANING	"migration"
PRONUNCIATION	ASH-kuh-lon
SITE AND LOCATION	A city on the coast of the Mediterranean Sea
	Map 2, area A-5

This city sat right in the middle of Philistine territory during the days of Saul, first king of Israel, and his successor, King David. The Philistines migrated to this territory from the island of Crete about 1200 BC. They settled along the Mediterranean coast and eventually pushed as far north as Ekron. The Israelites often clashed with the Philistines to keep them from taking over their territory in the interior of the country. The five major cities of the Philistines were Ashkelon, Ashdod, Ekron, Gath, and Gaza (see 1 Samuel 6:17).

Ashkelon is mentioned in connection with the judge Samson's exploits (see "Timnah," p. 73 and "Zorah," p. 72). He killed thirty Philistines at Ashkelon and took their clothes to give to thirty of his friends. Samson had bet his companions that they couldn't solve his riddle about a dead lion that he had killed with his bare hands (see Judges 14:8–14; see sidebar, "The Ricochet Effect of Samson's Riddle," p. 62).

Even before the time of Samson and the Philistines, Ashkelon was an important city. Excavations show that it was destroyed and rebuilt several times and that it was inhabited successively by the Canaanites, Philistines, Israelites,

Modern Ashkelon.

Persians, and Romans. Ashkelon's natural harbor and its location on the main road from Egypt to Mesopotamia made it an important trade center. At one point in its long history, it was surrounded by a huge defensive wall with a vaulted gate complex—one of the largest archaeologists have ever discovered.

The excavated ruins of ancient Ashkelon are preserved today in Ashkelon National Park. This park adjoins the beach, so many visitors come to view remnants from the city's past as well as take a swim in the Mediterranean Sea. The modern city of Ashkelon, located not far away, has a population of more than 100,000 people.

Samson wrestling the lion in an engraving by Gustave Dore.

THE RICOCHET EFFECT OF SAMSON'S RIDDLE

Later. . .he [Samson]. . .turned off the path to look at the carcass of the lion. And he found that a swarm of bees had made some honey in the carcass. He scooped some of the honey into his hands and ate it along the way.

Samson said to them [his friends], "Let me tell you a riddle. If you solve my riddle during these seven days of the celebration, I will give you thirty fine linen robes and thirty sets of festive clothing. But if you can't solve it, then you must give me thirty fine linen robes and thirty sets of festive clothing."

"All right," they agreed, "let's hear your riddle."

So he said: "Out of the one who eats came something to eat; out of the strong came something sweet.". . .

Before sunset of the seventh day, the men of the town came to Samson with their answer: "What is sweeter than honey? What is stronger than a lion?" . . . Then the Spirit of the Lord came powerfully upon him. He went down to the town of Ashkelon, killed thirty men, took their belongings, and gave their clothing to the men who had solved his riddle (Judges 14:8–9, 12–14, 18–19).

ASHDOD

MEANING "fortress"

PRONUNCIATION ASH-dahd

SITE AND LOCATION A city on the coast of the Mediterranean Sea
Map 2, area A-5

Modern Ashdod, with a population of more than 200,000 people, is one of the largest cities in southern Israel. It has sprung up on the Mediterranean coast since 1956, when the Israeli government established it as a planned city. Ashdod has a large port, through which much of the country's imported and exported goods pass each year. This modern city was built not far from the ruins of ancient Ashdod, one of the five main cities of the Philistines during Old Testament times.

According to the book of 1 Samuel, the Philistines captured the ark of the covenant from the Israelites during a fierce battle (see 1 Samuel 4:10–11). They carried it to Ashdod, where they put it on display in the temple of their pagan god Dagon. This was probably their way of showing that their god was superior to this religious icon of the Israelites. But they were not prepared for what they discovered when they went into the temple the next day

Sail Square in modern Ashdod.

(see sidebar, "Dagon Falls before the Ark in Ashdod," below).

During New Testament times, the city of Ashdod was known as Azotus. Philip the evangelist was miraculously transported by the Spirit of God to Azotus after the conversion of the Ethiopian eunuch on the road to Gaza. From Azotus he launched a preaching tour that took him all the way up the coast of the Mediterranean Sea to the city of Caesarea (see Acts 8:39–40).

DAGON FALLS BEFORE THE ARK IN ASHDOD

Dagon.

When the citizens of Ashdod went to see it [the ark of the covenant] the next morning, Dagon had fallen with his face to the ground in front of the Ark of the LORD! So they took Dagon and put him in his place again. But the next morning the same thing happened—Dagon had fallen face down before the Ark of the LORD again. This time his head and hands had broken off and were lying in the doorway. Only the trunk of his body was left intact. That is why to this day neither the priests of Dagon nor anyone who enters the temple of Dagon in Ashdod will step on its threshold.

Then the LORD's heavy hand struck the people of Ashdod and the nearby villages with a plague of tumors. When the people realized what was happening, they cried out, "We can't keep the Ark of the God of Israel here any longer! He is against us! We will all be destroyed along with Dagon, our god." So they called together the rulers of the Philistine towns and asked, "What should we do with the Ark of the God of Israel?" (1 Samuel 5:3–8).

EKRON

MEANING "barren place"

PRONUNCIATION ECK-rahn

SITE AND LOCATION A city about midway between Jerusalem and the Mediterranean Sea   Map 2, area B-5

Ekron was the northernmost city of the Philistine pentapolis ("five cities"—the others were Ashdod, Ashkelon, Gath, and Gaza). Before the Philistines occupied the city in the twelfth century BC, it was a Canaanite stronghold. The Bible does not say whether Ekron was one of the cities the Israelites conquered when they invaded the land of Canaan.

Ruins from ancient Ekron.

What we do know about Ekron is that it was the last city where the Philistines placed the ark of the covenant after they captured it from the Israelites (see 1 Samuel 5:10–12). The ark's reputation as a troublemaker in Ashdod had preceded it, and the citizens of Ekron wanted nothing to do with it (see sidebar, "Send the Ark Back," below). Eventually, after the ark had caused havoc in Ekron, the Philistines sent the ark back to the Israelites at Beth-shemesh (see p. 70).

Ekron was also known as a site of pagan worship in Bible times. We learn this from an event in the life of King Ahaziah of the northern kingdom of Israel (ruled about 853–852 BC). At some time during his brief reign, he suffered a serious injury from a fall. Rather than consulting the Lord, he sent messengers to ask priests of the pagan god Baal-zebub at Ekron whether he would recover (see 2 Kings 1:2). The prophet Elijah delivered the bad news that the king would soon die from his injuries (see sidebar, "Bad News for King Ahaziah," above right).

The word *Baal-zebub* means "lord of the fly." This pagan god was worshipped as the producer of flies and apparently as the deity that was able to protect people from these troublesome insects. Ekron may have been a place where swarms of flies made life miserable for its residents.

William Thomson visited the site of ancient Ekron in the mid-1800s. He was struck by the rudeness of the people and the swarms of pestilent flies in the area. "There would be some excuse for these modern Ekronites if they could secure deliverance from these pesky flies by calling on the power of Baal-zebub," he observed. "We were so persecuted by them that it was difficult to get a photograph of this place where their god was supposed to dwell."

The site of ancient Ekron has been identified with a mound known as Tel Mikne. Here archaeologists have discovered iron tools that verify this city's association with the Philistines, who were known for their production of this metal (see 1 Samuel 13:19–22). At one time, the city was also a center of olive oil production.

BAD NEWS FOR KING AHAZIAH

Elijah said to the king [Ahaziah], "This is what the LORD says: Why did you send messengers to Baal-zebub, the god of Ekron, to ask whether you will recover? Is there no God in Israel to answer your question? Therefore, because you have done this, you will never leave the bed you are lying on; you will surely die."

So Ahaziah died, just as the LORD had promised through Elijah (2 Kings 1:16–17).

"SEND THE ARK BACK"

They sent the Ark of God to the town of Ekron, but when the people of Ekron saw it coming they cried out, "They are bringing the Ark of the God of Israel here to kill us, too!" The people summoned the Philistine rulers again and begged them, "Please send the Ark of the God of Israel back to its own country, or it will kill us all."

For the deadly plague from God had already begun, and great fear was sweeping across the town. Those who didn't die were afflicted with tumors; and the cry from the town rose to heaven (1 Samuel 5:10–12).

GATH

MEANING "wine press"

PRONUNCIATION gath

SITE AND LOCATION A city about twenty miles northeast of Ashkelon
Map 2, area B-5

The city of Gath, a Philistine stronghold, is thought to be one of the places where the descendants of a giant named Anak lived during Old Testament times. The size of these people struck fear into the hearts of ten of the spies Moses had sent to explore the land of Canaan. "All the people we saw were huge," they reported to Moses. "We even saw giants there, the descendants of Anak. Next to them, we felt like grasshoppers, and that's what they thought, too!" (Numbers 13:32–33).

About three hundred years after the spies trembled at the sight of these giants, a teenage boy named David faced one in a valley not far from David's

Excavations at Gath, as viewed from the east.

home in Bethlehem (see "Valley of Elah," p. 59). Goliath of Gath was more than nine feet tall, but David felled him with a single stone from his sling. His victory proved that the Lord didn't need weapons to rescue His people. David succeeded because he faced the giant in the name of "the God of the armies of Israel" (1 Samuel 17:45). He prevailed where the spies had failed because of his great faith in God and in His awesome power.

Biblical Gath is identified with Tel es-Safi, where an archaeological dig has been going on for several years. One of the most interesting finds at the site is a piece of pottery inscribed with a name similar to "Goliath." This has been dubbed the "Goliath Shard." It doesn't prove the giant's existence, but it does give evidence of the culture of the Philistines who lived here during David's time.

Gath may have been the most important city of the five the Philistines occupied. It is mentioned more times in the Bible than any other Philistine site.

GATH: A BIBLICAL SNAPSHOT

- The giant David killed was from Gath (see 1 Samuel 17:4).
- David and his warriors killed other Philistine giants from Gath (see 2 Samuel 21:22).
- David sought sanctuary from King Saul at Gath (see 1 Samuel 27:2–4).
- After David learned that the Philistines had killed King Saul, he declared that news of his death event should not be announced in Gath (see 2 Samuel 1:20).
- After David became king of Israel, he captured Gath (see 1 Chronicles 18:1).
- In later years, King Rehoboam of Judah fortified Gath for the defense of his kingdom (see 2 Chronicles 11:5–10).

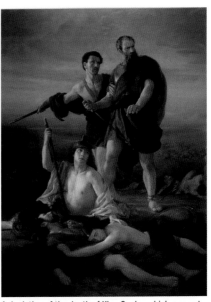

A depiction of the death of King Saul—which was not to be announced in Gath.

GAZA

MEANING	"stronghold"
PRONUNCIATION	GAY-zuh
SITE AND LOCATION	A city just inland of the Mediterranean Sea

Map 2, area A-6

Gaza will always be known as the place where the judge Samson demonstrated his superhuman strength. Once, his enemies thought they had him trapped inside the city walls. Samson ripped the gate out of the wall and carried it all the way to Hebron, about fifty miles away! (see Judges 16:1–3).

Later, Samson's girlfriend Delilah betrayed him by revealing the secret of his strength—his long hair—to the Philistines. They gave him a haircut and took him to prison. When his hair grew back and his strength returned, he took revenge against his enemies and committed suicide at the same time by toppling the temple of their pagan god Dagon (see sidebar, "Samson's Revenge at Gaza," p. 69).

A peaceful day in a troubled city—photo taken on a Gaza beach.

It's been many centuries since Samson beat up on the city of Gaza. But it's still a place marred by violence and revenge. Now the conflict is between the Jewish people and the Palestinian residents of Gaza, known today as Gaza City. Terrorist attacks against Israel often originate inside the Gaza Strip, where decades of economic hardship have taken their toll. Many of these residents blame Israel for their plight, going back to the days when Palestinian refugees fled to this place for sanctuary during the Arab-Israeli War of 1948.

Gaza is also associated with the evangelist Philip and a more pleasant incident from New Testament times. The Lord commanded Philip to "go south down the desert road that runs from Jerusalem to Gaza" (Acts 8:26). Somewhere on this road Philip met a man from Ethiopia who was reading about the Suffering Servant from the book of Isaiah. The evangelist helped him understand that he was reading about the Messiah. After the Ethiopian professed faith in Christ, Philip baptized him in a nearby pool of water (see Acts 8:36–37).

Today there is a site near this ancient road known as Philip's Spring, reputed to be the very place where this baptism took place. Its sparkling waters flow into a pool large enough for Philip and this new convert to have stood in. The nearby remains of an ancient church give evidence that early Christians considered this a sacred site.

SAMSON'S REVENGE AT GAZA

Samson said to the young servant who was leading him by the hand, "Place my hands against the pillars that hold up the temple. I want to rest against them." Now the temple was completely filled with people. All the Philistine rulers were there, and there were about 3,000 men and women on the roof who were watching as Samson amused them.

Then Samson prayed to the LORD, "Sovereign LORD, remember me again. O God, please strengthen me just one more time. With one blow let me pay back the Philistines for the loss of my two eyes." Then Samson put his hands on the two center pillars that held up the temple. Pushing against them with both hands, he prayed, "Let me die with the Philistines." And the temple crashed down on the Philistine rulers and all the people. So he killed more people when he died than he had during his entire lifetime (Judges 16:26–30).

Samson destroying the temple of Dagon.

BETH-SHEMESH

MEANING "house of the sun" or "temple of the sun"

PRONUNCIATION beth-SHEH-mesh

SITE AND LOCATION A town about twelve miles southwest of Jerusalem
Map 4, area D-4

This ancient town lay on the border between the territory of Israel and the region the Philistines occupied. At one time, as its name implies, it was associated with Canaanite worship of the pagan sun god. It apparently fell into the hands of the Israelites during Joshua's conquest of the promised land.

Beth-shemesh is best known as the town where Israel's ark of the covenant was lodged for a time. How it came to be placed here is one of the strangest stories in the Bible.

The Philistines from the territory south and east of Beth-shemesh captured the ark in a battle. But they decided to send it back to the Israelites after the ark caused confusion and disease in the Philistine towns where they placed it (see 1 Samuel 5:1–12). They put the ark on a cart, hitched two cows to it, and sent the cart away with no human driver. The cows pulled the ark

The remains of old Beth-shemesh, with the modern city in the background.

straight to Beth-shemesh, in Israelite territory (see sidebar, "A Cart with No Driver," below).

During a later period in Israel's history, Beth-shemesh was the scene of a senseless conflict between the southern and northern factions of the Israelite people. King Amaziah of Judah (ruled about 796–767 BC) challenged King Jehoash of Israel (ruled about 798–782 BC) with this cryptic message: "Come and meet me in battle" (2 Kings 14:8). He gave no reason why he wanted to fight with Jehoash. As it turned out, Amaziah should have held his tongue. His forces were roundly defeated, and the Israelites sacked his capital city of Jerusalem and looted its treasures (see 2 Kings 14:8–14).

Excavations at the site of Beth-shemesh have uncovered the ruins of an ancient city from the time of the judges up to about 800 BC. A huge iron workshop operated here during the time of David about 1000 BC. Also discovered was a huge underground reservoir that provided water for the residents of the town. An impressive system of pipes from the streets above channeled water into this huge cistern.

A modern town of the same name has grown up close to the ancient town of Beth-shemesh. Established in 1950, it has grown quickly to a population of more than one hundred thousand with the influx of Jewish immigrants from Africa, Ethiopia, Russia, and several European nations.

A CART WITH NO DRIVER

Two cows were hitched to the cart, and their newborn calves were shut up in a pen. Then the Ark of the Lord and the chest containing the gold rats and gold tumors were placed on the cart. And sure enough, without veering off in other directions, the cows went straight along the road toward Beth-shemesh, lowing as they went. The Philistine rulers followed them as far as the border of Beth-shemesh.

The people of Beth-shemesh were harvesting wheat in the valley, and when they saw the Ark, they were overjoyed! The cart came into the field of a man named Joshua and stopped beside a large rock. So the people broke up the wood of the cart for a fire and killed the cows and sacrificed them to the Lord as a burnt offering.

Several men of the tribe of Levi lifted the Ark of the Lord and the chest containing the gold rats and gold tumors from the cart and placed them on the large rock. Many sacrifices and burnt offerings were offered to the Lord that day by the people of Beth-shemesh (1 Samuel 6:10–15).

People of Beth-shemesh look up from harvesting to see the ark of the covenant returning to them.

ZORAH

MEANING "place of hornets"

PRONUNCIATION ZOE-rah

SITE AND LOCATION A city about fifteen miles southwest of Jerusalem
Map 5, area B-5

The supposed tomb of Samson and his father in Tel Zorah.

Not far from Beth-shemesh is the site where Samson, the famous strong man of the Bible, is buried. The ruins of the city are known today as Tel Zora. This site is also memorialized in the Bible as the place where Samson was born (see Judges 13:24; 16:31).

Visitors climb the mound that marks the site of the city to view Samson's tomb on the summit. Also on this spot is a rock called the Altar of Manoah. This is said to be the spot where Samson's father offered a sacrifice to the Lord when an angel announced that his barren wife would give birth to a son (see sidebar, "Manoah's Altar and Samson's Birth," below).

MANOAH'S ALTAR AND SAMSON'S BIRTH

The angel departs after telling Manoah his wonderful news.

Then Manoah took a young goat and a grain offering and offered it on a rock as a sacrifice to the LORD. And as Manoah and his wife watched, the LORD did an amazing thing. As the flames from the altar shot up toward the sky, the angel of the LORD ascended in the fire. When Manoah and his wife saw this, they fell with their faces to the ground. . . . When her son was born, she named him Samson. And the LORD blessed him as he grew up (Judges 13:19–20, 24).

TIMNAH

MEANING "allotted portion"

PRONUNCIATION TIM-nuh

SITE AND LOCATION An unidentified city in southern Israel
Map 3, area B-5

Samson, the judge of Israel with superhuman strength, was born and buried at Zorah. But some of his most famous exploits took place in the territory around Timnah (see sidebar, "Samson's Exploits Near Timnah," below).

Before Samson was born, an angel announced to his parents that he would be "dedicated to God as a Nazirite" (Judges 13:7). A Nazirite was a person especially consecrated to God for a divine purpose. He was expected to stay away from worldly influences. As one of the judges, Samson's role was to protect the Israelites from their enemies.

Instead, Samson let anger and pride motivate his actions. Rather than protecting Israel from the Philistines, he seemed determined to wage a personal vendetta against them. Eventually, God abandoned him to his own selfish desires, and he died a violent death in the Philistine city of Gaza (see p. 68).

SAMSON'S EXPLOITS NEAR TIMNAH

- He wanted to marry a Philistine woman from this city (see Judges 14:1–4).
- With his bare hands, he killed a young lion near here (see Judges 14:5–7).
- He posed a riddle about the lion's carcass to thirty of his friends at Timnah (see Judges 14:10–15).
- He killed thirty Philistines to pay off his thirty friends who solved the riddle (see Judges 14:16–19).
- He burned the crops of the Philistines near Timnah (see Judges 15:3–5).
- Somewhere near this city, he killed a thousand Philistines with the jawbone of a donkey (see Judges 15:14–17).

Samson showing a spectacular physique over the body of the lion.

LACHISH

MEANING unknown

PRONUNCIATION LAY-kish

SITE AND LOCATION A city about thirty miles west of the Dead Sea
Map 4, area B-5

The ancient city of Lachish is one of the most significant archaeological sites in Israel. Evidence uncovered here shows that the Canaanites inhabited Lachish at least three centuries before Joshua and the Israelites entered their land about 1400 BC. Joshua destroyed the city and killed all its inhabitants (see Joshua 10:31–33).

Discoveries at the site also show that Lachish remained virtually uninhabited for about four hundred years after Joshua's time. Then King Rehoboam (ruled about 931–913 BC), Solomon's successor, rebuilt Lachish and fortified it with a massive protective wall. This was one city among several in southern Judah that Rehoboam strengthened to protect his nation from attack along its southwestern flank (see 2 Chronicles 11:5–12).

During the next three or four centuries, Lachish underwent several other improvements until it became a formidable fortress city. Under King Jehoshaphat of Judah (ruled about 870–846 BC), a huge outer wall was added to the existing wall. This outer wall was eighteen feet thick and fourteen feet high. Both

Modern Lachish (Moshav Lachish) from the air.

walls had their own massive gates, adding an extra measure of security in the event of a siege against the city.

The fortress of Lachish was put to the test in 701 BC when King Sennacherib of Assyria invaded the kingdom of Judah during King Hezekiah's administration (ruled about 716–686 BC). Lachish and several other cities in southern Judah fell to the Assyrian onslaught. Hezekiah knew that his capital city would be next, so he offered to pay protection money if Sennacherib would leave Jerusalem alone (see sidebar, "King Hezekiah's Protection Money," right).

The Assyrian ruler took the money and prepared to advance against Jerusalem anyway. Then the Lord stepped in and struck the Assyrian army with a mysterious illness that killed thousands of its soldiers, causing Sennacherib to withdraw (see 2 Kings 19:35–36).

The Assyrian siege of Lachish and other southern Judean cities is documented by a source outside the Bible. Sennacherib portrayed the event on a stone slab and had it mounted in his royal palace in his capital city of Nineveh. It was discovered when archaeologists unearthed this city in the 1800s. The Lachish excavations verify the events shown on this Assyrian engraving, including siege ramps against the double defensive walls of Lachish, the battering rams that broke through the walls, and the piles of debris following the destruction of the city.

Sennacherib also couldn't resist bragging about his defeat of Lachish and other cities in Hezekiah's kingdom. In a stone relief near the drawing, he left this record of his victory: "I besieged and conquered (46 walled cities of Judah) by stamping down earth ramps and then by bringing up battering rams, by the assault of foot soldiers, by breaches and tunneling. Young and old, male and female, were the spoils of war. . . . Hezekiah, the Jew (in Jerusalem), was shut up like a caged bird within Jerusalem, his royal city."

But the Assyrian king had nothing to say about the mysterious and miraculous disease that left thousands of his troops dead in the territory around Lachish. Perhaps he didn't want to remind his people about all these battle-field casualties. Several years after returning to Nineveh from Judah, two of his own sons assassinated him and a third, Esarhaddon, succeeded him as king (see 2 Kings 19:35–37).

KING HEZEKIAH'S PROTECTION MONEY

King Hezekiah sent this message to the king of Assyria at Lachish: "I have done wrong. I will pay whatever tribute money you demand if you will only withdraw." The king of Assyria then demanded a settlement of more than eleven tons of silver and one ton of gold.

To gather this amount, King Hezekiah used all the silver stored in the Temple of the Lord and in the palace treasury. Hezekiah even stripped the gold from the doors of the Lord's Temple and from the doorposts he had overlaid with gold, and he gave it all to the Assyrian king (2 Kings 18:14–16).

GERAR

MEANING "halting place" or "lodging place"

PRONUNCIATION GEE-rar

SITE AND LOCATION A settlement and city about fifteen miles west of Beersheba

Map 2, area A-6

Gerar is one of those places in the Bible that presents a dilemma for archaeologists and serious students of the scriptures alike.

We know that a place called Gerar existed about 2000 BC when Abraham first entered the land of Canaan (see Genesis 20:1). A city identified as Gerar has been excavated in modern times. But evidence at this site shows that the town came into being about 1200 BC, about 800 years later than Abraham's time. How do we explain this discrepancy?

It's possible that Gerar was little more than a crossroads settlement when Abraham arrived at this place. Then, in later years, it developed into a larger city—the one archaeologists explored.

Bedouin women approach ruins at a place identified as ancient Gerar—Tel Haror.

Another strange thing about Gerar is that Abraham and his son Isaac committed the same blunder here. Both told the king of Gerar, a man named Abimelech, that their wives were their sisters. Both were afraid the king would kill them and take their wives—Sarah and Rebekah, respectively—into his harem because they were so beautiful. In each case, this didn't happen. The king discovered the truth and scolded Abraham and Isaac for their deceit (see Genesis 20:1–16; 26:1–11).

Still another strange thing about Gerar is that the Abimelech Isaac encountered is called a Philistine (see Genesis 26:1). Most scholars believe the Philistines didn't settle in Palestine until about 800 years after Abraham's time. This is a mystery that is not easily solved. But the Philistines could have arrived in Canaan in two distinctive waves—the first before Abraham's arrival and the second about eight centuries later.

In spite of these questions, there is one thing about Gerar that we know for sure: it was located in the hot and dry area of Israel known as the Negev. Here Abraham and Isaac wandered from place to place with their flocks and herds, just as many Arab Bedouins still do today in this section of Israel.

Rainfall was sparse in the Negev, so water was always a problem here. After Abraham died, Isaac and the Philistines squabbled over the rights to several wells in the region around Gerar. Isaac was a foreigner who owned no property in this region. This meant he had to settle for a well in an undisputed plot of grazing land (see sidebar, "Isaac's Dispute Over Wells Near Gerar," above right).

ISAAC'S DISPUTE OVER WELLS NEAR GERAR

So Isaac moved away to the Gerar Valley, where he set up their tents and settled down. He reopened the wells his father had dug, which the Philistines had filled in after Abraham's death. Isaac also restored the names Abraham had given them.

Isaac's servants also dug in the Gerar Valley and discovered a well of fresh water. But then the shepherds from Gerar came and claimed the spring. "This is our water," they said, and they argued over it with Isaac's herdsmen. So Isaac named the well Esek (which means "argument"). Isaac's men then dug another well, but again there was a dispute over it. So Isaac named it Sitnah (which means "hostility"). Abandoning that one, Isaac moved on and dug another well. This time there was no dispute over it, so Isaac named the place Rehoboth (which means "open space"), for he said, "At last the Lord has created enough space for us to prosper in this land" (Genesis 26:17–22).

BEERSHEBA

MEANING   "well of the seven" or "well of an oath"

PRONUNCIATION   BEE-ur-SHEE-buh

SITE AND LOCATION   A city about midway between the southern section of the Dead Sea and the Mediterranean Sea   Map 2, area B-6

Modern Beersheba is a city of more than 200,000 people that has grown up not far from the ruins of the old city mentioned several times in the Old Testament. A settlement has existed at this site in the Negev for thousands of years. The patriarchs Abraham, Isaac, and Jacob lived here, probably because it offered good grazing lands for their flocks and herds. Surface water was in short supply in this hot, dry region. But this problem was solved by digging deep wells and tapping into the groundwater.

The biblical record shows that these deep wells played an important role in Beersheba's early history. Soon after settling here, Abraham dug a well to provide water for his cattle. Then he complained to Abimelech, the Philistine ruler of the region, that the king's servants had confiscated the well for their own use. Abimelech promised to return the well. Then he pledged that

Excavated ruins of ancient Beersheba.

both of them would live together as friends and share the water supply. To seal the agreement, Abraham gave Abimelech seven lambs from his flock. This is why the site is called Beersheba, a name meaning "well of an oath" or "well of the seven" (see Genesis 21:22–33).

On this site Abraham planted a tamarisk tree, a species similar to an oak. Here he also built an altar and kneeled down to worship the Lord (see Genesis 21:34).

The site of ancient Beersheba is about three miles outside the modern city. Here visitors are shown a tamarisk tree planted beside an ancient well. Of course, the tree can't be the one Abraham planted about four thousand years ago. But it's possible this is the same well he dug at that time. The curbstone has grooves four to five inches deep, worn by the friction from ropes being pulled up with heavy buckets of water.

J. W. McGarvey, a Bible scholar from the United States, visited ancient Beersheba in the 1880s. At that time, several wells were still in operation at this site. He was convinced these wells went all the way back to Abraham's time (see sidebar, "The Testimony of Beersheba's Ancient Wells," above right).

But another traveler at about the same time as McGarvey offered a different view on these wells. James Finn, in his book *Byeways in Palestine*, pointed out that Isaac reopened several wells that had been dug by Abraham, then filled in by the Philistines after Abraham's death (see Genesis 26:17–18). Several filled-in wells were evident on the site of ancient Beersheba when Finn visited. This indicated to him that the wells of Abraham's time may have been filled in long ago.

Ancient Beersheba is known today as Tel es-Saba, and its excavation and reconstruction are ongoing. One of the most interesting discoveries at the site is a large four-horned stone altar from the time of King Hezekiah of Judah (ruled about 716–686 BC). Apparently Beersheba has been destroyed and rebuilt several times throughout its long history.

Visitors to the nearby Negev Museum are able to view a collection of archaeological artifacts from this region. Here they also learn about the culture of the Arab Bedouins, who have lived and worked in this part of the Holy Land for hundreds of years.

THE TESTIMONY OF BEERSHEBA'S ANCIENT WELLS

Cities have risen and fallen and nations and religions have come and gone since Abraham lived here. But these silent wells have remained, through all the fluctuations of human society, the same as when they were first dug. Today they are the most ancient and the best-preserved relics of antiquity to be found in all Palestine. It awakens emotions to be experienced only once in a lifetime to draw and drink water from a well that Abraham dug, and from which he and his family drank, nearly four thousand years ago.

—J. W. McGarvey, *Lands of the Bible*

HEBRON

MEANING "alliance"

PRONUNCIATION HEE-bruhn

SITE AND LOCATION A city about twenty miles west of the middle section of the Dead Sea

Map 2, area C-6

Perhaps the most unusual thing about this ancient city is that it has been inhabited on the same spot for thousands of years. Hebron is one of the oldest continually inhabited cities in the world. Excavations at the site have yielded evidence of buildings that were built before the pyramids were erected in Egypt.

This means that Hebron had already existed for more than one thousand years when Abraham lived here about 2000 BC. When his wife died, Abraham faced a dilemma. Since he was a foreigner in the land, he owned no property on which to bury Sarah. So he approached the officials of the city of Hebron about buying a specific plot of land for this purpose. This property contained a cave, and it belonged to a man named Ephron. The bargaining between Abraham and the landowner and his representatives is a classic illustration of how land transactions were conducted in this part of the world in Old Testament times (see sidebar, "Abraham and Ephron Strike a Deal," p. 81).

In modern Hebron, old buildings are built atop generations of older buildings—with a security tower overlooking all.

This burial plot Abraham purchased is known as the cave of Machpelah (pronounced mock-PEE-luh). After Abraham died, he was also buried here (see Genesis 25:7–10). In later years, four other members of his family were also laid to rest in this cave—Abraham's son Isaac and Isaac's wife, Rebekah, and Abraham's grandson Jacob and Jacob's wife, Leah (see Genesis 49:29–33).

Today, a modern city with the Arabic name el-Khalil has built up around the cave of Machpelah. Entrance to the actual burial cave is forbidden. The spot above the cave is enshrined by a Muslim mosque. The entire compound is surrounded by a high wall. Herod the Great built the lower part of this wall. Over the centuries, this wall has been enlarged and rebuilt several times.

Once inside the wall and the mosque, visitors are shown not only the tombs of these three couples—Abraham and Sarah, Isaac and Rebekah, and Jacob and Leah—but the tomb of Jacob's son Joseph as well. The Bible tells us that Joseph was buried at Shechem after he died in Egypt (see Joshua 24:32). But according to a Muslim tradition, Joseph's bones were later removed from his original burial site and placed in the cave at Machpelah.

Hebron is associated with several other important events in the Bible. David made this his capital city for the first seven and one-half years of his reign (see 2 Samuel 2:1–4, 11). Here all the tribal leaders met and proclaimed David king of all Israel (see 2 Samuel 5:1–5). From Hebron Absalom plotted his rebellion against his father, David. And even before David's time, Caleb received Hebron as part of his share of the land of Canaan (see Joshua 14:13–15; Judges 1:20).

Modern Hebron is a predominantly Muslim city inhabited by more than 200,000 Palestinians and a few Jewish families. This city on the West Bank often erupts into conflict between these two factions. When this happens, tours of Hebron are not permitted until order is restored.

ABRAHAM AND EPHRON STRIKE A DEAL

Ephron was sitting there among the others, and he answered Abraham as the others listened, speaking publicly before all the Hittite elders of the town. "No, my lord," he said to Abraham, "please listen to me. I will give you the field and the cave. Here in the presence of my people, I give it to you. Go and bury your dead."

Abraham again bowed low before the citizens of the land, and he replied to Ephron as everyone listened. "No, listen to me. I will buy it from you. Let me pay the full price for the field so I can bury my dead there."

Ephron answered Abraham, "My lord, please listen to me. The land is worth 400 pieces of silver, but what is that between friends? Go ahead and bury your dead."

So Abraham agreed to Ephron's price and paid the amount he had suggested—400 pieces of silver, weighed according to the market standard. The Hittite elders witnessed the transaction.

So Abraham bought the plot of land belonging to Ephron at Machpelah, near Mamre. This included the field itself, the cave that was in it, and all the surrounding trees. It was transferred to Abraham as his permanent possession in the presence of the Hittite elders at the city gate (Genesis 23:10–18).

MAMRE

MEANING "firmness" or "lusty"

PRONUNCIATION MAM-reh

SITE AND LOCATION A place about two miles northeast of Hebron
Map 4, area C-5

The ruins of ancient Mamre near Hebron are known by the modern Arabic name Ramet el-Khalil. Here is where Abraham sat at the entrance of his tent when he was assured that Sarah would give birth to a son. This good news came from three strangers to whom Abraham served a meal when they appeared mysteriously at his door. His wife, Sarah, found it hard to believe what they told Abraham (see sidebar, "Good News for Sarah at Mamre," below).

At Mamre, Abraham also learned from the Lord that He planned to destroy the cities of Sodom and Gomorrah because of their wickedness. He tried without success to get God to spare Sodom (see Genesis 18:23–33). Long after Abraham's time, a pagan shrine was built at the site of Mamre. This was eventually torn down and replaced by a church, the remains of which are still visible today.

GOOD NEWS FOR SARAH AT MAMRE

Abraham and Sarah were both very old by this time, and Sarah was long past the age of having children. So she laughed silently to herself and said, "How could a worn-out woman like me enjoy such pleasure, especially when my master—my husband—is also so old?"

Then the Lord said to Abraham, "Why did Sarah laugh? Why did she say, 'Can an old woman like me have a baby?' Is anything too hard for the Lord? I will return about this time next year, and Sarah will have a son" (Genesis 18:11–14).

The Oak of Mamre is said to mark the spot where Abraham pitched his tent before his encounter with the angels. The tree is said to be 5,000 years old.

ARAD

MEANING "fugitive"

PRONUNCIATION AY-rad

SITE AND LOCATION A city about ten miles west of the southern tip of the Dead Sea

Map 2, area C-6

City gates of Arad, estimated to date to perhaps 3000 BC.

This city receives only a passing mention or two in the Bible. The king of Arad led his people into battle against Joshua and the Israelites in their southern campaign to conquer the land of Canaan. The Israelites defeated the warriors of Arad, along with those from other cities in southern Canaan (see Joshua 12:7–14). Apparently Joshua's forces destroyed the city (see Joshua 12:24).

Years before the Israelites entered the promised land, they also encountered the king of Arad, who tried to prevent them from crossing into his territory. The Israelites were also victorious in this conflict (see Numbers 21:1–3).

Excavations at the site of ancient Arad have failed to yield any trace of the city from Joshua's time. It was apparently destroyed and abandoned long before the Exodus, then rebuilt as a Jewish city during the time of David and Solomon. This is one of those mysteries that archaeology has failed to solve.

Near the ancient ruins, known as Tel Arad, a modern planned city of the same name has grown up within the past forty years. Its location in the Judean Desert makes it an ideal spot for "desert tourism." Arad offers hiking trails, eco-tours of the desert, mountain biking, and side trips to nearby Masada (see p. 51) and the Dead Sea (see p. 40).

Also nearby is Israel's largest wooded area, known as Yatir Forest, where several species of trees thrive. Tourists find it hard to believe that a desert and a forest can exist so close together.

VALLEY OF ESHCOL

MEANING "cluster" or "cluster of grapes"

PRONUNCIATION ESH-cuhl

SITE AND LOCATION An unidentified valley in the vicinity of Hebron

Map 3, area B-6

The valley of Eshcol is famous because of a bunch of grapes. Here is where the spies Moses sent into Canaan cut down a large cluster of grapes. They carried these grapes back to Moses in the wilderness (see "Kadesh," p. 30) to show the fertility of the land.

This valley has never been identified with certainty. But we know from the Bible that it was somewhere in the vicinity of Hebron (see sidebar, "Grapes on a Pole," below). Grape vineyards still grow today in this section of the Holy Land.

The soil and climate of Israel were ideal for growing grapes, and vineyards abounded here in Bible times. For every person to sit "under his vine and under his fig tree" (Micah 4:4 KJV) was a symbol of peace and prosperity.

GRAPES ON A POLE

So they [the spies] went up and explored the land from the wilderness of Zin as far as Rehob, near Lebo-hamath. Going north, they passed through the Negev and arrived at Hebron. . . . When they came to the valley of Eshcol, they cut down a branch with a single cluster of grapes so large that it took two of them to carry it on a pole between them! They also brought back samples of the pomegranates and figs. That place was called the valley of Eshcol (which means "cluster"), because of the cluster of grapes the Israelite men cut there (Numbers 13:21–24).

Harvesting grapes from a vineyard.

TEKOA

MEANING   "trumpet blast"

PRONUNCIATION   tuh-KOE-uh

SITE AND LOCATION   A city about ten miles south of Jerusalem

Map 5, area D-5

The city of Tekoa was built near the Judean Desert on a mountain about 2,800 feet above sea level. From this high plateau, the Mount of Olives, just outside Jerusalem ten miles to the north, was visible. Thus, Tekoa could warn officials at the Holy City about an attack from enemies to the south. In Bible times, trumpets were often sounded to rally warriors to their battle stations—thus the meaning of Tekoa's name, "trumpet blast."

The Lord called the prophet Jeremiah to sound a trumpet of warning for a different reason. He was concerned about the nation's sin. Unless the people stopped their idolatry and turned to the Lord, He would send a foreign nation to take them into exile. It's interesting that the prophet included Tekoa in his call for the people to change their ways: "Run for your lives, you people of Benjamin! Get out of Jerusalem! Sound the alarm in Tekoa! . . . A powerful army is coming from the north, coming with disaster and destruction" (Jeremiah 6:1).

Another prophet of the Old Testament is also associated with Tekoa. This was the hometown of Amos, a shepherd from the southern kingdom of Judah whom the Lord called to deliver His message of judgment against the northern kingdom of Israel. A priest named Amaziah rejected Amos's message and told him that he was out of his jurisdiction. But Amos never lost confidence in his divine call.

Tekoa is also mentioned during the time of David. Joab, one of David's military officers, summoned a wise woman from Tekoa to Jerusalem. With a story about her own family's broken relationships, she tried to convince the king to make amends with his own son Absalom (see 2 Samuel 14:1–24). But her efforts were only partially successful. The bad blood between father and son continued, and Absalom eventually tried to take over David's kingship by force (see 2 Samuel 15:13–14).

The Muslim Dome of the Rock is perhaps the most recognized feature of modern Jerusalem.

CHAPTER 4

JERUSALEM: THE HOLY LAND'S HOLY CITY

Jerusalem is such an important city in the Holy Land that it takes a full chapter to do it justice. In and around this Jewish capital are dozens of places where great biblical events took place. These sites are featured in chapters 5 and 6. But here we focus on Jerusalem as an entity all its own—the place of which the Lord said, "In Jerusalem will I put my name" (2 Kings 21:4 KJV).

A close look at a Bible concordance will convince you that Jerusalem was, indeed, an important city to the Lord and His people. The city is mentioned more than eight hundred times in the Bible—more than any other place in the scriptures (see sidebar, "Jerusalem: A Biblical Snapshot," p. 88). And unlike many other biblical cities, Jerusalem is not in ruins. You can visit it today on essentially the same site it occupied in Abraham's time. It has been inhabited continually for more than five thousand years.

The city has always been a source of pride and joy for the Jewish people. During the exile, when they were forcibly removed from their homeland and taken to the pagan nation of Babylonia, the Jews longed to return to their beloved city. "If I forget you, O Jerusalem," one homesick Jerusalemite lamented, "let my right hand forget how to play the harp. May my tongue stick to the roof of my mouth if I fail to remember you, if I don't make Jerusalem my greatest joy" (Psalm 137:5–6).

While the Jewish people love their capital city with a special passion, they do not have a monopoly on affection for Jerusalem. People from all over the world have been visiting this ancient city for centuries. Most of them return to their homes convinced that it lives up to its reputation as "the Holy City."

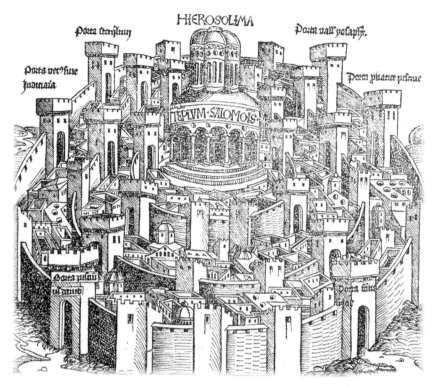

One of the oldest-known printed images of Jerusalem, from the late fifteenth century. King Solomon's Temple occupies the central location.

JERUSALEM: A BIBLICAL SNAPSNOT

- David captures Jerusalem from the Jebusites (see 1 Chronicles 11:4–9).
- David relocates the ark of the covenant to its permanent home in Jerusalem (see 2 Samuel 6:12–15).
- Solomon builds the temple in Jerusalem (see 1 Kings 6:1–13).
- Nebuchadnezzar of Babylon destroys Jerusalem (see Jeremiah 52:1–16).
- After the exile, Nehemiah rebuilds the walls of Jerusalem (see Nehemiah 2:11–18; 6:15).
- As an infant, Jesus is recognized as the Messiah in the temple at Jerusalem (see Luke 2:21–38).
- As a boy, Jesus talks with the teachers of the law in the temple at Jerusalem (see Luke 2:41–47).
- The fickle crowds at Jerusalem hail Jesus as a hero (see Mark 11:7–10).
- Jesus grieves over Jerusalem's hostility and unbelief (see Matthew 23:37–39).
- On the day of Pentecost in Jerusalem, the Holy Spirit fills believers (see Acts 2:1–6).
- Stephen, the first Christian martyr, is stoned in Jerusalem (see Acts 7:54–60).
- The apostle Paul is falsely accused of bringing a Gentile into the temple at Jerusalem (see Acts 21:26–29).
- The apostle John foresees in the end times a New Jerusalem, a beautiful city without sin (see Revelation 21:1–4).

Perhaps the most unusual thing about Jerusalem is that three of the world's major religions—Judaism, Christianity, and Islam—consider it a holy site. Each has its own reasons for holding the city in such high esteem.

JUDAISM

For Jews, Jerusalem is the city where their beloved temple once stood. Actually, three separate temples have existed at various periods of Jerusalem's history. The first, which Solomon built about 960 BC, was destroyed when the Babylonians overran Jerusalem in 587 BC. A second temple was built on the same site about 515 BC, after the Jews returned from the Babylonian exile. This structure was not as large and ornate as Solomon's original temple.

Herod the Great enlarged and renovated Jerusalem's second temple into a more impressive structure. This temple was under construction during Jesus' earthly ministry. His disciples were impressed with this ornate structure built from huge stones, but Jesus foresaw its bleak future. "Yes, look at these great buildings," He told them. "But they will be completely demolished. Not one stone will be left on top of another!" (Mark 13:2).

Just as Jesus predicted, Herod's temple was soon destroyed. This happened in AD 70 when the Roman army put down a revolt by Jewish zealots. No temple of the Jews has existed in Jerusalem since that time. But the Jewish people look upon the spot where their temple stood as a holy site. Many of them

gather for prayer at a place in Jerusalem known as the Western Wall (see chapter 5, p. 118), the foundation and retaining wall of the temple that Herod built on this site almost two thousand years ago.

The Western Wall.

CHRISTIANITY

Christians consider Jerusalem a holy city because of its association with Jesus Christ, God's Anointed One and our personal Savior. He proved His God-given authority by making His triumphal entry into the very heart of Jerusalem and cleansing the temple, the center of Jewish worship and tradition (see sidebar, "Jesus Shows His Superiority to the Temple," below). Here, just outside the city several days later, He was also crucified and resurrected.

Not far from Jerusalem, Jesus also ascended to heaven (see Acts 1:6–12). He had commissioned His disciples in Galilee several days before to continue the work He had started (see Matthew 28:18–20). God infused the church in Jerusalem with His strength and vision on the day of Pentecost (see Acts 2:1–6). After gaining its legs in Jerusalem, the church grew into a worldwide movement that brought people of all nations into the kingdom of God.

JESUS SHOWS HIS SUPERIORITY TO THE TEMPLE

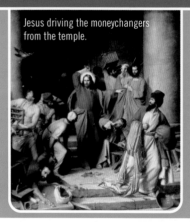

Jesus driving the moneychangers from the temple.

Then Jesus entered the Temple and began to drive out the people selling animals for sacrifices. He said to them, "The Scriptures declare, 'My Temple will be a house of prayer,' but you have turned it into a den of thieves."

After that, he taught daily in the Temple, but the leading priests, the teachers of religious law, and the other leaders of the people began planning how to kill him. But they could think of nothing, because all the people hung on every word he said (Luke 19:45–48).

ISLAM

Modern Muslims, adherents of a religion known as Islam, revere Jerusalem because of its association with Muhammad, their chief prophet. According to Islamic tradition, from Jerusalem Muhammad was taken on a spiritual trip known as the Nocturnal Journey. During this trip he was taken through all the heavens—or higher states of being—until he was joined with the Divine Presence itself. While in this exalted state, he was given revelations from the supreme god Allah that became the basis of all Islamic beliefs.

The very spot from which Muhammad was launched on this nighttime journey is the site where the Islamic Dome of the Rock (see chapter 5, p. 125)

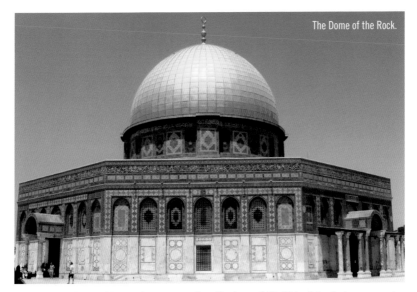

The Dome of the Rock.

in the Old City of Jerusalem sits today. Built in AD 691, this shrine occupies the site where the Jewish people believe Solomon built their beloved temple many centuries ago. This is one of the reasons the Jewish temple has never been rebuilt. The Jews cannot imagine that a temple could be built anywhere but on this sacred site. So they content themselves with praying at the Western Wall adjacent to the Dome of the Rock. This is as close as they can get to the spot where their beloved temple once stood.

While Muslims consider Jerusalem a sacred site, two other cities, both of which are in Saudi Arabia, eclipse its importance in their belief system. Mecca is where Muhammad was born, and Medina is where he died and is buried. All Muslims are expected to make a pilgrimage to Mecca during their lifetimes, if physical and financial circumstances permit. About two million Muslims visit Mecca every year—about the same number of Christian and Jewish pilgrims who make their way to Jerusalem.

A CITY ON A MOUNTAIN

In His Sermon on the Mount, Jesus compared believers to "a city on a hilltop that cannot be hidden" (Matthew 5:14). It's possible He had Jerusalem in mind when He made this comparison, because the city fits this description perfectly. Built on a plateau about 2,500 feet above sea level, ancient Jerusalem and its residents had a panoramic view of all the surrounding territory.

- **Salem**: The city where Melchizedek was a king and priest when he met Abraham (see Genesis 14:18).
- **Jebus**: A Jebusite fortress city David captured and turned into his capital city (see 1 Chronicles 11:4 KJV).
- **Jebusi**: A variation of the name Jebus that appears in the King James Version (see Joshua 18:16 KJV).
- **Zion**: A name for the hill on which the Jebusite fortress of Jebus stood (see 2 Samuel 5:7). This name was eventually applied to the entire city of Jerusalem (see Psalm 87:2 KJV).
- **Ariel**: A symbolic name the prophet Isaiah used for Jerusalem (Isaiah 29:1). It means "lion of God."

The city's high and lifted-up location explains why the Bible speaks several times of people going "up" to Jerusalem (see Luke 2:42 KJV). No matter what direction a person came from when traveling to the Holy City, he was always on an upward climb.

Deep valleys surrounded the city. Along its eastern side lay the Kidron Valley. Running along its western border was a deep gorge known as the Hinnom Valley. These two valleys ran together on Jerusalem's southern side, forming another deep trench. Thus, the city was cut off from the outside world by deep canyons—a natural defense against enemy attack from these directions. Only on the north, where the ground was level, did the city lack a natural defensive barrier.

King David recognized that Jerusalem's location between these valleys made it an ideal candidate for his capital city. Soon after all the tribes proclaimed him king, he moved his army against the fortified city, then known as Jebus and occupied by the Jebusites (see sidebar, "Other Names for Jerusalem," left). He succeeded in capturing the city by sending some of his warriors inside its walls through a water shaft (see sidebar, "How David Captured Jerusalem from the Jebusites," p. 93).

Today, of course, Jerusalem has outgrown its need for the natural defenses it required to protect itself from an enemy siege in Bible times. The walls of the Old City still exist, but modern Jerusalem has spilled outside these borders to become a busy urban center of more than 800,000 residents. Its outlying suburban growth has tended to blur Jerusalem's distinction as "a city set on a hill." But the Old City behind its ancient walls still impresses modern visitors, just as it struck Bayard Taylor in the mid-1800s when he saw the city for the first time (see sidebar, "First View of Jerusalem in 1863," p. 93).

When you visit Jerusalem's Old City today, you will see essentially the same walls, ancient buildings, and narrow streets that Bayard Taylor viewed in 1863. But don't jump to the conclusion that ancient Jerusalem has always looked this way. Across the centuries, the city has been destroyed and rebuilt several times. It would expand during one era, only to be leveled and the walls rebuilt at a later time to include a different plot of ground than it did before.

For example, the city known as the City of David that David captured and enlarged is outside the walls of the Old City today. The current walls around the Old City were rebuilt by the Ottoman Turks in the 1500s—more than 2,500 years after David's time—and they did not take in David's original city. But inside the walls of the Old City today you will find Mount Moriah, the site where Solomon built the temple and where the Muslim Dome of the Rock stands.

This mixture of sites can be confusing unless you remember that Jerusalem has been through many upheavals across its lifetime of more than five thousand years. Considering its violent history, it is indeed ironic that the name Jerusalem means "possession of peace" or "founded peaceful."

HOW DAVID CAPTURED JERUSALEM FROM THE JEBUSITES

David then led his men to Jerusalem to fight against the Jebusites, the original inhabitants of the land who were living there. The Jebusites taunted David, saying, "You'll never get in here! Even the blind and lame could keep you out!" For the Jebusites thought they were safe. But David captured the fortress of Zion, which is now called the City of David.

On the day of the attack, David said to his troops, "I hate those 'lame' and 'blind' Jebusites. Whoever attacks them should strike by going into the city through the water tunnel." . . .

So David made the fortress his home, and he called it the City of David. He extended the city, starting at the supporting terraces and working inward (2 Samuel 5:6–9).

FIRST VIEW OF JERUSALEM IN 1863

We urged our horses forward and reached the ruins of a garden, surrounded with hedges of cactus. Over these I could see domes and walls in the distance. Soon we reached another slight rise in the rocky plain. We dashed on at a gallop around the corner of an old wall on the top of the hill, and there it was—the Holy City!

From the descriptions of travelers, I had expected to see an ordinary Turkish town. But what lay before me—with its walls, fortresses, and domes—was it not still the City of David? I saw the Jerusalem of the New Testament as I had imagined it—long lines of walls crowned with a notched parapet and strengthened by towers, a few domes and spires above them, and clusters of cypress and olive trees here and there.

Now I knew for sure I was in Palestine, the Holy Land. My sight grew weak, and all objects trembled and wavered in a watery film. Since I arrived, I have viewed Jerusalem from many different angles. But I have not been able to recover the joy of that first view of the Holy City.

—Bayard Taylor, *The Lands of the Saracen*

JERUSALEM'S MAJOR VALLEYS

The two deep valleys that surround Jerusalem on three sides have played a major role in its history. Both are mentioned several times in the Bible.

The view along the Kidron Valley from Jerusalem's Old City.

KIDRON VALLEY
(pronounced KIH-drun)

This valley (see Map 8, areas D-4 and E-3) runs along the eastern edge of Jerusalem's Old City between the city wall and the Mount of Olives. Its name means "gloomy" or "dusky place," perhaps derived from the many tombs that have existed here for many centuries. The most famous burial site in this valley is Absalom's Tomb or Absalom's Pillar. This conical structure is named for the son of King David who tried to take over the kingdom by force and was killed by David's army (see 2 Samuel 15–18).

It is doubtful that Absalom is actually buried here, since the monument was erected many centuries after his death. But to the Jewish people, the structure represented everything they hated about Absalom and his revolt against their hero, King David. Generations of Jews threw rocks at the monument as they passed by, until the entire area was totally covered. Finally, in 1925, the area was cleaned and the stones removed to make Absalom's Tomb accessible for viewing by modern tourists.

Several other burial sites of notable biblical personalities may be seen near Absalom's Pillar in the Kidron Valley. These include the tomb of Zechariah, a priest stoned to death in the temple on orders from King Josiah (ruled about 640–609 BC) of Judah (see 2 Chronicles 24:20–22), and the tomb of Saint James, one of Jesus' disciples.

In addition to its function as a burial site, parts of the Kidron Valley were also used as a dumping ground in Bible times. Priests during the time of King Hezekiah (ruled about 716–686 BC) removed pagan objects from the temple and piled them outside in the temple courtyard. Then the Levites, assistants to the priests, "carted it all out to the Kidron Valley" (2 Chronicles 29:16). This dumping continued across the centuries until the debris piled up to an estimated fifty to one hundred feet. Tourists today marvel at the depth of the Kidron gorge, but how much more impressive it would be if they could see all the way to the original valley floor.

In Bible times, a dry streambed, or wadi, known as the Kidron Brook flowed through the Kidron Valley. The bed of this stream is not visible today, since it has been replaced with an underground drainage culvert beneath a modern road. But this is the very stream that King David and his aides crossed when they evacuated Jerusalem to escape Absalom's rebellion (see sidebar, "David Flees across the Kidron Brook," above).

DAVID FLEES ACROSS THE KIDRON BROOK

And there came a messenger to David, saying, The hearts of the men of Israel are after Absalom. And David said unto all his servants that were with him at Jerusalem, Arise, and let us flee; for we shall not else escape from Absalom: make speed to depart, lest he overtake us suddenly, and bring evil upon us, and smite the city with the edge of the sword (2 Samuel 15:13–14 KJV).

And all the country wept with a loud voice, and all the people passed over: the king also himself passed over the brook Kidron, and all the people passed over, toward the way of the wilderness (2 Samuel 15:23 KJV).

HINNOM VALLEY (pronounced HEN-nahm)

Of the two valleys that bordered ancient Jerusalem, the Hinnom—also called the valley of Ben-Hinnom—had by far the worst reputation. In this valley (see Map 8, area B-6), long before the Israelites arrived in Canaan, the Canaanites sacrificed their children as acts of worship in order to placate their pagan god Moloch, also known as Molech. The Lord had expressly forbidden this ghastly ritual, and it was not to be practiced among His people (see sidebar, "God's

King David's Citadel seen from the Hinnom Valley.

GOD'S PROHIBITION AGAINST HUMAN SACRIFICE

Offerings to Molech.

Prohibition against Human Sacrifice," left).

In spite of God's law against it, child sacrifice sometimes took place among the Israelites. The Bible tells us that two kings of Judah—Ahaz (ruled about 742–727 BC) and his grandson Manasseh (ruled about 687–642 BC)—were guilty of this form of idolatry. And the place where they committed it was the valley of Hinnom (see 2 Chronicles 28:1–3; 33:6).

Like its sister valley, Kidron, the valley of Hinnom was also a garbage dump for the city of Jerusalem. Here the carcasses of dead animals and household wastes were left for vultures to pick over. Sometimes the huge piles of waste caught fire and smoldered for days, emitting foul odors and clouds of smoke. To the Jewish people, the valley became an image of hell, the place of eternal punishment for the wicked. The Greek word for Hinnom is *Gehenna*, the word Jesus used when He declared that the scribes and Pharisees would not escape "the judgment of hell" (Matthew 23:33).

Another word for the valley of Hinnom is Topheth or Tophet, a term meaning "inferno" derived from the burning garbage piles on this site. The prophet Jeremiah declared that Topheth would be renamed the Valley of Slaughter because of the huge number of Israelites who would be buried here when a foreign power overran the nation of Judah. The prophet's prediction was fulfilled when the Babylonian army defeated Judah and destroyed Jerusalem in 587 BC.

A CITY OF MUSEUMS

While Jerusalem is known as the Holy City, it could just as appropriately be called the Museum City. Whether you're interested in archaeology, animals, plants, or history, you are sure to find here a museum or similar attraction that caters to your tastes. The nation of Israel boasts that it has more museums per capita than any other country in the world. And you won't have to go any farther than Israel's cultured capital city to find many of these excellent places to visit.

ISRAEL MUSEUM

At the top of the list of "must-see" places to visit in Jerusalem is the Jewish nation's pride and joy—the Israel Museum. Founded in 1965, it houses

the world's most extensive collection of biblical and Holy Land artifacts—a total of more than 500,000 objects. Its most famous exhibit consists of fragments of writings known as the Dead Sea Scrolls (see "Qumran" in chapter 3, p. 43). These manuscripts are housed in a special section of the museum, the Shrine of the Book. Other early manuscripts of the Bible are also displayed in this area.

Near the Shrine of the Book is another exhibit that never fails to captivate visitors—a model of ancient Jerusalem. This intricately detailed reproduction on a scale of 1:50 shows the city in all its glory from the Herodian temple era of its history (about AD 64). Visitors can view the city's walls, defense towers, palaces, houses, courtyards, markets, and gardens, along with the impressive temple, the spiritual center of the Jewish people. A related film depicts what life was like in Jerusalem during that time.

The Shrine of the Book at the Israel Museum.

Discoveries from archaeological digs all over Israel have found their way to the Israel Museum. For example, an inscription known as the Pilate Stone was found at Caesarea, capital of the Roman province of Judea during the time of Jesus. This inscription marked the residence of Pontius Pilate, the Roman ruler who pronounced the death sentence against Jesus (see Matthew 27:24–26). This is the only evidence of Pilate's rule, outside the New Testament, that has ever been discovered.

The Hall of Names in the Holocaust Memorial Museum.

HOLOCAUST MEMORIAL MUSEUM

This unusual museum on the slopes of a hill commemorates the six million Jewish victims of the Holocaust in Nazi Germany during World War II. It exists to call attention to this tragedy and to educate the public about its causes and results to make sure that it never happens again. Established in 1953, the museum contains the world's largest collection of material about the Holocaust.

The most impressive part of the museum consists of documentation of the personal feelings and experiences of the Holocaust victims themselves. This is communicated through photos, films, personal letters, works of art, and personal items from the death camps. In a special section called the Hall of Remembrance, ashes of some of the dead are buried and an eternal flame burns to perpetuate their memory.

On the site, visitors may view an actual railroad car that was used to haul Jews to the Nazi concentration camps. Another impressive part of this memorial is the Avenue of the Righteous among the Nations. Here more than two thousand trees have been planted in honor of non-Jews who risked their lives to protect Jews from the Nazi death squads.

DAVIDSON CENTER IN JERUSALEM ARCHAEOLOGICAL PARK

This unique attraction is near the Western Wall in Jerusalem's Old City. Here you will find some artifacts from excavations in the nearby sections of the Holy City. But the most popular exhibit is a three-dimensional virtual reconstruction of Herod's temple from the first Christian century. High-speed photos in a simulation mode make you feel as if you are actually walking up a stairway to the temple and standing before its towering columns.

TOWER OF DAVID MUSEUM

Located in the Tower or Citadel of David in the Old City, this museum specializes in the history of Jerusalem. Different sections of the citadel are dedicated to different periods of the city's history, from ancient to modern times. Visitors may view artifacts that demonstrate each historical period as well as a short film that serves as an introduction to the checkered history of the Holy City.

The Tower of David.

BIBLE LANDS MUSEUM

This museum is unique because it contains artifacts and exhibits from all the lands mentioned in the Bible, not just Israel. Here you will learn about the civilizations and way of life of many ancient cultures, including the Egyptians, Philistines, Hittites, Phoenicians, Babylonians, Assyrians, Persians, Greeks, and Romans. Pottery, paintings, and weavings show the skills of all the ethnic groups that lived in the ancient world.

The Bible Lands Museum is right next door to the Israel Museum. This is a convenience for pilgrims who want to maximize their time by visiting both places on the same day.

ROCKEFELLER MUSEUM OF ARCHAEOLOGY

Opened in 1938, this is one of the oldest museums in Israel. Most of the artifacts in its collection were unearthed during the British Mandate over Palestine (1919–1948). It occupies a beautiful building of white limestone in one of the newer sections of Jerusalem.

MARDIGIAN MUSEUM

If you visit the Armenian section of the Old City, you will find this quaint museum that specializes in the history of the Armenian people. The nation of Armenia adopted Christianity as its official religion early in the fourth Christian century. The Armenian Church has maintained a presence in the Holy Land for many centuries. Near the museum is its beautiful old church known as the Cathedral of Saint James and an Armenian monastery.

MUSEUM OF PSALMS

Where else but in Jerusalem would you expect to find a combination museum and art gallery devoted exclusively to the book of Psalms? The paintings in this museum are the work of one artist, Moshe Berger, who created them across a period of fifteen years. A survivor of the Holocaust, he used vivid colors in a semi-abstract style to render his artistic impression of each of the 150 psalms. Each painting also contains a single verse from the appropriate psalm rendered in the Hebrew alphabet.

JERUSALEM BIBLICAL ZOO

The full name of this attraction is the Tisch Family Zoological Garden, but most visitors refer to it as Jerusalem's Biblical Zoo. This popular family attraction opened in 1928 as a small animal park for children, but it has expanded in recent years into a first-class urban zoo with more than twelve hundred animals. Here you will see animals that are native to Israel as well as others from around the world. Many visitors to Israel find the zoo with its lake and greenery a refreshing change of pace after several days of hectic traveling throughout the country.

Syrian brown bears in the Jerusalem Biblical Zoo.

JERUSALEM BOTANICAL GARDENS

In addition to the Biblical Zoo, another soothing and relaxing place to visit in Jerusalem is its Botanical Gardens. You will find it in a quiet residential neighborhood not far from downtown Jerusalem. As you walk through the gardens—featuring six thousand species of plants, a lake, a waterfall, and two small ponds—you will find it easy to forget that you are surrounded by a busy city.

The Botanical Gardens contains plants from all over the world, organized according to geographic zones—the Mediterranean Basin, North America, Australia, Europe, South Africa, Central Asia, and Southwest Asia. Jerusalem's climate, with its hot, dry summers and cold, rainy winters, is ideal for the cultivation of such a wide variety of plants.

HERZL MUSEUM

This museum is for those who have an interest in modern Jewish history. It memorializes the role that Hungarian journalist Theodore Herzl played in bringing about the reestablishment of Israel as a sovereign and independent nation in 1948. As early as 1897, he gathered Jews from sixteen countries to support his vision of a reborn and unified Jewish state. Near the museum is a military cemetery known as Har Herzl (Mount Herzl) where he is buried, along with other notable Israeli leaders.

The walls of Jerusalem at night.

CHAPTER 5

To fully appreciate the Old City of Jerusalem, you have to approach it with a sense of wonder. Use your imagination to put yourself in the right frame of mind with the following mental exercise:

Imagine turning back the calendar by four or five centuries and strolling through a medieval city with high walls and massive defense towers. Visualize its ancient churches, mosques, and houses. Imagine its narrow, cramped streets with no traffic except people on foot and an occasional donkey cart. Now think as small as you can about this imaginary city. Then reduce its size again in your mind to no more than fifty streets—most of them no longer than a block or two.

By running these scenes through your imagination, perhaps you can get a glimmer of what the Old City of Jerusalem was like several centuries ago. Indeed, even today, it still looks a lot like it did to Mark Twain, American humorist and author, who visited Jerusalem in the mid-1800s (see sidebar, "Jerusalem: A Nobby City," p. 104). Twain's observation that a person could walk around the Old City in an hour is an accurate assessment of its size. The ancient walls extend for about three miles around the city. This is just about the distance that an adult can walk at a brisk pace in one hour.

Over the years, ancient Jerusalem has evolved into a city with four distinct sections or quarters—Christian, Jewish, Armenian, and Muslim. This "zone" system is a helpful tool for getting around the city, but it also has its drawbacks. The problem is that not all Christian sites are found within the Christian Quarter. For example, the Via Dolorosa—the "Way of Sorrows" that Jesus followed on His way to the cross—winds through the Muslim Quarter at some places.

In the following pages, you will find summaries of the most important sacred sites within the walls of the Old City. These descriptions will include the specific quarters or zones of Jerusalem in which these sites are located. Don't be upset or confused when you discover that some Christian sites are inside the Jewish Quarter or the Muslim Quarter of the city.

JERUSALEM: A KNOBBY CITY

A fast walker could go outside the walls of Jerusalem and walk entirely around the city in an hour. I do not know how else to emphasize how small it is. When you look down from a hill upon the compact mass of houses (so closely crowded together that there is no appearance of streets at all, so the city looks solid), you see the knobbiest town in the world, except Constantinople. It looks as if it might be roofed with inverted saucers.

The rough, crooked streets of the Old City are paved with stone. From the top of the lower story of many of the houses, narrow roofs like those over porches or sheds project over the streets. These overhangs have no supports from below. Several times I have seen a cat jump from one of these roofs to another on the other side of the street.

I mention these things to give you an idea of how narrow the streets are. Since a cat can jump across them, it is hardly necessary to state that Jerusalem's streets are too narrow for carriages. These vehicles cannot navigate the Holy City.

—Mark Twain, *Innocents Abroad*

The author Mark Twain, photographed in Constantinople on his way to Palestine.

POOL OF BETHESDA

MEANING "house of grace"

PRONUNCIATION buh-THEZ-duh

SITE AND LOCATION Twin water storage reservoirs in the Muslim Quarter of the Old City

Map 8, area D-1

Ancient Jerusalem had several cisterns or reservoirs for the storage of water, but this pool is one of the most famous in the Bible. In his Gospel, the apostle John immortalized this pool by naming it as the place where Jesus performed one of His healing miracles (see sidebar, "Jesus Heals a Man at the Pool of Bethesda," p. 106).

Extensive excavations and restorations at the site have revealed that two pools existed here during the time of Jesus' earthly ministry. They were apparently built at two different times during Jerusalem's long history. The first pool was constructed sometime after King Solomon built the temple. Its purpose was to provide water for the temple's sacrificial rites. Later, perhaps during the 200s BC, a second pool was added next to the first to increase the temple's

Ruins of the Pool of Bethesda.

water supply. The two separate pools—"upper" and "lower" or "northern" and "southern"—were connected by a trench that ran between them.

The area these pools covered was larger than a football field, and they were hollowed out to a depth of about forty-five feet. They were fed by an ingenious system of aqueducts that channeled runoff water from the nearby Kidron Valley. Once we realize the immense scope of this water collection system, we can better understand John's statement in his Gospel that "five covered porches" were a part of the Pool of Bethesda.

But then another question arises about John's account of Jesus' healing miracle at this pool. Why were crowds of sick people lying on the porches waiting to be healed? It's obvious they were not waiting for Jesus, because the sick man was surprised when Jesus restored him to health. John's account shows clearly that the people thought the waters themselves had miraculous healing power. Perhaps they believed this because of a pagan statue that stood nearby. The Romans had erected here a statue of Asclepius, the Greek god of medicine and healing.

But Jesus healed the man with words rather than water. His command was more powerful than the mysterious bubbling of the pool by an agent of healing. This proved that the false gods and superstitious beliefs of His time were weak and ineffective in comparison to His God-given authority and power.

JESUS HEALS A MAN AT THE POOL OF BETHESDA

Jesus at Bethesda

Afterward Jesus returned to Jerusalem for one of the Jewish holy days. Inside the city, near the Sheep Gate, was the pool of Bethesda, with five covered porches. Crowds of sick people—blind, lame, or paralyzed—lay on the porches, waiting for a certain movement of the water, for an angel of the Lord came down from time to time and stirred up the water. And the first person to step in after the water was stirred was healed of whatever disease he had. One of the men lying there had been sick for thirty-eight years. When Jesus saw him and knew he had been ill for a long time, he asked him, "Would you like to get well?"

"I can't, sir," the sick man said, "for I have no one to put me into the pool when the water bubbles up. Someone else always gets there ahead of me."

Jesus told him, "Stand up, pick up your mat, and walk!"

Instantly, the man was healed! He rolled up his sleeping mat and began walking! (John 5:1–9).

VIA DOLOROSA

MEANING "way of sorrows"

PRONUNCIATION VEE-uh dole-uh-ROW-suh

SITE AND LOCATION The route Jesus purportedly followed through the Old City of Jerusalem on His way to the cross

Visualize this scenario: You are sentenced to die after a rigged trial in first-century Jerusalem. You know you are innocent of the charges that were brought against you. In this situation, what would it be like to walk to your execution site along the city's narrow streets?

It's impossible to know, of course, since none of us will ever actually face this situation. But walking Jesus' path to His crucifixion site on Jerusalem's Way of Sorrows may be as close as we will ever come to feeling what that was like. Generations of pilgrims have testified that their walk along the Via Dolorosa was the most moving experience of their entire Holy Land trip.

Let's admit before we begin our journey that it's impossible to follow the exact path that Jesus walked. To do that, we would have to dig up the streets of the Old City and go down several feet to the street level that existed in His time almost two thousand years ago. So we will have to settle for the route that has been mapped out for us by many centuries of Christian tradition—not all of which is supported by scripture.

For example, we could quibble over the fact that three of the fourteen stations on the Via Dolorosa are said to be places where Jesus fell. How could this be, when two of these falls are said to occur after Simon of Cyrene carried the cross of Jesus? Perhaps it's best to put our critical faculties on the back burner before setting out on this walk. We will try to focus instead on the spiritual benefits of the journey.

STATION 1: JESUS IS CONDEMNED TO DEATH

This is the place where Pontius Pilate pronounced the death sentence against Jesus. On the site you will see Pilate's judgment hall where he finally gave in to the demands of the crowd, even though he knew Jesus was innocent of the charges against Him (see Luke 23:13–25).

A convent owned by the Sisters of Zion stands over a part of this hall where

The Sisters of Zion convent.

Jesus faced Pilate. In the church's basement, you will be shown ancient flagstones that are identified as the Stone Pavement mentioned as the place of judgment in the Gospel of John: "Then Pilate sat down on the judgment seat on the platform that is called the Stone Pavement (in Hebrew, *Gabbatha*)" (John 19:13).

Also inside this convent is the base of an ancient arch called the Ecce Homo Arch. This is identified as the spot where Pilate presented Jesus to His accusers with the words, "Behold the man!" (John 19:5 KJV). Pilate's words in their Latin equivalent are "Ecce homo."

STATION 2: JESUS RECEIVES HIS CROSS

The spot where the vertical beam of the cross was placed on Jesus' shoulders (see John 19:17) is marked by the Church of Condemnation. Also on this site is the Church of Flagellation, which commemorates the Roman soldiers' flogging of Jesus. Here they also placed a mock crown on His head and dressed Him in a purple robe to poke fun at His claim to be a king (see sidebar, "Jesus' Humiliation by Roman Soldiers," p. 110). Inside the Church of Flagellation are several beautiful stained glass windows that portray Jesus' mistreatment by Pilate and the Roman guard.

STATION 3: JESUS FALLS UNDER THE CROSS THE FIRST TIME

This station is marked by a stone tablet that shows Jesus falling under the weight of the cross. Another marker at this station is a small Polish Catholic chapel with a painting showing Him stumbling under the cross.

STATION 4: JESUS MEETS HIS MOTHER, MARY

According to the Gospel of John, Jesus saw His mother just before His death while He was hanging on the cross—not while He was on His way to the execution site. Nevertheless, this station commemorates that poignant time when He told His mother that His beloved disciple John, author of the Gospel of John, would take care of her after He died (see John 19:26–27). This station is marked by a beautiful little Armenian church with a silver dome. Over the church door is a carving showing Jesus and His mother at the cross.

STATION 5: SIMON OF CYRENE HELPS JESUS CARRY HIS CROSS

A small church dedicated to Simon the Cyrenian stands at this station. Established in 1229, it belongs to the Franciscans—Catholic caretakers of numerous sites in the Holy Land. In the church wall is a small cavity that is said to be an imprint made by the hand of Jesus.

Why was Simon forced to carry the cross of Jesus? (See Mark 15:21.) No one knows for sure. But the traditional view is that Jesus was weak from loss of blood caused by the Roman soldiers' flogging, so He could not carry it all the way to the execution site. But none of the Gospels actually say that Jesus fell while carrying the cross. The Via Dolorosa route claims that He fell three times.

STATION 6: VERONICA WIPES THE FACE OF JESUS

This station is based on Luke 23:27: "A large crowd trailed behind, including many grief-stricken women." According to an early Christian legend, one of these women was Veronica, who wiped Jesus' bleeding face with a silk veil. Miraculously, the image of His face was permanently imprinted on this cloth, and—so the legend goes—it is preserved today in the Basilica of Saint Peter in Rome.

A small Greek Catholic chapel is located at this station. It is named, appropriately, "The Holy Face."

STATION 7: JESUS FALLS THE SECOND TIME

A small Catholic chapel marks this site. Under its altar is a wall painting portraying Jesus' second fall.

STATION 8: JESUS SPEAKS TO THE WOMEN OF JERUSALEM

Among the Gospels, only Luke records the words of Jesus commemorated at this station (see sidebar, "Jesus' Words to the Women of Jerusalem," p. 110). His message to them was they should not pity Him but should feel sorry for themselves because of the coming destruction of Jerusalem. This happened in AD 70 when the Roman army sacked the city. A Greek Orthodox monastery marks this station.

STATION 9: JESUS FALLS THE THIRD TIME

This station brings you to the courtyard of the Church of the Holy Sepulchre. At this site are several interesting landmarks, including the Ethiopian

Station 9.

Church of Saint Michael and the Coptic Church of Saint Helen. Inside Saint Helen's is a large underground cistern that served at one time as a water source for the Church of the Holy Sepulchre. After walking the entire length of the Via Dolorosa, many Holy Land visitors take a much-needed break by visiting this cool, enchanting place.

STATIONS 10–14

The last five stations on the Via Dolorosa are located inside the Church of the Holy Sepulchre. These are discussed in the article on this church beginning on page 111.

JESUS' HUMILIATION BY ROMAN SOLDIERS

Some of the governor's soldiers took Jesus into their headquarters and called out the entire regiment. They stripped him and put a scarlet robe on him. They wove thorn branches into a crown and put it on his head, and they placed a reed stick in his right hand as a scepter. Then they knelt before him in mockery and taunted, "Hail! King of the Jews!" And they spit on him and grabbed the stick and struck him on the head with it. When they were finally tired of mocking him, they took off the robe and put his own clothes on him again. Then they led him away to be crucified (Matthew 27:27–31).

JESUS' WORDS TO THE WOMEN OF JERUSALEM

But Jesus turned and said to them, "Daughters of Jerusalem, don't weep for me, but weep for yourselves and for your children. For the days are coming when they will say, 'Fortunate indeed are the women who are childless, the wombs that have not borne a child and the breasts that have never nursed.' People will beg the mountains, 'Fall on us,' and plead with the hills, 'Bury us.' For if these things are done when the tree is green, what will happen when it is dry?" (Luke 23:28–31).

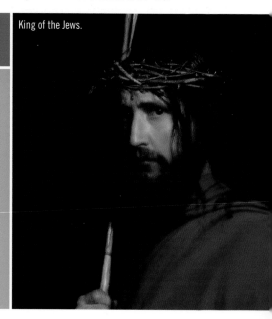
King of the Jews.

CHURCH OF THE HOLY SEPULCHRE

SEP-uhl-cur

A church in the Christian Quarter of the Old City

Many Christian pilgrims are a little disappointed at their first glimpse of this huge church. They were expecting a beautiful structure with perfect form. But it seems gangly and unplanned—as if an architect with no sense of taste had designed it. It is certainly not the most beautiful church in the city, but it is second to none in its significance and history. Known to locals as the Church of the Resurrection, it has been venerated for more than 1,600 years as the site where Jesus was crucified, buried, and resurrected.

Whether the Church of the Holy Sepulchre does, indeed, mark the exact site where Jesus was crucified has been debated for many years. Traditionalists insist that it does. They point out that it is the latest in a series of churches built on this authentic site since the fourth Christian century. The first church was constructed on this spot in AD 335 after Helena, mother of the Roman emperor Constantine, visited the Holy Land. Her mission was to identify all the sites associated with the life and ministry of Jesus.

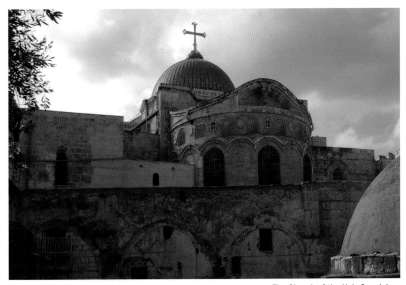

The Church of the Holy Sepulchre.

According to the traditionalists, Helena succeeded in finding the exact spot in Jerusalem where the cross had stood and where Jesus was buried. The modern Church of the Holy Sepulchre is the direct descendant of the original church built by Constantine and several other church buildings that have stood on this site throughout the centuries.

Those who question these claims believe Jesus was crucified and buried outside the walls of Jerusalem. They point to a skull-shaped hill outside the Old City called Gordon's Calvary as the actual place of the crucifixion. Nearby is a site known as the Garden Tomb where they think He was buried (see "Gordon's Calvary and the Garden Tomb" in chapter 6, p. 138).

The traditionalists respond to these claims by pointing out that the walls of Jerusalem have been destroyed and rebuilt several times during its long history. Thus, the traditional site marked by the Church of the Holy Sepulchre may have been outside the city walls when Jesus was crucified. And Gordon's Calvary was not identified until the 1800s. The traditionalists believe the 1,600-year tradition behind the Church of the Holy Sepulchre gives them an edge in this debate.

Perhaps the best approach to this question is the one Mark Twain, who visited this famous old church in the late 1800s, took. He was known to be a skeptic about some religious matters. But Twain focused on the spiritual lessons to be learned from an encounter with the site of the cross inside the Church of the Holy Sepulchre (see sidebar, "Mark Twain's Take on the Site of the Cross," p. 114).

Still another perspective on the actual site of the crucifixion was spelled out by William Thomson, who visited this church about the same time as Mark Twain. He declared that the actual place where Jesus died is not as important as what He accomplished through His death (see sidebar, "Jesus, Not His Sepulchre," p. 114).

Now that we have set the stage for your visit, let's focus on the organization of the Church of the Holy Sepulchre itself. It's best to think of it not as a single

The Tomb of Jesus Christ in the Church of the Holy Sepulchre.

structure but as several smaller chapels or churches under one roof. Several different Christian groups have jurisdiction over the holy sites that are scattered throughout the building.

Once you get inside, you will encounter representatives of its three major occupants or caretakers: Roman Catholic, Eastern Orthodox, and Armenian Orthodox. Three other groups that maintain a presence here are the Coptic Church (national Church of Egypt), the Syrian Orthodox Church, and the Ethiopian Orthodox Church. These groups are very possessive of their assigned spaces within the building, so don't be surprised if you detect a spirit of rivalry among them as you move from site to site.

In the courtyard of the church, you will find a small Catholic chapel called the Chapel of the Franks. This chapel commemorates the stripping off of Jesus' clothes by Roman soldiers (Station 10 on the Via Dolorosa; see John 19:23–24).

Station 11 on the Via Dolorosa (Jesus is nailed to the cross) is marked by a Catholic chapel with an altar known as the Nails of the Cross. On the ceiling of this chapel is a mosaic illustrating the crucifixion. Station 12 (Jesus dies on the cross) is commemorated by an Eastern Orthodox chapel that is reputed to sit on the exact site of the cross. This spot is marked by a silver disk. On each side of this disk are black disks that represent the crosses of the two criminals who were executed with Jesus (see Matthew 27:38).

Station 13 on the Via Dolorosa commemorates the removal of Jesus' body from the cross. This site is marked by a stone slab known as the Stone of Unction or the Stone of the Anointing. This is venerated as the place where Jesus' body was placed for anointing with spices before being placed in the tomb (see sidebar, "Jesus' Body Is Prepared for Burial," p. 114).

The Via Dolorosa comes to an end at Station 14 (Jesus is laid in the tomb) inside the Church of the Holy Sepulchre. The tomb is enclosed in a small chapel that sits beneath the central dome of the church. Visitors have to stoop to enter the tomb, which is only about six feet long by six feet wide. Only three or four visitors are admitted at a time. Visitors are usually standing in line waiting their turn to enter this sacred site.

Other interesting sites inside the Church of the Holy Sepulchre include the Jacobite Chapel, the place where Syrian Orthodox Christians claim the bodies of Nicodemus and Joseph of Arimathea are buried; the Chapel of Mary Magdalene, devoted to the Mary who came to the tomb on the morning of Jesus' resurrection (see John 20:11–18); and the Chapel of Saint Longinus. According to Greek Orthodox tradition, Saint Longinus was the Roman soldier who declared of Jesus just after He died, "Truly this was the Son of God" (Matthew 27:54 KJV).

MARK TWAIN'S TAKE ON THE SITE OF THE CROSS

The crucifixion of Christ was too notable an event in Jerusalem, and the Hill of Calvary made too celebrated by it, to be forgotten in the short space of three hundred years. I climbed the stairway in the church which brings one to the top of the small enclosed pinnacle of rock. Then I looked upon the place where the true cross once stood. I did so with a far more absorbing interest than I had ever felt in any thing earthly before. I could not believe that the three holes in the top of the rock were the actual ones the crosses stood in. But I felt satisfied that those crosses had stood so near the place now occupied by them that the few feet of possible difference were a matter of no consequence.

—Mark Twain, *Innocents Abroad*

JESUS, NOT HIS SEPULCHRE

There is no need to search for a site that the providence of God has rendered it impossible to discover. It is far better to rest contented with the fact that somewhere, near the walls of this very limited platform of the Holy City, the Son of Man was lifted up, "that whosoever believeth in him should not perish, but have eternal life." It is himself that men must believe in, not his sepulchre. It is not on Golgotha we must look for salvation, but to the precious blood of the Lamb of God that taketh away the sins of the world.

—William Thomson, *The Land and the Book*

JESUS' BODY IS PREPARED FOR BURIAL

Afterward Joseph of Arimathea, who had been a secret disciple of Jesus (because he feared the Jewish leaders), asked Pilate for permission to take down Jesus' body. When Pilate gave permission, Joseph came and took the body away. With him came Nicodemus, the man who had come to Jesus at night. He brought seventy-five pounds of perfumed ointment made from myrrh and aloes. Following Jewish burial custom, they wrapped Jesus' body with the spices in long sheets of linen cloth.

The place of crucifixion was near a garden, where there was a new tomb, never used before. And so, because it was the day of preparation for the Jewish Passover and since the tomb was close at hand, they laid Jesus there (John 19:38–42).

BROAD WALL

A section of Jerusalem's defensive wall in the Jewish Quarter of the Old City

This section of the wall around Jerusalem from the eighth century BC is an object lesson in how the city has grown and changed over the years. Uncovered by archaeologists in 1970, it was built by King Hezekiah of Judah (ruled 716–686 BC) to provide protection for a newer part of the city in the event of an attack by the Assyrian army.

The Broad Wall is named appropriately, since it was almost twenty-three feet thick at its base. It was probably not that wide at the top. Archaeologists estimate that it was about as tall as its thickness at the bottom—more than twenty feet high.

This huge wall was needed because the Assyrians were on the prowl in the ancient world. They were noted for their expertise in battering down the city walls of any nation that resisted their advance. It took a big wall to stand up to their attack. Besides that, the city of Jerusalem had grown outside the walls of the original City of David during the three centuries since David had captured it from the Jebusites. The wall around this newer section may have been substandard. So the Broad Wall was Hezekiah's ambitious attempt to shore up the defenses around the entire city.

Excavations at the Broad Wall revealed that some houses that stood in the path of the wall were demolished. Archaeologists theorize that the stones from these houses were used in the construction of the wall. The prophet Isaiah, who ministered in Jerusalem during Hezekiah's time, seems to support this theory. Here is how Isaiah described Hezekiah's preparation for the Assyrian threat: "You inspect the breaks in the walls of Jerusalem. You store up water in the lower pool. You survey the houses and tear some down for stone to strengthen the walls" (Isaiah 22:9–10).

As it turned out, the Assyrians never put this Broad Wall to the test. Their army withdrew after God intervened to save Jerusalem (see 2 Kings 19:29–36). But just over one hundred years later, the Babylonians battered this wall down. After a period of exile in Babylon, the Jewish people returned to their beloved city to rebuild its walls and the temple.

The Bible tells us that a group of workmen, under the supervision of Nehemiah, repaired a section of Jerusalem's defenses "as they built the Broad Wall" (Nehemiah 3:8). This is probably the same massive wall whose remains you can view today in Jerusalem's Old City.

BURNT HOUSE

SITE AND LOCATION Excavated remains of an ancient house in the
Jewish Quarter of the Old City

Like the Broad Wall (see p. 115), the Burnt House tells the story of Jerusalem's
destruction—but at a different time in its history. This house reveals evidence of
the Romans' burning of the city, more than six centuries after the Babylonians
destroyed Jerusalem in 587 BC.

Archaeologists uncovered the Burnt House in 1970. For almost two
thousand years, it lay under a layer of ashes and charred wood that preserved
its remains. Several coins discovered in the rubble were dated from AD 67 to
69, but none later than this time were found. This led archaeologists to the
logical conclusion that the Burnt House was a victim of the wrath of Rome
when it put down a Jewish revolt and sacked the city in AD 70.

Enraged by the rebellious Jews, Rome showed no mercy when it finally
battered down Jerusalem's walls and swarmed into the city. The Jewish historian Josephus recorded the atrocities Roman soldiers committed against its
residents, including women and children (see sidebar, "Jerusalem's Bloodbath of
AD 70," p. 117).

A human bone found in the remains of the Burnt House bears out Josephus's report. It was the lower arm and hand of a young woman in her twen-
ties. All five fingers, still attached to the hand, seemed to be reaching out and
grasping at something. In his book *Discovering Jerusalem*, archaeologist Nahman

The Burnt House
on display in a
modern museum.

Avigad described this bone as a disturbing image of Jerusalem's tragic fall to the Romans. "We could visualize a young woman working in the kitchen when the Roman soldiers broke into the house and put it to the torch," he observed. "She tried to flee, but collapsed near the doorway, to perish in the flames" (p. 137).

Visitors can see this arm bone in a small museum located next to the Burnt House. Here you will also find other objects discovered at the site, including coins, stone water jars, inkwells, lamps, jugs, measuring cups, and iron nails.

JERUSALEM'S BLOODBATH OF AD 70

When they [Roman soldiers] went into the lanes of the city with their swords drawn, they slew those whom they overtook and set fire to the houses whither the Jews were fled. They burnt every soul in them and laid waste a great many of the rest. When they were come to the houses to plunder them, they found in them entire families of dead men, and the upper rooms full of dead corpses—that is, of such as died by the famine. They then stood in a horror at this sight, and went out without touching any thing.

Although they had this sympathy for such as were destroyed, yet had they not the same for those that were still alive. They ran every one through whom they met with, and obstructed the very lanes with their dead bodies. They made the whole city run down with blood to such a degree that the fire of many of the houses was quenched with these men's blood.

—Flavius Josephus, *The Jewish War*

CARDO MAXIMUS

MEANING "the main line"

PRONUNCIATION car-DOE MAX-ih-muss

SITE AND LOCATION An excavated street in the Jewish Quarter of the Old City

This section of an ancient street from about 1,400 years ago gives you a glimpse of what Jerusalem would have looked like at the height of its glory as a Roman city. The Cardo was typical of the main boulevards that spanned the grand Roman cities of that time. Lined with tall marble columns, it was the approximate width of a modern six-lane highway.

Archaeologists uncovered a five-hundred-foot-long section of this street in the 1970s. It sits about eight feet below the level of the modern streets of the Old City. This shows dramatically how Jerusalem has been destroyed several times, then rebuilt on the ruins from a previous period of its history.

WESTERN WALL

SITE AND LOCATION **A place of prayer before the remains of Herod's temple in the Jewish Quarter of the Old City**

The Western Wall.

There are plenty of walls in the Holy Land. Everywhere you look you see them around cities, churches, and mosques. But the Western Wall in Jerusalem's Old City stands above all others in importance. The Jews consider it their most sacred site and the heart of their religion. To them, the Western Wall represents their beloved temple that once stood on this site.

To understand the significance of this wall, you have to go back to the time of Herod the Great, Roman ruler over Palestine (ruled 37–4 BC). He rebuilt and renovated the Jewish temple into a magnificent structure in order to curry the favor of the Jewish people. He began the construction project by building a four-sided rectangle of huge stones to serve as the temple foundation—what is referred to today as the Temple Mount.

Eventually, the Roman army destroyed this temple. But some of its massive foundation stones remained intact and are still visible today. The Jews specially venerate the Western Wall of this Herodian structure because they believe it was the closest to the Holy of Holies—the most sacred inner sanctuary of the temple.

In the past, the Western Wall was sometimes referred to as the Wailing Wall. This name was more appropriate when Palestine was under the thumb of foreign oppressors. Groups of Jews would gather here to lament the destruction of the temple and pray for the day when the temple would be rebuilt. This was the situation Don Carlos Janes found when he visited

Jerusalem in the early 1900s. He recorded a chant that Jewish worshippers repeated at the Wailing Wall under the leadership of a rabbi (see sidebar, "A Jewish Lament at the Wailing Wall in 1905," below).

Today, the scene at the Western Wall is not as lament-oriented as it was when Janes visited. But this wall is still a place of prayer for all people—not just the Jews. Thousands of pilgrims gather here to offer their silent prayers or to slip their prayer requests written on small pieces of paper into the crevices in the wall. The broad courtyard in front of the wall also serves as a swearing-in place for inductees into the Israeli military forces. Jewish parents also bring their children here for their traditional Bar Mitzvah (coming of age) ceremonies.

The part of the modern Western Wall where people gather for prayer is 187 feet long. But the entire length of the wall is about 1,600 feet. Of the remaining 1,400 feet that extend beyond the Prayer Plaza, 262 feet have been excavated in a project known as the Western Wall Tunnels. More than one thousand feet of the wall remain undisturbed, running silently beneath the streets and buildings of the Old City.

The section of the Western Wall visible today at the Prayer Plaza is about sixty-two feet high. But archaeologists believe parts of the wall of Herod's time may have been as high as two hundred feet. Massive building stones were quarried from solid rock and carved for exact fit, then stacked on top of one another to create the wall.

One stone uncovered during the excavation of the Western Wall Tunnels is forty-four feet long by ten feet wide, and its estimated weight is 570 tons—the largest building stone ever discovered in the Holy Land. How Herod's engineers managed to cut, transport, and lift these giant stones in place remains a mystery to this day.

A JEWISH LAMENT AT THE WAILING WALL IN 1905

Leader: For the place that lies desolate,
People: We sit in solitude and mourn.

Leader: For the place that is destroyed,
People: We sit in solitude and mourn.

Leader: For the walls that are overthrown,
People: We sit in solitude and mourn.

Leader: For our majesty that is departed,
People: We sit in solitude and mourn.

Leader: For our great men who lie dead,
People: We sit in solitude and mourn.

Leader: For the precious stones that are buried,
People: We sit in solitude and mourn.

Leader: For the priests who have stumbled,
People: We sit in solitude and mourn.

—Don Carlos Janes, *A Trip Abroad*

CATHEDRAL OF SAINT JAMES

A church in the Armenian Quarter of the Old City

The ornate interior of the Cathedral of Saint James.

This church, parts of which were built in the AD 1100s, is one of the most beautiful in the Holy Land. Visitors are awestruck by the ancient oil-burning lamps that shed a soft glow throughout the space beneath its vaulted dome. Its beautiful carpets reflect the light in a brilliant tapestry of colors. Many Holy Land visitors can't resist comparing the cheerfulness of this church to the dark and somber atmosphere of the Church of the Holy Sepulchre (see p. 111).

According to Armenian tradition, this church was built on the site where in AD 44 King Herod Agrippa I killed James, one of Jesus' disciples and the brother of John (see Acts 12:2). Inside the church is a little chapel with a shrine where they believe the head of James the apostle is entombed. This church also commemorates the other notable James in the New Testament—the half brother of Jesus. Armenian Christians claim that this James, a leader of the early church (see Acts 21:17–18), is also buried in the cathedral that bears his name.

The Armenian Quarter of the Old City has several interesting places to visit besides the Cathedral of Saint James. These include a library with thousands of rare and beautifully illuminated biblical manuscripts, a museum of Armenian history and culture, and a chapel identified as the site of the house of the high priest Annas, father-in-law of Caiaphas—before whom Jesus appeared after His arrest (see Matthew 26:57).

The Armenian Orthodox Church, an independent branch of the Eastern Orthodox Church, is one of the smallest Christian groups in the world. But it has had an important presence in the Holy Land since the AD 600s. Its position in Jerusalem is all out of proportion to its size. About twenty-five hundred Armenian Christians live in the Armenian Quarter, which occupies about one-sixth of the Old City's total area.

TOWER OF DAVID OR THE CITADEL

SITE AND LOCATION **Remains of a massive defensive tower inside the Jewish Quarter of the Old City**

This is one of those sites within the Old City that is guaranteed to produce confusion. For starters, this structure has nothing to do with David; it didn't even exist in David's time. Second, what used to be called the Tower of David is referred to today as the Citadel. And third, the name "Tower of David" is generally applied now to a Muslim mosque that stands close to the Citadel. Welcome to the wacky world of evolving Holy Land sites and migrating names!

Let's begin with the Citadel, the massive structure that used to be called the Tower of David. It is the remains of a huge defensive tower that Herod the Great built in the first Christian century to provide extra protection against an enemy attack on Jerusalem's northwest side. One of Herod's palaces was also built close to this tower. When the Romans destroyed the city in AD 70, they apparently left part of this tower standing as a testimony to their conquest of the city. Today a museum on the history of Israel is located in one of the many compartments inside the Citadel.

As for the Muslim mosque referred to as the Tower of David, it is one of many Muslim places of worship scattered throughout the city. Its distinctive round, slender tower is called a minaret. From this tower the Muslim call to prayer is sounded five times per day.

The Citadel.

CHURCH OF SAINT JOHN THE BAPTIST

A church in the Christian Quarter of the Old City

The Church of Saint John has two distinct personalities, and both of them are old. The "modern" church—the one visible at street level—was built in the eleventh century AD. But you can go downstairs and see the remains of a church that is five hundred years older. The present Church of Saint John was built over the remains of this earlier structure.

Dedicated to John the Baptist, the forerunner of Jesus, this Eastern Orthodox church claims that John's head is buried here. The Church of Saint John has carried on the forerunner's tradition of service and sacrifice across its long history. John is certainly worthy of such honor; even Jesus Himself praised John for his faith and commitment.

During the Crusades—a Christian campaign to take the Holy Land from the Muslims—an order known as the Knight Hospitallers of Saint John grew out of this church and its monastery. This group was also known as the Hospitallers. Their mission was to care for the sick and wounded participants in the Crusades in a hospital that they built next to the church. This tradition of Christian service and compassion continues today through the Sovereign Order of Saint John, a worldwide charitable and relief organization of the Eastern Orthodox Church.

The silver domed Church of Saint John the Baptist in the crowded Christian Quarter.

SAINT STEPHEN'S GATE

SITE AND LOCATION **A gate in the wall of the Old City that leads into the Muslim Quarter**

This is one of the eight gates in the wall of the Old City. According to tradition, this gate is near the site where an angry mob dragged Stephen out of the city and stoned him to death (see sidebar, "The Death of Stephen," below). They were enraged at Stephen's accusation that Jesus was the Messiah whose own people, the Jews, rejected and executed.

This gate is also known as the Lions' Gate, so called because of the engravings of two lions on the stone wall on both sides of the gate. The Muslims put them here to honor one of their leaders whose symbol was the lion.

Saint Stephen's Gate.

THE DEATH OF STEPHEN

Then they [Jewish religious leaders] put their hands over their ears and began shouting. They rushed at him [Stephen] and dragged him out of the city and began to stone him. His accusers took off their coats and laid them at the feet of a young man named Saul.

As they stoned him, Stephen prayed, "Lord Jesus, receive my spirit." He fell to his knees, shouting, "Lord, don't charge them with this sin!" And with that, he died (Acts 7:57–60).

CHURCH OF SAINT ANNE

SITE AND LOCATION **A church in the Muslim Quarter of the Old City**

Jerusalem is full of churches, but the Church of Saint Anne is special because it has survived relatively unchanged in its basic structure since it was built about 1138. Ironically, it owes its existence to the Muslims. They captured the church from the Crusaders in 1192. Rather than tearing it down, they decided to put it to use. Still visible over one of its doors today is an Arabic description that tells how Saladin, the Muslim conqueror of Jerusalem, converted the church into a school.

Eventually the Muslims abandoned the school, and the building was neglected for many years. It was finally restored and turned into a church again in the late 1800s.

Saint Anne's Church is reputed to be built over the home of Joachim and Anna, the parents of the virgin Mary. Here visitors are shown a cave twenty feet beneath the church floor where Mary was supposedly born. Inside the cave is a mural that portrays Joachim and Anna with their newborn baby daughter.

This tradition has no scriptural basis. The Bible is clear that Mary was from the village of Nazareth in Galilee (see Luke 1:26–27). And nothing is known about her parents—not even their names.

Inside the Church of Saint Anne.

DOME OF THE ROCK

SITE AND LOCATION **A Muslim shrine in the Muslim Quarter of the Old City**

The Dome of the Rock with the Old Town and the modern city behind it.

You have probably seen photographs of this beautiful building with its golden dome. Its image seems to appear in every book or magazine article written about Jerusalem. Because of its striking appearance, it has become an icon—a symbol of the ancient city.

The Dome of the Rock has been around for centuries, and it has always impressed visitors to Jerusalem. In the late 1800s, J. W. McGarvey —a Bible professor from the United States—said about it: "From whatever point it is viewed—from the city wall, the Mount of Olives, or any other height about the city— it is the most prominent and pleasing object in Jerusalem."

It upsets some Christian and Jewish pilgrims that the most prominent building in the Old City is a Muslim shrine. But this is just another example of the convoluted history of Jerusalem. The Muslims took over this site in the AD 600s when they became a strong force in the Holy Land. In 691 they built the Dome of the Rock over a huge outcropping of rock reputed to be the site of Mount Moriah where Abraham, at God's urging, prepared to sacrifice his son Isaac (see sidebar, "A Stopped Sacrifice on Mount Moriah," p. 126).

According to the Muslim account of this event, it was Abraham's son Ishmael—not Isaac—whom Abraham almost sacrificed on Mount Moriah. And the Jewish people believe it was on this very site that Solomon later built the temple. When the Muslims took over this location after the Jewish temple was destroyed, they showed their conviction that their religion was superior to Judaism by building this shrine where the temple had stood.

The Muslims also believe the rock inside the Dome of the Rock has a direct tie to their major prophet, the Messenger Muhammad. This huge formation of limestone is about sixty feet long by forty feet wide, and its rises about six feet above the ground. From this rock, they believe, Muhammad ascended to heaven for an encounter with Allah, their one and only true god. Allah revealed to Muhammad the doctrines and principles of Islam that are contained in the Muslim's holy book, the Koran.

So powerful and miraculous was Muhammad's ascent, they claim, that the rock began to go up with him. But the angel Gabriel stopped it, leaving two rough impressions on the rock from his hands. They also point out another depression in the rock's surface that was reputedly left by Muhammad's foot.

The inside of the Dome of the Rock is closed to Christian and Jewish pilgrims, but you can admire the building from the outside. It is an octagonal (eight-sided) structure adorned with colorful tiles. Below the 24-carat gold dome is an Arabic inscription from the Koran that describes Muhammad's miraculous "Nocturnal Journey" to Jerusalem from his birthplace in Mecca.

Jerusalem's Muslim Quarter is the largest of its four sections, or quarters. The Dome of the Rock with its fenced enclosure takes up about one-sixth of the entire Old City. Other attractions in the Muslim Quarter include the El Aksa Mosque and the Muslim Museum.

A STOPPED SACRIFICE ON MOUNT MORIAH

Abraham gives thanks to God for his son.

When they arrived at the place where God had told him to go, Abraham built an altar and arranged the wood on it. Then he tied his son, Isaac, and laid him on the altar on top of the wood. And Abraham picked up the knife to kill his son as a sacrifice. At that moment the angel of the LORD called to him from heaven, "Abraham! Abraham!"

"Yes," Abraham replied. "Here I am!"

"Don't lay a hand on the boy!" the angel said. "Do not hurt him in any way, for now I know that you truly fear God. You have not withheld from me even your son, your only son."

Then Abraham looked up and saw a ram caught by its horns in a thicket. So he took the ram and sacrificed it as a burnt offering in place of his son. Abraham named the place Yahweh-Yireh (which means "the LORD will provide"). To this day, people still use that name as a proverb: "On the mountain of the LORD it will be provided" (Genesis 22:9–14).

CHURCH OF THE REDEEMER

A church in the Christian Quarter of the Old City

This Lutheran church is the only Protestant church in the Old City and one of the few Protestant congregations in the entire Holy Land. It was built in the late 1800s and dedicated by Kaiser Wilhelm II, emperor of Germany. He was one of the first Western rulers of modern times to make a pilgrimage to Jerusalem.

Located next to the Church of the Holy Sepulchre, Redeemer Church has the tallest bell tower in the Old City. After climbing the 177 steps to the top of this tower, visitors are rewarded with a spectacular view of the city, surrounded by its ancient walls.

The dome of a Russian Orthodox church on the Mount of Olives.

CHAPTER 6

JUST OUTSIDE THE WALLS OF JERUSALEM'S OLD CITY

A visit to the sacred sites inside the Old City of Jerusalem (see chapter 5) is an unforgettable experience. But outside its ancient walls are many other places of interest to Holy Land travelers. On many of these sites, churches have been built in an unbroken chain that extends back for hundreds of years.

Most of the holy sites just outside Jerusalem's walls are clustered around three major focal points: Mount Zion (also called Sion), the City of David, and the Mount of Olives. A few facts about these three places should sharpen your focus on the major sites outside the city walls.

MOUNT ZION/SION

Early Jerusalem, the city David captured and later enlarged (see 1 Chronicles 11:4–9), was built on two hills—Mount Zion and the Ophel ridge. Mount Zion was the hill on the west, while Ophel was on the east. Originally both hills were designated as the site of the City of David. But in modern times, Zion has received its own separate designation. Zion is sometimes called the "upper city" (see Map 8, area B-4) because this hill was higher than the Ophel ridge.

The two hills were separated in David's time by a small valley known as the Tyropoeon Valley, but this landmark is barely visible today. It has been filled in across the centuries by the constant dumping of garbage and debris by the city's residents. Mount Zion is on the Old City's southwestern side.

CITY OF DAVID

Southeast of the city walls is the site known as the City of David. This name designates the part of David's original city that sits on the Ophel ridge between the Kidron Valley on the east and the Tyropoeon Valley on the west.

At one time, this part of Jerusalem—sometimes called the "lower city"—was included inside the walls of the Old City. But it was left out when the walls were rerouted and rebuilt in the AD 1500s.

This part of Jerusalem should not be confused with another "city of David" mentioned in the New Testament: "And Joseph also went up from Galilee. . .unto the city of David, which is called Bethlehem" (Luke 2:4 KJV). Bethlehem was called the city of David because this is where David was born and where he grew up (see 1 Samuel 17:15).

MOUNT OF OLIVES

The third landmark outside the city walls stands on Jerusalem's eastern side. It is called the Mount of Olives because of the olive trees that grew here in Bible times. This mountain—actually a high hill—rises more than two hundred feet above the city, with the Kidron Valley between it and the city walls.

From the top of this overlook, visitors can look down into the ancient city about half a mile away and make out most of its holy sites. On the opposite side of the peak, tourists can also view the bleak landscape of the Judean Desert that falls away to the Dead Sea about fifteen miles in the distance. William Thomson had an interesting observation about this "double view" from the Mount of Olives when he visited Jerusalem in the mid-1800s (see sidebar, "Two Views from the Mount of Olives," p. 131).

The Mount of Olives is mentioned several times in the New Testament, always in connection with the visits of Jesus to Jerusalem (see Matthew 24:3;

The Mount of Olives has been a Jewish burial site for over 3,000 years.

26:30; John 8:1). But the Old Testament refers to it only a couple of times. One of these recounts a critical time during the reign of King David. The king and his aides climbed the Mount of Olives as they fled Jerusalem to escape his son Absalom's rebellion. Looking down on the city, David decided to send his aide Hushai back into the heart of the rebellion as a spy (see sidebar, "David's Crucial Decision on the Mount of Olives," below).

Hushai succeeded in gaining Absalom's trust. Then he fed Absalom bad advice that brought David the precious time he needed to regroup his forces (see 2 Samuel 17:5–14). David eventually prevailed in this struggle. So the king's "Mount of Olives" decision may have saved his kingdom.

Now that you have these prominent landmarks in mind, let's begin our tour of the holy sites just outside the Old City. We will use these three focal points to identify the location of each site. This should make it easy for you to find your way around in the area just outside the city walls.

TWO VIEWS FROM THE MOUNT OF OLIVES

I was struck by the extreme contrast between the two views from the Mount of Olives. Facing eastward, my eye fell over leagues of hopeless desert—"the Wilderness of Judea"—ending in the Dead Sea. When I turned to the west, at my feet lay the Holy City with its sacred sites, symbolic names, and precious memories—suggestive of peace with God and life eternal in the Jerusalem on high.

It seemed not accidental that the Creator had placed here upon this hill one view against the other. Look to the left, and nothing appears but evil and cursing, all the way down to the bitter lake of Sodom. But on the right hand you behold with delight the symbols of life, goodness, and blessing. This was a vivid reminder of the words of Moses to the Israelites: "I have set before you life and death, blessing and cursing: therefore choose life, that both thou and thy seed may live" (Deuteronomy 30:19 KJV).

—William Thomson, *The Land and the Book*

DAVID'S CRUCIAL DECISION ON THE MOUNT OF OLIVES

David walked up the road to the Mount of Olives, weeping as he went. His head was covered and his feet were bare as a sign of mourning. And the people who were with him covered their heads and wept as they climbed the hill. When someone told David that his adviser Ahithophel was now backing Absalom, David prayed, "O LORD, let Ahithophel give Absalom foolish advice!"

When David reached the summit of the Mount of Olives where people worshiped God, Hushai the Arkite was waiting there for him. Hushai had torn his clothing and put dirt on his head as a sign of mourning. But David told him, "If you go with me, you will only be a burden. Return to Jerusalem and tell Absalom, 'I will now be your adviser, O king, just as I was your father's adviser in the past.' Then you can frustrate and counter Ahithophel's advice. . . . So David's friend Hushai returned to Jerusalem, getting there just as Absalom arrived (2 Samuel 15:30–37).

David grieves over his son's treachery.

POOL OF SILOAM

MEANING "sent"

PRONUNCIATION sigh-LOW-um

SITE AND LOCATION Storage pool in the City of David

Map 8, area C-5

This large water reservoir—along with its adjoining tunnel—is one of the most interesting sites in the Holy Land. King Hezekiah (ruled about 716–686 BC) of Judah constructed the Pool of Siloam, also known as Hezekiah's Pool, about 650 BC. He built it to store water for Jerusalem in case of a prolonged siege by the Assyrian army. This is the same king who shored up other defenses around the city, including the construction of the Broad Wall (see chapter 5, p. 115).

When Hezekiah built this storage pool, it was inside the walls of Jerusalem. But the city's main water source—the Gihon Spring—was outside the city walls. He dealt with this problem by constructing a tunnel to bring water from the spring to the reservoir inside the city. His engineers must have gasped when he

A photograph of the Pool of Hezekiah, dated around 1870.

ordered them to dig this tunnel for more than 1,700 feet through solid rock. This project is considered one of the most remarkable engineering achievements of Bible times.

One group of workmen began digging at the spring, and another group started work at the opposite end near the Pool of Siloam. After what was probably months of back-breaking labor, they met in the middle more than one hundred feet beneath the city. An inscription chiseled into the wall of the tunnel was discovered several years after the tunnel itself was uncovered. This inscription describes the time when the two groups of laborers finally met face-to-face (see sidebar, "A Joyful Meeting in Hezekiah's Tunnel," right).

One puzzling thing about this channel is that it is almost twice as long as the straight-line distance between the spring and the storage pool. Did the workmen take this circuitous route to avoid burial chambers in this section of the city? Did they follow a vein of softer rock to simplify the task? Or did they just dig in a random fashion, since they didn't have modern surveying methods to rely on? No one knows. This remains one of the mysteries of Hezekiah's Tunnel.

If this tunnel impresses modern visitors, just think how people of Hezekiah's time viewed it. The writer of 2 Chronicles ends his summary of this godly king's accomplishments like this: "He blocked up the upper spring of Gihon and brought the water down through a tunnel to the west side of the City of David. And so he succeeded in everything he did" (2 Chronicles 32:30). This seems to imply that the tunnel was considered one of Hezekiah's greatest achievements.

Modern visitors to the Holy Land can walk through this tunnel—if they aren't claustrophobic about tight spots and don't mind wading in knee-deep water. The space is confining—only six feet high by two feet wide—so you have to stay in single file. And be sure to bring an extra pair of shoes to slip on after your forty-five-minute slog through this remarkable shaft.

About seven hundred years after Hezekiah's time, the Pool of Siloam and its tunnel were still in use. One of Jesus' healing miracles took place here. To a pool whose name meant "sent," Jesus sent a blind man for washing and healing after He covered his eyes with mud mixed with His

A modern worker attempts to restore the work of his counterparts from 2,600 years earlier.

own saliva (see sidebar, "Saliva, Mud, and the Pool of Siloam," below).

King Hezekiah built this pool to provide physical water during a national emergency. But Jesus appropriated it for His own purposes. He used it to open the eyes of a blind man and give him living water.

SALIVA, MUD, AND THE POOL OF SILOAM

As Jesus was walking along, he saw a man who had been blind from birth. "Rabbi," his disciples asked him, "why was this man born blind? Was it because of his own sins or his parents' sins?"

"It was not because of his sins or his parents' sins," Jesus answered. "This happened so the power of God could be seen in him. We must quickly carry out the tasks assigned us by the one who sent us. The night is coming, and then no one can work. But while I am here in the world, I am the light of the world."

Then he spit on the ground, made mud with the saliva, and spread the mud over the blind man's eyes. He told him, "Go wash yourself in the pool of Siloam" (Siloam means "sent"). So the man went and washed and came back seeing!

His neighbors and others who knew him as a blind beggar asked each other, "Isn't this the man who used to sit and beg?" Some said he was, and others said, "No, he just looks like him!"

But the beggar kept saying, "Yes, I am the same one!"

They asked, "Who healed you? What happened?"

He told them, "The man they call Jesus made mud and spread it over my eyes and told me, 'Go to the pool of Siloam and wash yourself.' So I went and washed, and now I can see!" (John 9:1–11).

BAHURIM

MEANING "young men"

PRONUNCIATION bah-WHO-rim

SITE AND LOCATION An unidentified village east of Jerusalem near the Mount of Olives

King David passed through this little village on his way out of Jerusalem as he escaped his son Absalom's rebellion. The king was already in a sorrowful mood because of Absalom's attempt to kill him and take over the kingship. But a man named Shimei added insult to injury by cursing and insulting David and throwing rocks at him and his officials.

David's men wanted to kill Shimei because of his slander and disrespect. But David showed remarkable restraint by ignoring the insults. "Leave him alone and let him curse, for the LORD has told him to do it," he replied. "And perhaps the LORD will see that I am being wronged and will bless me because of these curses today" (2 Samuel 16:11–12).

The village of Bahurim has never been identified, but we know that it had a huge well that supplied its inhabitants with water. Two of David's officials hid in this well when Absalom sent out a search party to capture them (see sidebar, "Safe in Bahurim's Well," below).

Some people identify this water source with a modern site known as Job's Well. This shaft, about 125 feet deep, sits at the junction of the Kidron and Hinnom Valleys not far from the walls of the Old City.

SAFE IN BAHURIM'S WELL

Jonathan and Ahimaaz had been staying at En-rogel so as not to be seen entering and leaving the city. Arrangements had been made for a servant girl to bring them the message they were to take to King David. But a boy spotted them at En-rogel, and he told Absalom about it. So they quickly escaped to Bahurim, where a man hid them down inside a well in his courtyard. The man's wife put a cloth over the top of the well and scattered grain on it to dry in the sun; so no one suspected they were there.

When Absalom's men arrived, they asked her, "Have you seen Ahimaaz and Jonathan?"

The woman replied, "They were here, but they crossed over the brook." Absalom's men looked for them without success and returned to Jerusalem.

Then the two men crawled out of the well and hurried on to King David. "Quick!" they told him, "cross the Jordan tonight!" And they told him how Ahithophel had advised that he be captured and killed. So David and all the people with him went across the Jordan River during the night, and they were all on the other bank before dawn (2 Samuel 17:17–22).

CHURCH OF THE PATER NOSTER

| MEANING | "our Father" |

| PRONUNCIATION | PAH-tur NOH-stur |

| SITE AND LOCATION | A church on the Mount of Olives |

This church is built over a cave where Jesus is believed to have taught His disciples the prayer known as the "Lord's Prayer" or the "Model Prayer." It takes its name from the first two words of this prayer in Latin—*Pater Noster* ("our Father").

The tiles on the walls of this cave and the church impress visitors. These tiles feature the Lord's Prayer from Luke 11:2–4 rendered in more than fifty different languages. Almost all known languages appear on these tiles, including little-known dialects such as Aramaic, Chaldean, Guarani, Icelandic, Maltese, Ojibway, Pampango, and Tagalog.

Two versions of the Lord's Prayer appear in the Gospels—a short one in Luke (see sidebar, "Luke's Version of the Model Prayer," below) and a longer one in Matthew (see Matthew 6:9–13). The Luke version appears in the Church of the Pater Noster because it is believed that Jesus taught His disciples this prayer on the Mount of Olives. The setting for Matthew's version was the region of Galilee, where Jesus included the Lord's Prayer in His teachings known as the Sermon on the Mount.

Church of the Pater Noster.

LUKE'S VERSION OF THE MODEL PRAYER

And it came to pass, that, as he was praying in a certain place, when he ceased, one of his disciples said unto him, Lord, teach us to pray, as John also taught his disciples. And he said unto them, When ye pray, say, Our Father which art in heaven, hallowed be thy name. Thy kingdom come. Thy will be done, as in heaven, so in earth. Give us day by day our daily bread. And forgive us our sins; for we also forgive every one that is indebted to us. And lead us not into temptation; but deliver us from evil (Luke 11:1–4 KJV).

DOMINUS FLEVIT CHURCH

MEANING "the Lord wept"

PRONUNCIATION DOME-ih-nus FLEH-vit

SITE AND LOCATION A church on the western slope of the Mount of Olives

This little Roman Catholic church is one of the newest in the city. Built in 1954 in the shape of a teardrop, it commemorates Jesus' weeping over Jerusalem during the closing days of His earthly ministry (see sidebar, "Jerusalem's Plight Moves Jesus to Tears," right). He knew the city would be destroyed in the years to come. This happened in AD 70, about thirty-five years after His crucifixion and resurrection, when the Roman army sacked and burned the city.

The Gospel of Luke tells us that Jesus also wept over Jerusalem for another reason—because of its unbelief and the refusal of its citizens to accept Him as the Messiah. "O Jerusalem, Jerusalem," He cried, "the city that kills the prophets and stones God's messengers! How often I have wanted to gather your children together as a hen protects her chicks beneath her wings, but you wouldn't let me" (Luke 13:34). When Jesus uttered these words, He knew that the Holy City was the place where He would be arrested and executed.

In front of the altar of the Dominus Flevit Church is a mosaic that illustrates these words of Jesus. It shows a mother hen gathering her baby chicks under her wings. The church also has a huge picture window that allows visitors to look out over the Old City below. This panoramic view is similar to what Jesus would have seen from the Mount of Olives when He entered Jerusalem for the last time, just a few days before His death.

One of the most unusual things about the Dominus Flevit Church is that it is surrounded by thousands of ancient tombs. For many centuries the slopes of the Mount of Olives have served as a Jewish cemetery. But this teardrop-shaped building is more than a memorial to bitter tears and the anguish of death. It reminds us of a Savior who was both fully human and fully divine. His tears for Jerusalem were real, but so was the divine power that brought Him out of the grave. He bled real blood like any man, but this blood atoned for our sins and gave us eternal life in His kingdom.

JERUSALEM'S PLIGHT MOVES JESUS TO TEARS

But as he came closer to Jerusalem and saw the city ahead, he began to weep. "How I wish today that you of all people would understand the way to peace. But now it is too late, and peace is hidden from your eyes. Before long your enemies will build ramparts against your walls and encircle you and close in on you from every side. They will crush you into the ground, and your children with you. Your enemies will not leave a single stone in place, because you did not accept your opportunity for salvation" (Luke 19:41–44).

Jesus Wept by Tissot.

GORDON'S CALVARY AND THE GARDEN TOMB

A rocky hill with a nearby burial cave just outside the northern section of the walls of the Old City

The Garden Tomb.

Sometimes feelings are just as important as facts and ancient tradition when it comes to deciding on the authenticity of sacred sites in the Holy Land. At least, this seems to be the case with Gordon's Calvary and the Garden Tomb. Many Christians believe these sites—both outside the city walls—are the places where the crucifixion and resurrection of Jesus took place. This view challenges the 1,600-year-old tradition that these sites are marked by an ancient church that sits inside the walls of the Old City (see "Church of the Holy Sepulchre," chapter 5, p. 111).

For years many Protestant and evangelical Christians came away disappointed after viewing these sites within the Church of the Holy Sepulchre. They were turned off by the church's ritualistic tone. Also troubling was the competitive spirit among the six religious groups assigned jurisdiction over these holy sites. To the Protestant and evangelical mind, there had to be another site—quiet, serene, and simple—where Jesus died for our sins and burst the bonds of the grave.

The answer to the longing of these people came in the form of a British general named Charles Gordon. While visiting Jerusalem in 1863, he spotted a rocky hill just outside the walls of the Old City. Noting that this hill resembled a human skull, he remarked to his traveling companion, "That looks just like Calvary." Gordon knew his Bible. According to the Gospel writers, the Latin word *Calvary* and its Aramaic equivalent, *Golgotha*—the site where Jesus was crucified—mean "place of the skull" (see Mark 15:22; Luke 23:33; John 19:17).

Other Holy Land visitors before Gordon had noticed this hill and recognized its unusual features. But Gordon popularized the site through his writing and lectures, so it came to be called "Gordon's Calvary." The rocky hill is about fifty feet high. It has two deep crevices that resemble eye sockets, particularly when the light hits the hill just right. Just below the "eye sockets" is another formation that resembles a human nose.

So much for the place of Jesus' crucifixion, but what about the site where He was buried and resurrected? The Gospel of John tells us that His tomb was "close at hand" (John 19:42), possibly near the execution site. After the discovery and popularization of Gordon's Calvary, excavations were conducted around the hill. Here the remains of a garden with an empty tomb were discovered. Immediately, eager Protestants and evangelicals accepted this as Jesus' burial site, and it was dubbed the "Garden Tomb."

Thousands of pilgrims visit Gordon's Calvary and the Garden Tomb every year. Unlike the dim, cramped interior of the Church of the Holy Sepulchre, these sites have the setting of a beautiful garden to commend them as places of prayer and meditation. The broad courtyard around the Garden Tomb also makes it an ideal place where large groups can gather for Bible study, prayer, and singing.

But before we get too carried away with these two sites, let's set our emotions aside and face a few facts. Nowhere do the Gospels say specifically that Jesus was crucified on a hill. They refer to the execution site only as "a place" or "the place" (see Matthew 27:33; Mark 15:22; Luke 23:33; John 19:17). And scientific study of the Garden Tomb shows that it was used as a burial site in

NO RELICS NEEDED

In all probability, the actual spot where Jesus died lies buried several feet under the accumulated ruins of the city of Jerusalem. The rugged mountain represented in sacred pictures is as purely imaginary as the skull of Adam, which is often painted lying at the foot of the cross. This goes for all the other legends that have gathered around this most stupendous and moving scene in the history of the world.

All that we know about Golgotha is that it was outside the city gate. The religion of Christ is spiritual; it needs no relic; it is independent of holy places; it says to each of its children, not "Lo, here" and "Lo, there" but "The kingdom of God is within you."

—Frederic W. Farrar, *The Life of Christ*

Gordon's Calvary.

Old Testament times. The Gospel of John says clearly that Jesus' body was placed in a new tomb where no person had ever been buried (see John 19:41).

Perhaps we are majoring on minors when we try to pinpoint the exact site of Jesus' death, burial, and resurrection. After all, this is not as important as the fact that He died for us, rose from the grave, and continues to abide with us as our living Savior and victorious Lord. Frederic Farrar came to this conclusion in the late 1800s after visiting both sites in Jerusalem that claim to be the place where Jesus was lifted up on the cross (see sidebar, "No Relics Needed," p. 139).

TOMB OF KING DAVID

This holy site is located in one of the most interesting buildings in Jerusalem. It has something to offer Christians, Jews, and Muslims. David's tomb is considered a Jewish shrine, since he is one of Israel's great heroes. But his tomb sits in the lower floor of a Christian church that was built several centuries ago.

The supposed tomb of King David among the buildings of Jerusalem in 1903.

And the irony doesn't end there. Go up one floor, and you find yourself at the traditional site of the Upper Room, where Jesus celebrated the Memorial Supper with His disciples (see "The Upper Room," p. 141). And one floor higher will take you to a Muslim mosque! This is one of the few places in the world where sites that these three great religions consider sacred are grouped together under the same roof.

When you enter the ground floor of the building, you find yourself in an anteroom (a waiting room) decorated with colorful tiles. Beyond this area is another room where the actual tomb sits. But this is as close as you can get to it; this room is sealed off with iron bars. Draped in a red cloth, the tomb is inscribed with writings in the Hebrew language. This is your first hint that the Jewish people considered this an especially sacred site.

The second hint hits you when you enter an adjoining room known as the King David Museum. All the placards on the exhibits are written in Hebrew.

This is a departure from the English descriptions you will find in most of the other museums in Israel.

Experts agree that this tomb does not contain the remains of Israel's most popular king. It has never been subjected to scientific analysis to determine its age or whether it contains a corpse at all. They believe David's tomb was probably destroyed during a Jewish rebellion and that its exact location was forgotten. Over the centuries, popular tradition suggested various sites. Finally, this site on Mount Zion came to be accepted as David's burial site.

This beloved king of Israel died about 970 BC after leading his people for forty years (see 1 Kings 2:10–11). It's possible that the actual site of his tomb in Jerusalem was known for about one thousand years after that. In about AD 35, the apostle Peter preached a powerful sermon about the crucified Christ in Jerusalem. He told the crowd that David "died and was buried, and his tomb is still here among us" (Acts 2:29).

Did Peter mean that David's tomb was clearly visible at that time? No one knows. This is one of those mysteries that keeps Bible students from adopting a know-it-all attitude.

THE UPPER ROOM

SITE AND LOCATION **A large room in a three-story building on**
Mount Zion Map 8, area B-5

Inside the Cenoculum.

This site is on the second floor of a building that also houses the tomb of David (see p. 140). Here Jesus and His disciples ate the Last Supper together on the night before He was arrested (see sidebar, "A Final Meal with Jesus," p. 142).

The room where the Last Supper is reputed to have taken place is known as the Cenoculum, a Latin word meaning "dinner." It is a large, rectangular room with several floor-to-ceiling arches that sit on huge stone pillars. The structure was apparently built in the twelfth Christian century during the Crusades, a campaign by Christian pilgrims to take Jerusalem by force from the Muslims. It is the successor to several other buildings that have been erected on the site since at least the AD 300s.

A little shrine adjacent to the Upper Room is known as the Chapel of the Holy Spirit. An ancient Christian tradition claims that this room marks the place where the Holy Spirit descended upon early believers on the day of Pentecost (see Acts 2:1–12).

The Cenoculum is not the only place in Jerusalem reputed to be the site of the Upper Room. The little Church of Saint Mark inside the walls of the Old City also lays claim to this honor. It contains a stone inscription that testifies to early believers' reverence for this spot. The little church belongs to the Syriac Orthodox Church, a group with a presence in the Holy Land that dates back to the early centuries of the Christian movement.

A FINAL MEAL WITH JESUS

Jesus said, "I have been very eager to eat this Passover meal with you before my suffering begins. For I tell you now that I won't eat this meal again until its meaning is fulfilled in the Kingdom of God."

Then he took a cup of wine and gave thanks to God for it. Then he said, "Take this and share it among yourselves. For I will not drink wine again until the Kingdom of God has come."

He took some bread and gave thanks to God for it. Then he broke it in pieces and gave it to the disciples, saying, "This is my body, which is given for you. Do this to remember me."

After supper he took another cup of wine and said, "This cup is the new covenant between God and his people—an agreement confirmed with my blood, which is poured out as a sacrifice for you" (Luke 22:15–20).

SAINT PETER IN GALLICANTU CHURCH

MEANING   "the cock's crow"

PRONUNCIATION   gal-lee-CAN-too

SITE AND LOCATION   A church on the slopes of the Mount of Olives

The present church by this name has existed since 1931. But it is the successor to another church of the same name that stood on this site in the twelfth century. That church, in turn, was the successor to another church on the same site that was built in AD 475. Thus, Saint Peter's Church has occupied the same site for more than 1,500 years. Where but in Jerusalem would you expect to find such an unbroken succession of churches?

As its name implies, Saint Peter in Gallicantu claims to occupy the site where Peter denied Jesus on the night He was arrested. This disciple of Jesus had sworn just a few hours before that he would remain faithful to Jesus until the bitter end (see Matthew 26:33). At least he did follow Jesus to the courtyard of the high priest Caiaphas, where Jesus had been taken for trial. But when questioned about his association with Jesus, Peter denied that he knew Him. When he heard a rooster crow, Peter realized the bitter truth that he had failed to keep his promise (see sidebar, "Peter's Triple 'I Don't Know Him,'" right).

All four Gospels record Peter's infamous denial (see Matthew 26:69–75; Mark 14:66–72; Luke 22:54–62; John 18:15–27). In the courtyard of the Gallicantu church is a carving that shows the four major ingredients of this dramatic event: Peter, the rooster, the young girl, and the Roman soldier who questioned Peter.

Underneath the church are caves that were carved into the rock beneath the streets of the houses of Roman-era Jerusalem. These caverns were used as cisterns and storage compartments. On the north side of the church is an ancient stone stairway that leads down toward the Kidron Valley. This passage dates back to Old Testament times, but where it led and the reason for its existence are unknown.

Saint Peter in Gallicantu Church.

In Carl Bloch's painting Jesus looks on as Peter denies knowing Him.

PETER'S TRIPLE "I DON'T KNOW HIM"

So they arrested him [Jesus] and led him to the high priest's home. And Peter followed at a distance. The guards lit a fire in the middle of the courtyard and sat around it, and Peter joined them there. A servant girl noticed him in the firelight and began staring at him. Finally she said, "This man was one of Jesus' followers!"

But Peter denied it. "Woman," he said, "I don't even know him!"

After a while someone else looked at him and said, "You must be one of them!"

"No, man, I'm not!" Peter retorted.

About an hour later someone else insisted, "This must be one of them, because he is a Galilean, too."

But Peter said, "Man, I don't know what you are talking about." And immediately, while he was still speaking, the rooster crowed.

At that moment the Lord turned and looked at Peter. Suddenly, the Lord's words flashed through Peter's mind: "Before the rooster crows tomorrow morning, you will deny three times that you even know me." And Peter left the courtyard, weeping bitterly (Luke 22:54–62).

AKELDAMA

MEANING "field of blood"

PRONUNCIATION ah-kell-DAH-muh

SITE AND LOCATION A field in the Hinnom Valley near the City of David

This site is perhaps the most infamous place in Jerusalem because of its association with Judas, the disciple who betrayed Jesus (see Luke 22:1–6). Here on this site he committed suicide because of remorse over his heinous act (see sidebar, "How Judas's Blood Money Was Spent," p. 145).

Akeldama is an Aramaic word that means "field of blood." This word appears in the account of Judas's suicide in the book of Acts (see Acts 1:18–19).

The field bought with his blood money is also referred to as the potter's field, possibly because first-century potters in Jerusalem used it as a dumping ground.

Matthew's account of this event states that the Jewish religious leaders turned the property bought with this money into a cemetery for the burial of strangers. Excavations conducted on the site have revealed that it was, indeed, a burial site for many centuries, beginning with the first Christian century. These excavations were conducted in 1989, when construction workers on the site uncovered several huge caves that had been used as burial chambers.

On a cliff above the site of Akeldama stands a Greek Orthodox monastery that was built in the 1800s. It is dedicated to Saint Onuphrius, a monk who lived in the desert during the fourth century.

The entrance to the monastery at Akeldama.

HOW JUDAS'S BLOOD MONEY WAS SPENT

When Judas, who had betrayed him [Jesus], realized that Jesus had been condemned to die, he was filled with remorse. So he took the thirty pieces of silver back to the leading priests and the elders. "I have sinned," he declared, "for I have betrayed an innocent man."

"What do we care?" they retorted. "That's your problem."

Then Judas threw the silver coins down in the Temple and went out and hanged himself.

The leading priests picked up the coins. "It wouldn't be right to put this money in the Temple treasury," they said, "since it was payment for murder." After some discussion they finally decided to buy the potter's field, and they made it into a cemetery for foreigners. That is why the field is still called the Field of Blood. This fulfilled the prophecy of Jeremiah that says, "They took the thirty pieces of silver—the price at which he was valued by the people of Israel, and purchased the potter's field, as the LORD directed" (Matthew 27:3–10).

The pieces of silver, in this painting by Rembrandt, are on the floor. Judas is pleading with the priests to take them back—but no one wants to touch the tainted coins.

MONASTERY OF THE CROSS

SITE AND LOCATION A monastery near the Israel Museum in the southwestern section of modern Jerusalem

This Greek Orthodox monastery looks like a fortress from the Middle Ages. This imagery is all the more dramatic because of its contrast with its modern surroundings. When the monastery was first built more than eight hundred years ago, it was in a remote location about three miles from the Old City. But Jerusalem's modern suburban growth has surrounded it. Now it sits in one of the city's more affluent neighborhoods.

According to an ancient Eastern Orthodox tradition, this monastery marks the site of the tree that was made into Jesus' cross. They believe Abraham gave a seedling to Lot, who planted it here and nurtured it with water from the Jordan River. This seedling eventually grew into the tree used to create the cross on which Jesus was crucified.

Inside the monastery is a room that marks the site where the tree once stood. Several paintings around the room tell the story of what the monks refer to as the "holy tree."

CHURCH OF ALL NATIONS

SITE AND LOCATION **A church at the foot of the Mount of Olives**

No tour of the Holy Land is complete without a visit to this magnificent church. Its medieval-style architecture and beautiful mosaics have been compared to the grand cathedrals of Europe. And its association with Jesus' final hours before He was arrested makes it a rewarding stop for thousands of Christian pilgrims every year.

The popular name for this structure is the Church of All Nations. This title recognizes the contributions that came from several countries of the world to enable the Catholic order known as the Franciscans to build the church in 1924 (see sidebar, "Contributor Countries to the Church of All Nations," p. 147). But it is also known as the Church of the Agony or Basilica of the Agony. This name commemorates Jesus' agonizing prayer in the nearby Garden of Gethsemane (see p. 147) as He faced His impending death.

Above the painting of Jesus on the front of the church are two Greek letters, alpha and omega. These symbolize Jesus as the Lord of all creation, the first and the last, the beginning and the ending (see Revelation 1:8). Inside the church, a painting at the altar shows Jesus in prayer, flanked by ancient olive trees in the Garden of Gethsemane. On the front is a flat rock, said

A more modern Rock of the Agony at the Church of all Nations.

to be the holy rock of agony on which Jesus knelt to pray. The rock is surrounded by a wrought iron crown of thorns, symbolizing the mock crown Roman soldiers placed on His head (see Mark 15:17).

The ceiling of the church is painted a deep blue to simulate the night sky beneath which Jesus prayed. Adding to this effect are the violet-colored glass tiles used throughout the building and the unusual blue windows. These evoke Jesus' somber mood as He faced the cross.

While the modern Church of All Nations is less than one hundred years old, it rests on the foundations of two earlier churches—one built in the 1100s, preceded by another dating back to the fourth century.

CONTRIBUTOR COUNTRIES TO THE CHURCH OF ALL NATIONS

Argentina
Australia
Belgium
Brazil
Canada
Chile
France
Germany
Hungary
Ireland
Italy
Mexico
Poland
Spain
United Kingdom
United States

GARDEN OF GETHSEMANE

MEANING "oil press" or "olive press"

PRONUNCIATION geth-SIMM-uh-nee

SITE AND LOCATION A garden on the Mount of Olives

Map 8, area E-2

This tranquil garden occupies a section of the courtyard of the Church of All Nations (see p. 146). Most Christian pilgrims to the Holy Land visit both these sites at the same time. The garden with its ancient olive trees is reputed to be the site where Jesus agonized in prayer on the night when Judas betrayed Him and the Jewish Sanhedrin arrested Him.

A marker said to indicate the place where the disciples slept in Gethsemane.

The Gospels give us enough details to piece together the events of this Thursday night before Jesus' crucifixion the next day (see Matthew 26:14–56; Mark 14:10–50; Luke 22:1–53; John 13:1–38; 18:1–10). First, He ate the Passover meal with His disciples on Mount Zion, turning this into a memorial supper to mark His approaching death (see "The Upper Room," p. 141).

Then Jesus and His disciples left Jerusalem and walked across the Kidron Valley to the Mount of Olives (see Mark 14:26). Somewhere on this mountain, He went into a garden called Gethsemane, probably so named because of a nearby press for producing olive oil (see Matthew 26:36). It is possible that Jesus knew the owner of this garden and had his permission to use it as a place where He could withdraw for prayer and meditation.

The Garden of Gethsemane.

When we focus on Jesus in this garden, we get a full-blown look at the human side of His God-man nature. He knew the cross was His destiny and thus a part of God's plan for the salvation of the world. But He still shuddered at the thought of dying. He needed the support of His three closest disciples—Peter, James, and John—to help Him through this traumatic time. But they fell asleep without uttering a word of encouragement.

Jesus had to face His darkest hour without any help from His friends. But He conquered temptation and fear with the words that make Gethsemane one of the most sacred spots on earth. "If this cup cannot be taken away unless I drink it," He prayed to His Father, "your will be done" (Matthew 26:42).

To modern visitors, the most striking feature of this little garden is its ancient olive trees. These are probably not the actual trees that grew here in Jesus' time. But they could have sprung from the roots of old trees from that era. Whether or not they can be traced to the first century, their gnarled and weathered trunks remind us of the agony that Jesus experienced when He prayed on this site almost two thousand years ago. To visit Gethsemane is to reflect on the suffering that Jesus endured on our behalf.

This mood of reflection is how Henry van Dyke, an American Presbyterian minister, described his feelings when he visited the Garden of Gethsemane in the early 1900s (see sidebar, "Feeling the Presence of Jesus in Gethsemane," below).

FEELING THE PRESENCE OF JESUS IN GETHSEMANE

It is here, in this quaint and carefully tended garden, that we find for the first time what we have come so far to seek—the soul of the Holy Land, the sense of the real presence of Jesus. Nothing that we have yet seen in Palestine—no vision of wide-spread landscape, no sight of ancient ruin or famous building or treasured relic—comes as close to our hearts as this little garden sleeping in the sun.

Here Jesus learned the frailty of human friendship, the narrowness, dullness, and coldness of the very hearts for whom He had done and suffered most. His disciples could not even keep watch and pray with Him for one hour.

But Jesus met and overcame the spirit of despair in the Garden of Gethsemane. After that meeting the cross had no terror for Him because He had already endured it. The grave held no fear because He had already conquered it. How calm and gentle was the voice with which He awakened His disciples, how firm the step with which He went to meet Judas. He left the bitterness of death behind Him in the shadow of the olive trees. The peace of heaven twinkled above Him in the silent stars.

—Henry van Dyke, *Out of Doors in the Holy Land*

CHURCH OF MARY MAGDALENE

MEANING   Mary Magdalene = "Mary of Magdala"

PRONUNCIATION   mag-duh-LEE-nih

SITE AND LOCATION   A church near the base of the Mount of Olives

You may have to pinch yourself to make sure you are not in Russia when you see this church. It has seven gilded, onion-shaped domes that look just like those on the ancient churches in downtown Moscow. Its lavish architecture is unique to the Russian Orthodox Church, an independent branch of the Eastern Orthodox Church.

This church commemorates Mary Magdalene, the woman out of whom Jesus cast seven demons (see Mark 16:9). She was present at the crucifixion and was one of the first followers of Jesus to see Him after His resurrection (see sidebar, "Jesus Greets Mary Magdalene at the Empty Tomb," below).

JESUS GREETS MARY MAGDALENE AT THE EMPTY TOMB

She [Mary Magdalene] turned to leave and saw someone standing there. It was Jesus, but she didn't recognize him. "Dear woman, why are you crying?" Jesus asked her. "Who are you looking for?"

She thought he was the gardener. "Sir," she said, "if you have taken him away, tell me where you have put him, and I will go and get him."

"Mary!" Jesus said.

She turned to him and cried out, "Rabboni!" (which is Hebrew for "Teacher").

"Don't cling to me," Jesus said, "for I haven't yet ascended to the Father. But go find my brothers and tell them, 'I am ascending to my Father and your Father, to my God and your God.'"

Mary Magdalene found the disciples and told them, "I have seen the Lord!" Then she gave them his message (John 20:14–18).

The Church of Mary Magdalene.

CHURCH OF AUGUSTA VICTORIA

PRONUNCIATION Aw-GUSS-tuh Vic-TOE-rih-uh

SITE AND LOCATION A church on the northern side of the
Mount of Olives

This church, with its impressive bell tower, overlooks the Old City like a silent sentinel. It is interesting and unusual for two reasons. First, Augusta Victoria is one of the few Protestant churches in Jerusalem. And second, it is not dedicated to any saint, nor does it claim to occupy any holy site. After seeing so many churches named for saints or built on sacred soil, many visitors to Jerusalem find this a refreshing change of pace.

Like its sister church in the Old City (see "Church of the Redeemer," chapter 5, p. 127), the Church of Augusta Victoria is a Lutheran congregation.

It was built in the early 1900s and named for the wife of the German emperor Kaiser Wilhelm II.

This church's bell tower, a noted Jerusalem landmark, is almost two hundred feet tall. From its summit, hardy visitors who climb all the way up are rewarded with a beautiful view of the city and the surrounding countryside.

The Church of Augusta Victoria.

The dome of Bethlehem's Church of the Nativity.

CHAPTER 7

When you visit Jerusalem, you will see many holy places inside the walls of the Old City (see chapter 5) and several others just outside the city walls (see chapter 6). But only a few miles beyond the Holy City are several other key sites you shouldn't miss. These range from Bethlehem, just six miles south of Jerusalem, to Gibeon, about the same distance to the north (see map 5). Some of the most important events in the Bible took place in these towns that were within easy walking distance of Jerusalem.

BETHLEHEM

MEANING "house of bread"

PRONUNCIATION BETH-luh-him

SITE AND LOCATION A city about six miles south of Jerusalem
Map 5, area D-5

The birth of Jesus in Bethlehem was such an important event in world history that you would expect the Bible to devote a lot of attention to it. But only the Gospels of Matthew and Luke have anything to say about it. And the main account in Luke's Gospel in the King James Version contains fewer than 150 words (see sidebar, "Jesus Is Born in Bethlehem," p. 157).

This brief, to-the-point account shows that big things often come in small packages. This flies in the face of the worldly view that important events require a lot of hype. It's true, Luke's Gospel tells us, that Jesus was born in humble surroundings in a small, insignificant village. But this is just the beginning of the story. This little baby of Bethlehem was destined to change the world.

When Mary and Joseph arrived in Bethlehem, it was probably a village of

U.S. President Bush during a vist to the Church of the Nativity.

just a few hundred people. The town was packed with other descendants of David who had come to register for Caesar's taxation census, and no rooms were available in the village inn. So the young parents-in-waiting had to settle in with the animals in a nearby stable. Here is where Jesus was born, and here is where Mary placed Him in a feeding trough as a makeshift crib.

Most modern visitors to Bethlehem are surprised to learn that the stable said to be Jesus' birthplace is actually a cave. This birth cave is located beneath the fortress-like Church of the Nativity in the middle of the town.

This site is not as farfetched as it seems. The area around Bethlehem contains scores of caves. Caverns like this were often used to store goods and to shelter animals in Bible times. So it is possible that the stable in which Joseph and Mary lodged was an adjoining cave where the animals of the inn's guests were kept.

Early Christian tradition also holds that Jesus was born in a cave. As early as about AD 150, the Christian writer Justin Martyr stated that Joseph and Mary were staying in a cave on the night of Jesus' birth. Other Christian figures who followed Martyr supported this claim. The first church in Bethlehem was built in AD 335 over the cavern said to be the place where Jesus was born.

Whether or not this is Jesus' actual birth site, we do know that the present Church of the Nativity is one of the oldest churches in the world. Parts of the original structure built more than 1,600 years ago are still visible in the more "modern" church that was built about 200 years later. The second church—the current Church of the Nativity—incorporated elements from the original building on the site.

Both churches owe their longevity to a prominent mosaic on the outside of the current building. It shows the wise men from the East who brought gifts to Jesus, and they are depicted in Persian attire. This apparently caused Muslim invaders on several different occasions to pass up the Church of the Nativity while they were destroying other churches or turning them into Muslim mosques.

Like the Church of the Holy Sepulchre in Jerusalem (see chapter 5, p. 111), several different Christian groups administer Bethlehem's Church of the Nativity. Representatives of these various groups escort Holy Land pilgrims from one part of the church to another. In addition to the Grotto (Cave) of the Nativity, visitors are shown the cave where Jerome (c. AD 345–420) spent thirty years translating the Hebrew and Greek scriptures into his Latin Vulgate Bible. This version was the only Bible of Christians of the Middle Ages until John Wycliffe and others did their translation work on the English Bible, beginning in the late 1300s.

Several other sites near Bethlehem are also worth a visit. They include the following:

MILK GROTTO. This site, a short distance from the Church of the Nativity, is said to be the place where Jesus and His parents hid from the death order of King Herod before their flight into Egypt (see Matthew 2:13–16). Its name comes from the milk that dropped on the floor while Mary was nursing the infant Jesus.

The Milk Grotto.

SHEPHERDS' FIELDS AND FIELDS OF BOAZ. This plot of land on the outskirts of Bethlehem is reputed to be the place where angels announced the birth of Jesus to lowly shepherds (see Luke 2:8–14). This is the same field where Naomi gleaned behind the harvesters in the grain fields of Boaz (see Ruth 2:1–3).

RACHEL'S TOMB. This little shrine with a white dome sits beside the main road from Jerusalem to Bethlehem. It supposedly marks the spot where Rachel, one of Jacob's wives, was buried. Jacob placed a stone monument over her grave (see Genesis 35:19–20). The present building on the site was erected in the twelfth century AD.

MAR SABA MONASTERY. *Solitude* is the word that comes to mind when you see this monastery near Bethlehem. Greek Orthodox monks built it into the side of a high mountain so they could live a quiet life of prayer and contemplation. Founded about 1,500 years ago, it is one of the oldest still-inhabited monasteries in the world.

Mar Saba monastery.

POOLS OF SOLOMON. These ancient water reservoirs have nothing to do with King Solomon, but they are still an impressive engineering achievement. About two miles southwest of Bethlehem, they were built several centuries after Solomon's time to ensure an adequate supply of water for Jerusalem and Bethlehem. The entire complex—three huge storage pools fed by four different springs—covers about seven acres. Water was trapped and stored here, then channeled to its final destination by an ingenious system of aqueducts.

These pools take their name from their erroneous identification with these words of Solomon in the Bible: "I built reservoirs to collect the water to irrigate my many flourishing groves" (Ecclesiastes 2:6).

Solomon's Pools, pictured around 1930.

JESUS IS BORN IN BETHLEHEM

And it came to pass in those days, that there went out a decree from Caesar Augustus that all the world should be taxed. (And this taxing was first made when Cyrenius was governor of Syria.) And all went to be taxed, every one into his own city.

And Joseph also went up from Galilee, out of the city of Nazareth, into Judaea, unto the city of David, which is called Bethlehem; (because he was of the house and lineage of David:) to be taxed with Mary his espoused wife, being great with child.

And so it was, that, while they were there, the days were accomplished that she should be delivered. And she brought forth her firstborn son, and wrapped him in swaddling clothes, and laid him in a manger; because there was no room for them in the inn (Luke 2:1–7 KJV).

BETHLEHEM: A BIBLICAL SNAPSHOT

- Bethlehem was also known as Ephrath (Genesis 35:19), Bethlehem Ephratah (Micah 5:2), and Bethlehem-judah (see Judges 19:1 KJV).
- This town was the birthplace and home of King David. It was often referred to as "the city of David" (see 1 Samuel 17:15; Luke 2:4 KJV).
- Here Samuel anointed David to succeed Saul as king of Israel (1 Samuel 16:1–13).
- Naomi gleaned in the fields of Boaz near Bethlehem (see Ruth 2:1–3).
- The prophet Micah predicted that the Messiah would be born in Bethlehem (see Micah 5:2–5).
- Jacob's wife Rachel was buried somewhere near Bethlehem (see Genesis 35:16–20).
- Shepherds just outside Bethlehem journeyed to the town to see the newborn Messiah (see Luke 2:15–20).
- Wise men from the East brought gifts to Jesus in Bethlehem (see Matthew 2:1–12).

BETHANY

MEANING "house of unripe figs"

PRONUNCIATION BETH-ah-nee

SITE AND LOCATION A village about two miles east of Jerusalem
Map 6, area C-6

Bethany will always be remembered as the town where a man named Lazarus walked out of his tomb at a simple command from his friend Jesus (see sidebar, "Lazarus, Come Out!" p. 159). This event electrified the crowd, and news about it spread quickly to nearby Jerusalem. It was a happening that the religious elite of Israel could not ignore. From that day forward, they began to plot how they could have Jesus killed (see John 11:45–54).

It's interesting that Bethany is not mentioned in the Old Testament. It probably developed into a village in the shadow of Jerusalem just a few decades before Jesus was born.

And just as interesting is that Bethany is always mentioned in the New Testament in connection with a visit of Jesus to this little town. It was clearly a place where He withdrew for rest and relaxation. Here He probably spent many hours in the company of His close friend Lazarus and his two sisters, Mary and Martha. When He visited Jerusalem, He sometimes stopped in Bethany to spend the night, perhaps at their home (see Matthew 21:17).

At Bethany, Jesus delivered a gentle rebuke to Martha when she complained that her sister was talking to Him rather than helping her in the kitchen. "My dear Martha, you are worried and upset over all these details!" He told her. "There is only one thing worth being concerned about. Mary has discovered it, and it will not be taken away from her" (Luke 10:41–42).

According to the Gospel of John, it was this same Mary of Bethany who anointed Jesus with expensive perfume just a few days before His crucifixion (see John 12:1–8). Mark's Gospel also records this event. But according to Mark's account, a woman of

The supposed tomb of Lazarus in Bethany.

questionable reputation performed the anointing, and it took place in Bethany—and at the house of Simon the leper (see Mark 14:3–9).

Bethany is also a holy site because here is where Jesus gave the disciples His final blessing before He ascended into heaven (see Luke 24:50–51). The book of Acts also records this event, but it names the site of the ascension as the Mount of Olives only half a mile from the city of Jerusalem (see Acts 1:9–12). This is clearly not as far from the Holy City as from the town of Bethany. So the Mount of Olives site, marked by the Catholic Chapel of the Ascension, is accepted as the traditional site where Jesus ended His earthly ministry. Standing nearby on the Mount of Olives is a Russian Orthodox church that also claims to mark the place where Jesus ascended into heaven.

The town of Bethany today is known by its Arabic name, el Azariyeh—a name derived from Lazarus. Years ago it had only a few permanent residents. But it has grown in recent years into a town of more than fifteen thousand Muslims and Arab Christians. There is little doubt that this town is the successor to the small village of Bethany where Jesus raised Lazarus from the dead.

A Catholic Franciscan church, known as the Church of Saint Lazarus, which was built on the site in 1955, commemorates this famous biblical event. It sits on the remains of several other churches that were built successively on this spot across several centuries. Inside the church are mosaics depicting Jesus raising Lazarus, His anointing by Mary, and Lazarus with his two sisters.

Just up the hill from the church, visitors walk down several crude stone steps into a gloomy underground chamber that has been venerated for centuries as the tomb of Lazarus. This may not be the actual tomb, but it is typical of burial chambers from the time of Jesus.

LAZARUS, COME OUT!

When Jesus saw her [Mary] weeping and saw the other people wailing with her, a deep anger welled up within him, and he was deeply troubled. "Where have you put him?" he asked them.

They told him, "Lord, come and see." Then Jesus wept. The people who were standing nearby said, "See how much he loved him!" But some said, "This man healed a blind man. Couldn't he have kept Lazarus from dying?"

Jesus was still angry as he arrived at the tomb, a cave with a stone rolled across its entrance. "Roll the stone aside," Jesus told them.

But Martha, the dead man's sister, protested, "Lord, he has been dead for four days. The smell will be terrible."

Jesus responded, "Didn't I tell you that you would see God's glory if you believe?" So they rolled the stone aside. Then Jesus looked up to heaven and said, "Father, thank you for hearing me. You always hear me, but I said it out loud for the sake of all these people standing here, so that they will believe you sent me." Then Jesus shouted, "Lazarus, come out!" And the dead man came out, his hands and feet bound in graveclothes, his face wrapped in a headcloth. Jesus told them, "Unwrap him and let him go!" (John 11:33–44).

A very appreciative Lazarus greets his Savior in this painting by Jan Pynas.

BETHPHAGE

MEANING "house of unripe figs"

PRONUNCIATION beth-FAY-jeh

SITE AND LOCATION An unidentified village near Bethany about two miles south of Jerusalem
Map 6, area C-6

This may be the only village in the world made famous by a donkey. Jesus sent two of His disciples into Bethphage to find a young donkey on which He could make His triumphal entry into Jerusalem. Apparently He had made prior arrangements to borrow the animal from someone in this little town—perhaps one of His followers. He instructed His disciples to tell the owners, "The Lord needs it" (Luke 19:31), if they were asked why they were taking the animal. This reply seemed to satisfy the donkey's owners (see Luke 19:34).

The actual site of Bethphage is unknown. But tradition places it on the Mount of Olives near the town of Bethany. This traditional site is marked by a Catholic Franciscan chapel known as the Church of Bethphage. Inside the church is a beautiful painting depicting Jesus riding a donkey into Jerusalem while the crowds place palm leaves and items of clothing on the ground to form a path for His triumphal entry.

Also on this site is a relic called the Stone of Mounting, said to be the rock that Jesus stood on to mount the donkey. Actually, a stone like this would not have been necessary. Jesus could easily have gotten on the young animal from level ground without any assistance.

Inside the Church of Bethphage.

More important to the Gospel writers than the so-called Mounting Stone is that Jesus' ride into Jerusalem fulfilled biblical prophecy. Centuries before Jesus came into the world, the prophet Zechariah declared about the Messiah, "Rejoice, O people of Zion! Shout in triumph, O people of Jerusalem! Look, your king is coming to you. He is righteous and victorious, yet he is humble, riding on a donkey—riding on a donkey's colt" (Zechariah 9:9).

The Gospels of Matthew and John quoted this prophecy in connection with Jesus' triumphant but humble ride into the Holy City (see Matthew 21:5; John 12:15).

GIBEAH

MEANING "hill"

PRONUNCIATION gibb-ee-AH

SITE AND LOCATION A city about three miles northwest of Jerusalem
Map 5, area D-4

This city is notable because of its association with Saul, first king of Israel. Here he was born in the territory of the tribe of Benjamin, and here he established his headquarters after the prophet Samuel anointed him to lead the other tribes (see 1 Samuel 10:1–26; 15:34). Before Saul, the nation had no central ruler; each of the twelve tribes looked after its own affairs in a loose confederacy form of government.

Most scholars identify ancient Gibeah with the ruins known as Tel el-Ful. Excavations at this site have uncovered the remains of four fortresses, each built on the ruins of the others. Several tribes of Israel may have destroyed the original fortress during a civil war against the tribe of Benjamin (see Judges 20:12–48). Above these ruins were the remains of a later fortress that could be one King Saul built to provide protection against his Philistine enemies. During Saul's reign, he was at constant war with this aggressive people, who tried to extend their settlements into Israelite territory.

When modern Holy Land visitors see the ruins of Gibeah, they understand the meaning behind its name—"hill." The city's hilltop location made it easy to defend, and it gave its defenders a panoramic view of the surrounding countryside. On this hill, according to the Jewish historian Josephus, the Roman army camped in AD 70 on the night before it launched its siege against the nearby city of Jerusalem.

A hiker rests on ruins of Saul's fortress at Gibeah.

NOB

MEANING   unknown

PRONUNCIATION   nohb

SITE AND LOCATION   An unidentified town about two miles from Jerusalem

Map 5, area D-5

This town shows King Saul, the first king of Israel, at his worst. He ordered the slaughter of eighty-five priests who lived here because one of them had assisted David and his men as they fled from Saul's wrath (see 1 Samuel 22:9–18). But Saul didn't stop with this senseless slaughter. He wanted to send the message that anyone who assisted David would be dealt with as a traitor. So he sent his assassins to Nob to wipe out the families of these priests, as well as "all the cattle, donkeys, sheep, and goats" (1 Samuel 22:19).

The king was enraged because Ahimelech, one of the priests at Nob, had provided food for David and his men. Ahimelech also gave David a weapon—the sword David had used to kill the Philistine giant Goliath—to use in his defense (see 1 Samuel 21:6–9). These provisions allowed David to escape from Saul, who was determined to kill him because he represented a threat to his kingship.

Apparently the tabernacle was located in the priestly city of Nob at this time. The food Ahimelech gave David was sacred bread known as showbread. It consisted of twelve loaves placed in the sanctuary of the tabernacle every Sabbath to symbolize God's provision for His people. Normally the priests and their families ate the old loaves after they were replaced by fresh-baked bread. But Ahimelech felt that an exception to this ritual was justified because of David's need.

About a thousand years later, Jesus cited this principle of human need versus ritualism when He referred to Ahimelech's kindness to David at Nob. The Pharisees had criticized Jesus for violating the Sabbath by harvesting grain to feed His hungry disciples. "The Sabbath was made to meet the needs of people," He told them, "and not people to meet the requirements of the Sabbath" (Mark 2:27).

The precise location of Nob has never been identified. Some believe it was northwest of Jerusalem, while others place it on one of the ridges of the Mount of Olives northeast of the city.

MICHMASH

MEANING "a hidden place"

PRONUNCIATION MICK-mash

SITE AND LOCATION A town about seven miles northeast of Jerusalem
Map 5, area D-4

Just as the town of Nob showed the dark side of King Saul (see "Nob," p. 162), the village called Michmash demonstrated the good side of his son Jonathan.

While Saul and part of his fighting force cowered in fear at the might of the Philistine army (see 1 Samuel 13:5–7), Jonathan and his armor bearer took on the Philistines by themselves with a daring plan. They scaled the high cliff on which Michmash was perched and killed the sentries posted there. This threw the entire army into panic, making them easy prey for the army of Israel (see 1 Samuel 14:1–23).

No wonder Jonathan and David eventually became good friends. Both were intelligent and brave, and they had the ability to think outside the box. But beyond this, they depended on the Lord for strength and guidance (see 1 Samuel 20:9–17). After the Philistines killed Jonathan and his father, David composed a funeral song known as the Song of the Bow in which he lamented their deaths.

Caves pockmark the cliffs at Michmash.

ANATHOTH

MEANING   "answers" or "answered prayers"

PRONUNCIATION   AN-uh-tahth

SITE AND LOCATION   A town about three miles north of Jerusalem
Map 5, area D-4

Anathoth is one of hundreds of little towns mentioned in the Bible that we know very little about. But the one important thing we do know is that it was associated with one of the greatest spokesmen for God whom the world has ever known—the prophet Jeremiah. He was born in this small town not far from Jerusalem about 647 BC—the son of a priest named Hilkiah (see Jeremiah 1:1).

When Jeremiah was about twenty years old, God called him to deliver His message to the wayward nation of Judah. The people of the land had rejected the one true God and were worshipping false gods. Jeremiah's God-given task was to call them back to the Lord and to warn them that a foreign nation would overthrow them unless they turned from their sinful ways.

The prophet preached this harsh message for about forty years—in spite of criticism, condemnation, and charges of sedition and disloyalty by the leaders and priests of his country. Twice he was arrested and thrown into prison—once in an abandoned cistern with a layer of mud in the bottom. He would surely have died in this place, if not for the kindness of a royal official who pulled him out and put him in a regular prison (see Jeremiah 38:6–13).

Although the main theme of the prophet's preaching was approaching disaster, he mixed these messages with glimmers of hope. As the Babylonian army closed in to capture the city of Jerusalem in 587 BC, he told the people not to resist them but to go willingly into exile in this pagan nation. Jeremiah

Modern Anathoth, viewed from the north.

delivered God's promise to bring His people back to their homeland in about seventy years after their time of discipline and punishment was over (see Jeremiah 29:10–14).

Was Jeremiah just whistling in the dark, or did he really believe things would get better three generations down the road? The answer came when his cousin Hanamel from Anathoth showed up in Jerusalem where the prophet was preaching. Hanamel had a field to sell, and he wanted to know if Jeremiah was interested in buying it. Hanamel knew the conquering Babylonians would soon confiscate this property, along with the entire land of Judah. If the prophet was naïve enough to buy this property in nearby Anathoth, Hanamel probably had some oceanfront property in Arizona that he would be glad to throw in to seal the deal!

In a demonstration of his confidence that God would deliver on His promise, Jeremiah agreed to buy the field (see sidebar, "Jeremiah Shows His Faith in God's Promise," right). Apparently he and his cousin didn't even haggle over the price. The prophet paid for the property with his own money, had witnesses record and authenticate the deed, sealed the papers in an airtight jar, and placed them in a safe place for long-term protection.

This careful process is typical of the ministry of Jeremiah. He left nothing to chance when it came to following the Lord's commands. He will always be remembered as the small-town prophet who did big things for God—hanging in there for a lifetime to accomplish the tough task God called him to do.

JEREMIAH SHOWS HIS FAITH IN GOD'S PROMISE

Then, just as the LORD had said he would, my cousin Hanamel came and visited me in the prison. He said, "Please buy my field at Anathoth in the land of Benjamin. By law you have the right to buy it before it is offered to anyone else, so buy it for yourself." Then I knew that the message I had heard was from the LORD.

So I bought the field at Anathoth, paying Hanamel seventeen pieces of silver for it. I signed and sealed the deed of purchase before witnesses, weighed out the silver, and paid him. Then I took the sealed deed and an unsealed copy of the deed, which contained the terms and conditions of the purchase, and I handed them to Baruch son of Neriah and grandson of Mahseiah. I did all this in the presence of my cousin Hanamel, the witnesses who had signed the deed, and all the men of Judah who were there in the courtyard of the guardhouse.

Then I said to Baruch as they all listened, "This is what the LORD of Heaven's Armies, the God of Israel, says: 'Take both this sealed deed and the unsealed copy, and put them into a pottery jar to preserve them for a long time. . . . Someday people will again own property here in this land and will buy and sell houses and vineyards and fields'" (Jeremiah 32:8–15).

The modern Arabic village of Anata, not far from Jerusalem, probably preserves the name of Anathoth. But most scholars agree that the ruins known as Ras el-Kharrubeh, less than a mile from Anata, are the site of the biblical city where Jeremiah grew up.

EMMAUS

MEANING "warm wells"

PRONUNCIATION em-MAY-us

SITE AND LOCATION An unidentified village about seven miles from Jerusalem
Map 6, area C-6

This village is the place where Jesus revealed Himself to two of His followers on the day of His resurrection. They were walking from Jerusalem to their home in Emmaus. Suddenly a stranger fell in beside them and joined their conversation about the events that had taken place in Jerusalem over the past three days. This stranger was Jesus, but they didn't recognize Him because of His resurrection body. He accompanied them all the way to their home. Here He finally opened their eyes so they could recognize Him when they sat down for a meal together (see Luke 24:13–32).

The site of the village of Emmaus has never been identified with certainty. Luke in his Gospel tells us that it was seven miles from Jerusalem, but he didn't specify in which direction. Over the centuries, several sites have been suggested as the location of Emmaus, but none of these offers any scientific evidence to support these claims.

At the moment, a well-promoted site known as Emmaus/Nicopolis claims to be the site of this village. Here visitors are shown the remains of a church that was built on this site in the fifth century. But the problem with this place is that it is eighteen miles from Jerusalem. Even if Luke were giving an approximate distance from Jerusalem to Emmaus, it's hard to believe that he could have miscalculated by eleven miles.

Luke also reported that these two followers walked back to Jerusalem on the same day to tell Jesus' disciples that they had seen the Lord (see Luke 24:32–33). This would have required them to walk thirty-six miles in one day—an unlikely though not impossible accomplishment.

We may never know the exact site of Emmaus. But isn't it enough to know that we serve a living Lord whose presence gives meaning and purpose to our lives? We as believers can still feel what these two Emmaus followers experienced almost two thousand years ago as they walked along with Jesus: "Didn't our hearts burn within us as he talked with us on the road and explained the Scriptures to us?" (Luke 24:32).

GIBEON

MEANING "hilly"

PRONUNCIATION GIBB-eh-un

SITE AND LOCATION A city about six miles northwest of Jerusalem
Map 5, area C-4

This ancient Canaanite city is a case study in innovation, deception, and self-preservation. Other Canaanite strongholds near it—including Jericho and Ai—were falling to the invading Israelites. The leaders of Gibeon realized they would be next on Joshua's hit list unless they could fool him into giving them a pass. How they managed to trick the Israelites into making a peace treaty with them is one of the most interesting stories in the Bible (see sidebar, "How the Gibeonites Outflanked Joshua," p. 168).

In effect, the Gibeonites convinced Joshua that they were not Canaanites but residents of a distant land. Their peace treaty with Israel granted them exemption from the mass-extermination policy Joshua waged throughout the land of Canaan. Even when the truth came out, Joshua was bound by the terms of this agreement. He did save face to some degree by pressing the Gibeonites into service as lifelong woodcutters and water carriers for the nation of Israel (see Joshua 9:26–27).

Archaeologists have positively identified this city that hoodwinked Joshua. It occupied the site of a ruin known today as Tel el-Jib. Excavations here have uncovered wine jugs stamped with the name of the city. Several centuries after Joshua's time, it was the center of a commercial wine-making enterprise. Large underground cellars were dug for the storage of jars of wine. These storage vats could hold thousands of gallons of wine. Gibeon's farmers and merchants apparently marketed this valuable commodity throughout Israel, including nearby Jerusalem.

Al-Jib (Gibeon) in 1938.

But the most impressive find at ancient Gibeon was a huge well or cistern—one of the largest yet discovered in Israel. Measuring thirty-seven feet around, it descended through solid rock to a depth of eighty-two feet. At the bottom of the shaft, a tunnel about 180 feet long was dug to tap into the water from an underground spring. This ingenious water system probably served the same purpose for Gibeon that the Pool of Siloam and Hezekiah's Tunnel (see chapter 6, "Pool of Siloam," p. 132) did for Jerusalem. It guaranteed a supply of water for the city in the event of a prolonged siege by an enemy army.

This huge well may be the same as "the great waters. . .in Gibeon" the prophet Jeremiah mentioned (Jeremiah 41:12 KJV; see also 2 Samuel 2:12–13). After all these centuries, it is still in use today. Holy Land visitors marvel at its size and the back-breaking labor required to dig it through solid rock.

GIBEON: A BIBLICAL SNAPSHOT

- A large Canaanite city noted for its brave warriors (see Joshua 10:2).
- At Gibeon, Joshua's forces defeated Adoni-zedek, the Canaanite king of Jerusalem, and his allies (see Joshua 10:3–11).
- The sun and moon stood still at Gibeon until Joshua's forces defeated the Amorites (see Joshua 10:12–14).
- At Gibeon, Solomon offered sacrifices and prayed for wisdom at the beginning of his reign as king of Judah (see 1 Kings 3:3–15).
- After the Babylonian exile, residents of Gibeon helped Nehemiah rebuild the walls of Jerusalem (see Nehemiah 3:6–8).

The sun stands still for Joshua at Gibeon.

HOW THE GIBEONITES OUTFLANKED JOSHUA

When the people of Gibeon heard what Joshua had done to Jericho and Ai, they resorted to deception to save themselves. They sent ambassadors to Joshua, loading their donkeys with weathered saddlebags and old, patched wineskins. They put on worn-out, patched sandals and ragged clothes. And the bread they took with them was dry and moldy. When they arrived at the camp of Israel at Gilgal, they told Joshua and the men of Israel, "We have come from a distant land to ask you to make a peace treaty with us." . . .

"This bread was hot from the ovens when we left our homes. But now, as you can see, it is dry and moldy. These wineskins were new when we filled them, but now they are old and split open. And our clothing and sandals are worn out from our very long journey."

So the Israelites examined their food, but they did not consult the LORD. Then Joshua made a peace treaty with them and guaranteed their safety, and the leaders of the community ratified their agreement with a binding oath (Joshua 9:3–6, 12–15).

RAMAH

MEANING "height"

PRONUNCIATION RAY-mah

SITE AND LOCATION An unidentified city a few miles north of Jerusalem

Map 3, area C-5

In Bible times, many cities were built on mountains or high hills and were named "Ramah" because of their uplifted location. The most famous city with this name is the Ramah near Jerusalem. It was where the prophet Samuel was born (see 1 Samuel 1:1–2, 19–20) and where he was buried (see 1 Samuel 25:1).

Hannah, Samuel's mother, dedicated him to the Lord before he was born. When he was just a child, she took him to live with the priest Eli, who presided over the tabernacle at Shiloh (see chapter 8, p. 211). Samuel became one of the most beloved leaders of Israel, serving as prophet, priest, and judge. He served during the crucial time when the nation of Israel was moving away from a loose tribal confederacy form of government to the centralized rule of a king.

At Ramah, the elders of Israel approached Samuel and demanded that he appoint a king to rule over the tribes (see 1 Samuel 8:4–5). Samuel gave in and eventually anointed Saul as the first king of the nation—but not before warning the people of the dangers of a kingship (see 1 Samuel 8:10–18).

The site of Ramah has never been identified with certainty. But it must have been near the cities of Bethel (see chapter 8, p. 208) and Gilgal (see chapter 8, p. 188). Samuel traveled between his home at Ramah and these two cities, performing his duties as a judge among the Israelites (see 1 Samuel 7:15–17).

An aerial view of a suggested site of ancient Ramah.

MIZPAH

MEANING "watchtower"

PRONUNCIATION MIZ-pah

SITE AND LOCATION A city about four miles north of Jerusalem
Map 5, area D-4

This city, like Ramah (see p. 169), is also associated with the ministry of the prophet Samuel. Here he gathered the people of Israel to give thanks for the return of the ark of the covenant, which the Philistines had earlier captured (see 1 Samuel 7:1–6). Not far from Mizpah, he erected a stone to commemorate an Israelite victory over the Philistines. He named it *Ebenezer*, a Hebrew word meaning "the stone of help" (see 1 Samuel 7:10–12).

In later years, Mizpah's closeness to Jerusalem made it an important site for the protection of the Holy City. King Asa of Judah (ruled about 911–869 BC) fortified it as a defense outpost against invasion from the north (see 1 Kings 15:22).

Ruins of ancient Mizpah.

ZELAH

MEANING "side" or "slope"

PRONUNCIATION ZEE-luh

SITE AND LOCATION An unidentified town not far from Jerusalem
Map 5, area C-5

We know only two things about this town: (1) after the conquest of Canaan, it was allotted to the tribe of Benjamin (see Joshua 18:25–28), and (2) King Saul and his sons were buried here in the tomb of Saul's father, Kish (see 2 Samuel 21:10–14). Thus, it is likely that Zelah is where Saul was born and where he grew up.

It took awhile for Saul's body to make its way to its final resting place. After Philistines killed him and his sons in northern Israel, they hung his body on the wall of the city of Beth-shan (see chapter 9, p. 217) as an insult and a public example to the Israelites. But several brave men from the city of Jabesh-gilead east of the Jordan River rescued their bodies and gave them a decent burial in their city (see 1 Samuel 31:11–12).

Finally, King David retrieved the bones of Saul and his sons from Jabesh-gilead. Then he brought them to Zelah for their final entombment with Saul's ancestors. Even though David and Saul were enemies, David respected the kingly office and was grateful for Saul's service to his country.

King Saul died in the Battle of Gilboa—with ancient Israelites and Philistines here depicted in fifteenth-century armor—and was later buried at Zelah.

EIN KEREM

MEANING "spring of the vineyard"

PRONUNCIATION ahn-keh-RIM

SITE AND LOCATION A town about four miles southwest of Jerusalem
Map 6, area C-6

Holy Land pilgrims consistently rank this peaceful little town as one of their favorite places to visit. With its lovely gardens, huge shade trees, picturesque courtyards, and old Arabic-style houses, it is the perfect place for quiet prayer and meditation after days of hectic rushing from one Holy Land site to another.

Ein Kerem claims to be the town where John the Baptist was born. And there is no doubt that the quiet and reverent atmosphere of the town exudes John's spirit of humility and deference to Christ. "I am not the Messiah," he told the people of his time. "I am only here to prepare the way for him. . . . He must become greater and greater, and I must become less and less" (John 3:28, 30).

The Church of John the Baptist in Ein Kerem.

Whether this is the actual town where John was born is open to debate. We do know that the virgin Mary visited her relative Elizabeth—John's mother—during the time when both women were expectant mothers. But Luke's Gospel indicates only that "Mary hurried to the hill country of Judea, to the town where Zechariah [John's father] lived" (Luke 1:39–40). Luke did not tell us the exact name of the place where John was born. But early Christian tradition accepted Ein Kerem as the place of John's birth. The first churches dedicated to him were built here more than 1,500 years ago. The churches that mark the site today are successors of these earlier buildings.

One of these churches is the Church of Saint John the Baptist, which the Catholic Franciscan order operates. Its tall bell tower dominates the center of the little village. Underneath the church is a cave said to mark the spot where John was born in the home of Zechariah and Elizabeth. Here the relatives and friends of these new parents haggled over what to name this baby. Elizabeth insisted that his name was John, in accordance with an angel's declaration to his father that he was to be given this name (see Luke 1:13; see sidebar, "No! His Name Is John!" below).

Inside the church is a painting of John's baptism of Jesus in the Jordan River (see Matthew 3:13–15). Other paintings inside the church courtyard and the interior of the building depict Herod Antipas's beheading of John (see Mark 6:14–29) and John's preaching in the wilderness of Judea to prepare people for the coming of Jesus the Messiah (see Mark 1:1–8).

On a hillside overlooking Ein Kerem is another church known as the Church of Visitation. It commemorates Mary's visit to Elizabeth after Mary learned she would give birth to the Messiah. Her visit is captured in a beautiful mosaic inside the church. Another painting shows John's father, Zechariah, conducting his priestly duties in the temple at nearby Jerusalem (see Luke 1:8–10).

While in Ein Kerem, pilgrims visit a spring in the middle of the village. This is the spring that gives the town its name—Ein ("spring") Kerem ("vineyard")—or "spring of the vineyard." This water source is known as Mary's Spring because of a tradition that the virgin Mary stopped here for a drink while visiting Elizabeth.

The Virgin's Well in Ein Kerem.

NO! HIS NAME IS JOHN!

When it was time for Elizabeth's baby to be born, she gave birth to a son. And when her neighbors and relatives heard that the Lord had been very merciful to her, everyone rejoiced with her.

When the baby was eight days old, they all came for the circumcision ceremony. They wanted to name him Zechariah, after his father. But Elizabeth said, "No! His name is John!"

"What?" they exclaimed. "There is no one in all your family by that name." So they used gestures to ask the baby's father what he wanted to name him. He motioned for a writing tablet, and to everyone's surprise he wrote, "His name is John." Instantly Zechariah could speak again, and he began praising God.

Awe fell upon the whole neighborhood, and the news of what had happened spread throughout the Judean hills. Everyone who heard about it reflected on these events and asked, "What will this child turn out to be?" For the hand of the Lord was surely upon him in a special way (Luke 1:57–66).

Well-tended fields near Shechem.

CHAPTER 8

This large section of the Holy Land is about fifty-five miles wide (east to west) by about thirty-five miles long (north to south). It includes several significant sites from Jerusalem to Shechem, including Shiloh—the city where the ark of the covenant was kept for a time. The major river of Israel, the Jordan, runs north to south along the eastern edge of this territory. The area is bound on the west by the Mediterranean Sea, also referred to in the Bible as the "great sea" (see Numbers 34:7 KJV).

During the 1800s, most visitors to the Holy Land arrived by ship at the Mediterranean port city of Joppa. The distance from Joppa to Jerusalem was about forty-five miles, and it had to be traveled by horseback over a primitive road. This trip required about sixteen straight hours of riding if travelers wanted to get to Jerusalem in one day. In her memoirs from the 1800s, a German woman named Ida Pfeiffer described her tour guide's determination to do just that (see sidebar, "In the Saddle from Joppa to Jerusalem," p. 178).

Today, most Holy Land pilgrims fly into the modern Israeli airport near Tel Aviv—the site of ancient Joppa. Then they travel by air-conditioned bus over a modern highway from Joppa to Jerusalem in less than an hour. Some things do, indeed, change for the better.

Let's start our tour of this section of the Holy Land with the city where Ida Pfeiffer began her tiring ride. Here is where several important events in the Bible took place.

JOPPA

MEANING "beautiful"

PRONUNCIATION JAH-puh

SITE AND LOCATION A city on the coast of the Mediterranean Sea at the southern end of the Plain of Sharon
Map 6, area B-5

Change. Innovation. Revolution. No matter what word you use, it describes what happened at this ancient city in the early years of the Christian church. The apostle Peter at the time was the undisputed leader of the Christian movement. But Peter was a Jew, and he still held on to some of his views about what was acceptable and unacceptable to God. His famous vision at Joppa on the roof of Simon the tanner shook him up by challenging his cherished convictions about kosher and nonkosher foods (see sidebar, "Peter's Revolutionary Vision at Joppa," p. 178).

As it turned out, this vision was not about food at all, but about people. God used this vision to teach Peter that Gentiles were not second-class citizens, as the Jews believed, but people made in God's image who were welcome in God's kingdom.

And Peter, to his credit, was a fast learner. A few days after his "food vision," he told the Gentile Cornelius, "God has shown me that I should no longer think of anyone as impure or unclean" (Acts 10:28). Then Peter put his words into action by baptizing Cornelius and several members of his

The port of Jaffa (Joppa), perhaps the very place Jonah set sail from.

household upon their profession of faith in Christ (see Acts 10:44–48). From then on, the church was no longer restricted to people of Jewish background. It was open to all people, no matter what their race, creed, or national origin.

Before Peter's vision at Joppa, this city was also the site of another important event in his ministry. Here he raised Tabitha, also known as Dorcas, from the dead (see Acts 9:36–41). News of this miracle spread throughout the area around Joppa. This caused many people to turn to Jesus Christ (see Acts 9:42).

Today, these key events in Peter's ministry are commemorated in the old city of Joppa, also known as Jaffa and Yafo. Here visitors may view a shrine known as the House of Simon the Tanner, thought to be the place where Peter's life-changing event took place. The nearby Russian Orthodox Church of Tabitha's Tomb is said to mark the place where he brought Tabitha back to life.

Another memorial erected in the old city of Joppa in honor of the noted apostle is the Roman Catholic Church of Saint Peter. The original church by this name was built in 1654 on a medieval fortress near the sea. This building was replaced over the centuries by several others on the original site. The present Saint Peter's Church was built here in 1894. For many years, Joppa was the port of entry for tourists who traveled to the Holy Land by ship. This tall brick church looming on the horizon signaled to sea-weary pilgrims that their long voyage to the Holy Land was almost over.

In Bible times, Joppa was the only Israelite port on the Mediterranean Sea. Cedar logs from the mountains of Lebanon that were used in Solomon's temple were shipped by sea to Joppa. Then they were hauled overland to the temple site in Jerusalem about forty-five miles away. King Hiram of Tyre provided these logs (see 2 Chronicles 2:11–12, 16).

Joppa is also associated with one of the most famous runaways in history. Here is where the prophet Jonah caught a ship to escape God's command to preach in the city of Nineveh, Assyria. The last thing the prophet had in mind was a round trip, but that's exactly how it turned out. Tossed overboard into a stormy sea, Jonah was swallowed by a great fish, then spat out on the shoreline after three days—perhaps somewhere near Joppa (see Jonah 1:3, 17; 2:10).

The irony and humor of Jonah's "round trip" from Joppa were evident to Bayard Taylor, who visited the ancient city in the 1860s. "Our guide pointed out a hole in the city wall as the spot where Jonah was cast ashore by the great fish," he observed. "This part of the harbor is the place where all the garbage of the town is piled up. I fully understand why the fish's stomach would have turned on approaching this section of the city" (Bayard Taylor, *The Lands of the Saracen*).

Things have changed for the better in Joppa since Taylor visited here more than a century ago. Today, this ancient city by the sea has been totally surrounded by a modern metropolis known as Tel Aviv, a major economic and cultural center of Israel. These twin cities are known as Tel Aviv-Yafo. Together they have a population of more than 400,000, making it the second largest Israeli city, surpassed only by Jerusalem. Tel Aviv-Yafo's first-class hotels, restaurants, beaches, and shopping areas have turned it into a major resort city thousands of tourists visit every year.

Most modern Holy Land pilgrims fly into Israel's international airport, located in the city of Lod (see "Lydda," p. 179) just outside Tel Aviv-Yafo. In addition to visiting Joppa's holy sites, many tourists take in the area's fine museums, including the Old Jaffa Museum, Eretz Israel Museum, Museum of the Jewish Diaspora, and Ben Gurion Museum.

The Eretz Israel Museum focuses on the history and culture of the land of Israel. Its displays include olive oil and wine presses and tools people in Israel used in Bible times. Right in the center of the museum complex sits the excavated mound of an ancient city. Known as Tel Qasile, it was built in the twelfth century BC by the Philistines—a people who settled the coastal region of Palestine and often battled with the Israelites for control of a larger territory.

IN THE SADDLE FROM JOPPA TO JERUSALEM

We had been on horseback for eleven hours since leaving Joppa, and I was exhausted. But I was afraid that Mr. B. would consider me weak and ailing and change his intention of accompanying me from Jerusalem back to Joppa. So I refrained from telling him how I felt.

Finally, I dismounted and walked with tottering steps beside my horse until I felt better and could get back on. Mr. B. had determined to cover the distance from Joppa to Jerusalem (a ride of sixteen hours) at one stretch. He asked me if I thought I could go on. I was unwilling to abuse his kindness, so I assured him that I could manage to ride on for five or six hours longer.

Fortunately for my reputation, my companion was soon afterwards attacked with the same symptoms that troubled me. He began to think that it might be advisable to rest for a few hours in the next village. I felt silently thankful for this stroke of good luck.

—Ida Pfeiffer, *A Visit to the Holy Land, Egypt, and Italy*

PETER'S REVOLUTIONARY VISION AT JOPPA

The next day as Cornelius's messengers were nearing the town, Peter went up on the flat roof to pray. It was about noon, and he was hungry. But while a meal was being prepared, he fell into a trance. He saw the sky open, and something like a large sheet was let down by its four corners. In the sheet were all sorts of animals, reptiles, and birds. Then a voice said to him, "Get up, Peter; kill and eat them."

"No, Lord," Peter declared. "I have never eaten anything that our Jewish laws have declared impure and unclean."

But the voice spoke again: "Do not call something unclean if God has made it clean" (Acts 10:9–15).

LYDDA

MEANING unknown

PRONUNCIATION LID-uh

SITE AND LOCATION A city about eleven miles southeast of Joppa
Map 6, area B-5

The major event for which this city is known is a miraculous healing the apostle Peter performed. According to the book of Acts, Peter came to Lydda while he was visiting believers "from place to place" (Acts 9:32). Here he found a man named Aeneas, who had been lame and bedridden for eight years.

"Aeneas, Jesus Christ heals you!" Peter told him. "Get up, and roll up your sleeping mat!" (Acts 9:34). Aeneas was healed instantly, and this created quite a stir in Lydda. Many people in this city and the surrounding territory turned to the Lord because of this miraculous happening.

In Old Testament times, this city was known as Lod. Jews who returned here after the Babylonian exile repopulated it. Today the city is still known as Lod. With about 75,000 residents, it is one of the largest municipalities in the coastal region of Israel. The nation's major airport, Ben Gurion International, is located in Lod. Most Holy Land travelers land at this airport before beginning their tour of the sacred sites throughout Israel.

Lod is also proud to be the home of one of the newest archaeological museums in Israel. Known as the Lod Mosaic Archaeological Center, it opened in 2009. Here visitors view one of the largest and best-preserved mosaic floors ever discovered in Israel. Dating from the Roman period, it

features images of animals, plants, and Roman ships engraved in tiles that made up the floor of a Roman house. Construction workers excavating for a street-widening project uncovered the mosaic.

Modern Lod (Lydda).

PLAIN OF SHARON

MEANING unknown

PRONUNCIATION SHAR-uhn

SITE AND LOCATION A part of Israel's northern coastal plain along the Mediterranean Sea

Map 6, area B-5

This specific plain is the northern section of the part of Israel known as the coastal plain. Sharon's plain extends for about forty miles along the Mediterranean Sea, from Joppa up to Mount Carmel.

Only a few references to the Plain of Sharon appear in the Bible. Solomon's bride compared herself to "the spring crocus blooming on the Sharon Plain" (Song of Solomon 2:1). This probably referred to a wildflower that grew in this area's well-watered soil. The prophet Isaiah spoke of a time when the Lord would display His glory with the coming of the Messiah. In this time, the deserts of the land of Israel would be "as lovely as...the plain of Sharon" (Isaiah 35:2).

The Plain of Sharon was known for its beautiful wildflowers. One Holy Land pilgrim from the United States was struck by their beauty when he visited Israel during the springtime in the 1800s. "The silent declaration of ten thousand flowers is most beautiful and impressive," he wrote, "and I have seen it nowhere else in greater perfection than upon the sacred Plain of Sharon" (William Thomson, *The Land and the Book*).

Large sections of the Plain of Sharon were once covered with sand dunes and marshland. But the Israeli government's drainage projects in recent years have turned it into rich farmland where citrus orchards flourish. Other areas have been opened for settlement. Many Jews who returned to Israel when the nation was reestablished in 1948 now live in this area. Today the Plain of Sharon, with more than one million inhabitants, is one of the most populated districts of modern Israel.

Netanya, the largest city on the Plain of Sharon.

APHEK / ANTIPATRIS

MEANING "fortress"

PRONUNCIATION AY-feck / An-TIP-uh-tris

SITE AND LOCATION A city in the Plain of Sharon about eleven miles
northeast of Joppa

Map 6, area B-5

Where else but in Israel would you find a site with so many twists and turns as Aphek? This Canaanite city was already several centuries old when Joshua and the Israelites captured it about 1300 BC (see Joshua 12:18). Later it fell into Philistine hands and was one of the cities on its northern border.

Centuries later, Herod the Great rebuilt and enlarged Aphek and renamed it Antipatris in honor of his father, Antipater. This was the city that the apostle Paul passed through when he was transported under Roman guard from Jerusalem to the coastal city of Caesarea (see Acts 23:31).

The ruins of Aphek/Antipatris are a little off the beaten path today, but the city was strategically located in ancient times. Aphek stood on the main road known as the Way of the Sea that ran from Egypt into Syria. Along this

The tower of a sixteenth-century Turkish fort at Aphek.

route passed hundreds of camel caravans, carrying their goods for sale in these two major world markets.

Springs flowing from the nearby mountains converged at Aphek, forming the headwaters of the Yarkon River. Here weary travelers could stop to rest in a shaded area, water their camels, and replenish their water supply before continuing on their journey. Even today, Aphek's beautiful park along the Yarkon River offers jaded Holy Land visitors the same opportunity to rest and relax that appealed to ancient travelers.

At the ancient city of Aphek, the Israelites carried the ark of the covenant into battle against the Philistines. They must have thought that this symbol of God's presence with His people would give them an edge over their enemies. But just exactly the opposite happened. The Philistines defeated them and even captured the ark (see 1 Samuel 4:1–11). News of the ark's capture was such a shock to the high priest Eli that he fell from his seat, broke his neck, and died (see sidebar, "Shocking News about the Ark," below). This experience taught the Israelites that placing one's faith in a sacred object is not the same as trusting in God Himself.

The excavated ruins of Aphek/Antipatris, known as Tel Afek, are open to visitors. Sitting on the remains of the ancient cities is a huge fort from the AD 1500s, when the Ottoman Turks were the ruling power over Palestine. Many parts of this structure, including the gateway, walls, and corner towers, still remain intact after almost five hundred years.

The adjoining Yarkon National Park is also worth a visit. Its 3,200 acres feature five gardens with hundreds of species of plants, a lake, and broad expanses of green space with giant shade trees—the perfect setting for picnics or group Bible studies. The Yarkon River (not mentioned in the Bible) rises nearby and runs through the park, then continues for seventeen miles until running into the Mediterranean Sea near the modern city of Tel Aviv.

SHOCKING NEWS ABOUT THE ARK

Eli was waiting beside the road to hear the news of the battle, for his heart trembled for the safety of the Ark of God. When the messenger arrived and told what had happened, an outcry resounded throughout the town.

"What is all the noise about?" Eli asked.

The messenger rushed over to Eli, who was ninety-eight years old and blind. He said to Eli, "I have just come from the battlefield—I was there this very day."

"What happened, my son?" Eli demanded.

"Israel has been defeated by the Philistines," the messenger replied. "The people have been slaughtered, and your two sons, Hophni and Phinehas, were also killed. And the Ark of God has been captured."

When the messenger mentioned what had happened to the Ark of God, Eli fell backward from his seat beside the gate. He broke his neck and died, for he was old and overweight. He had been Israel's judge for forty years (1 Samuel 4:13–18).

GEZER

MEANING "portion" or "division"

PRONUNCIATION GEHZ-ur

SITE AND LOCATION A city about twenty-two miles west of Jerusalem
Map 4, area B-4

This city stood on the main road between Jerusalem and Joppa. Its occupants had a commanding view of the entire region along the coast of the Mediterranean Sea. This gave Gezer a strategic military importance. Thus, competing armies often fought over it.

The Canaanites held the city until Joshua dislodged them when he invaded the promised land (see Joshua 12:12). But the city must have fallen eventually into Philistine hands. The Bible records that David defeated the Philistines at Gezer some years after Joshua's time (see 1 Chronicles 20:4). Then the Egyptians apparently controlled the city for a time. Finally, King Solomon came into possession of the city when he married the daughter of the pharaoh of Egypt to seal an alliance with the Egyptians (see 1 Kings 9:16). Solomon rebuilt Gezer and turned it into a major fortress city to provide protection against his enemies.

Ancient Gezer is one of the most important archaeological sites in Israel. Excavations began here in the early 1900s, and they are still going on at this thirty-acre ruin at the present time. The persistence of several different archaeological teams over the years has been rewarded with significant finds at the site.

Perhaps the most interesting discovery at Gezer was the massive gate complex, along with sections of the city wall. For extra strength, Solomon built an inner wall and an outer wall. The space between them was fortified with stone partitions that ran from one wall to the other. Some of the spaces between these partitioned-off sections were used for storage. Others were filled with stones

The monoliths of Tel Gezer.

and rubble. These walls with the massive gate would have presented a challenge to any besieging army.

This double-wall-and-gate construction is the same as that found at the cities of Hazor (see chapter 10, p. 268) and Megiddo (see chapter 9, p. 241). This suggests strongly that Solomon fortified all three of these cities, as the Bible claims: "This is the account of the forced labor that King Solomon conscripted to build the LORD's Temple, the royal palace, the supporting terraces, the wall of Jerusalem, and the cities of Hazor, Megiddo, and Gezer" (1 Kings 9:15).

Other discoveries at Gezer include an ancient Israelite calendar based on the agricultural seasons, a tunnel about 150 feet long that led to a huge water storage cistern underneath the city, and eight huge stone pillars lined up in a row. These stones—perhaps part of a high place where people worshiped pagan gods—may go back to the Canaanite period of the city's history.

The site of Gezer today is an Israeli national park that attracts thousands of visitors every year.

JERICHO

MEANING	possibly "place of fragrance"
PRONUNCIATION	JEHR-ih-coe
SITE AND LOCATION	A city about twelve miles northeast of Jerusalem
	Map 6, area D-5

This was the first Canaanite city to fall to Joshua and the Israelites after they invaded the promised land. Jericho was located about eight miles west of the Jordan River. Its defeat paved the way for the Israelites to swarm into the interior of Canaan on a fierce military campaign to claim the land.

The method Joshua used to conquer this walled city is one of the most unusual strategies in military history. The plan came straight from the Lord Himself. Joshua marched the Israelites around the walls of Jericho for six consecutive days. On the seventh day, they marched around the city six times just as they had done before. But on the seventh time around, they made a lot of noise by blowing trumpets and yelling as loud as they could. At this great noise the walls collapsed, making the city and its defenders easy prey for the Israelites (see Joshua 6:12–21).

Many views about this famous battle have been expressed. Skeptics say it is just a made-up story that shouldn't be taken seriously. Others say the walls fell down because of a high wind or an earthquake. But the best explanation is exactly what the Bible says: the walls collapsed not because of the superior military tactics of the Israelites but because of the miracle-working power of the one true God. This sent a clear message that could not be ignored. When other Canaanites in the land heard about what happened at Jericho, they would grow fearful and wonder if they were next on Joshua's hit list. This would set them up for defeat by the army of Israel and the powerful God who led them into battle.

Cable cars heading to the Monastery of Temptation pass over the excavated ruins of Old Testament Jericho.

Archaeological digs at Old Testament Jericho—the site known as Tel es-Sultan—have shown that it was one of the oldest cities in the world. Debris from successive settlements on the site reached a depth of seventy feet. The most impressive feature archaeologists uncovered was a crude stone wall with a round defensive tower—the oldest city defense system discovered anywhere in the world. This relic from a past civilization never fails to impress modern visitors to the Holy Land.

But digging at Jericho has also raised a question about Joshua's relationship to the city. The problem is that there is no evidence of the ruins of the wall that fell to the Israelites. The wall that archaeologists uncovered predated Joshua's time by several centuries.

One possible explanation for this mystery is that the ruins of the wall from Joshua's time were carried away to be used in another building project. We know that this was often done in Bible times. For example, King Hezekiah of Judah (ruled about 716–686 BC) used the debris from demolished houses to shore up the wall of Jerusalem in the eighth century BC (see chapter 5, "Broad Wall," p. 115).

After Joshua destroyed Jericho, he pronounced a curse against the city. He declared, "May the curse of the LORD fall on anyone who tries to rebuild the town of Jericho" (Joshua 6:26). Several centuries later, a man named Hiel attempted to do just that. But the curse proved its effectiveness when his oldest son and his youngest son died (see 1 Kings 16:34). This is exactly what Joshua had predicted would happen to anyone who tried to rebuild the ancient city.

While the city Joshua destroyed was never rebuilt, a new city named Jericho was built about two miles away from the old site. At this new city, Roman ruler Herod the Great built his winter palace. This was an ideal place for his winter residence because of Jericho's warmer temperature. Excavations at this site have revealed that Herod also built beautiful pools and sunken gardens for the pleasure of himself and his guests.

This second city at the site is known as New Testament Jericho. Here Jesus healed blind Bartimaeus (see Mark 10:46–52) and confronted the unscrupulous tax collector Zacchaeus (see Luke 19:1–10). This Jericho was also the setting for Jesus' famous parable of the good Samaritan. This kind man came to the aid of a stranger who had been robbed, beaten, and left to die on the road from Jerusalem to Jericho (see Luke 10:30–37).

Along this ancient road today, visitors are shown a site known as the Inn of the Good Samaritan, referring to the inn where the kind Samaritan took the wounded man for healing (see Luke 10:34–35). An ancient building on the site has been turned into a tourist attraction known as the Museum of the Good Samaritan. On display here are mosaics, or tapestries with beautiful illustrations woven into the cloth. These mosaics were recovered from Christian churches and Jewish synagogues in the area. This is one of only a few mosaic museums in the world.

So far, we have counted two separate cities known as Jericho on this site. But there is still another. This is the modern village that preserves the name of Jericho in its Arabic equivalent, Eriha. This little town of only a few thousand people sits about a mile east of the site of Old Testament Jericho. Here visitors are shown a big spring known as Ein es-Sultan (Sultan's Spring) or Elisha's Spring. This is reputed to be the spring with bad water that the prophet Elisha turned into good water for the residents of Jericho (see sidebar, "Elisha Cleanses the Spring at Jericho," below).

Northwest of Old Testament Jericho is a high hill known as the Mount of Temptation, the traditional site of Satan's temptation of Jesus at the beginning of His public ministry (see Matthew 4:1–11). You can walk up to the site over a rough path or ride up by cable car. Built into this hill is an Eastern Orthodox monastery known as Qarantal (from a Greek word meaning "forty," the number of days that Jesus spent in the wilderness). This complex is supposedly built around a cave where Jesus stayed during His forty-day fast.

ELISHA CLEANSES THE SPRING AT JERICHO

One day the leaders of the town of Jericho visited Elisha. "We have a problem, my lord," they told him. "This town is located in pleasant surroundings, as you can see. But the water is bad, and the land is unproductive."

Elisha said, "Bring me a new bowl with salt in it." So they brought it to him. Then he went out to the spring that supplied the town with water and threw the salt into it. And he said, "This is what the LORD says: I have purified this water. It will no longer cause death or infertility." And the water has remained pure ever since, just as Elisha said (2 Kings 2:19–22).

AI

MEANING   "the ruin"

PRONUNCIATION   AY-eye

SITE AND LOCATION   An unidentified city about ten miles west of Jericho
Map 5, area D-4

This Canaanite city demonstrates the dangers of overconfidence and presuming on the blessings of the Lord. After their easy victory over the city of Jericho (see "Jericho," p. 184), Joshua and the invading Israelites expected the smaller city of Ai to roll over and play dead. Joshua's military scouts told him, "There's no need for all of us to go up there; it won't take more than two or three thousand men to attack Ai" (Joshua 7:3).

But it didn't turn out that way. The defenders of Ai put up a strong resistance, killed some of Israel's warriors, and even chased them from the field of battle. This humiliated Joshua's troops and paralyzed them with fear (see Joshua 7:4–5). Why had the Lord given them victory over Jericho and then turned His back on them when they advanced against this weak little city?

The problem was Israel's disobedience. A man named Achan had confiscated some of the spoils of war from Jericho and hidden them in his tent. This was a flagrant violation of God's command that all the booty was to be destroyed. Achan and his family were put to death for their deception (see sidebar, "An Extreme Penalty for a Property Crime," p. 188). After this, God gave the Israelites victory over the city of Ai (see Joshua 8:20–28).

Did Achan and his family deserve such harsh punishment for a property crime? Perhaps not, if judged from our modern cultural standards. But we must admit that God sent the message with their execution that absolute obedience and total honesty were demanded of His people. This was particularly important during the days when they were settling the land that God had promised to Abraham and his descendants.

Most archaeologists today identify the city of Ai with a site known as et-Tel, an Arabic word that means "ruins" or "the ruin." Several excavations have been conducted here. Evidence from these digs shows that a city existed on this site several centuries before Joshua's time and that another was built many years after his conquest of Canaan. But archaeologists have failed to find any evidence of an occupied city at the time when the Israelites invaded the land. How could Joshua destroy a city that didn't exist? This question is similar to one the city of Jericho poses (see p. 184).

Some people solve this mystery by claiming that the site of Ai is not et-Tel at all but a place not yet identified. Skeptics tend to say that the account of Ai and its conquest is just a fictional story—that it never happened. But Bible-believing students know that other difficulties like this in the past have been solved when further archaeological evidence came to light. It's just a matter of waiting for the final resolution of this "Ai problem."

Achan stoned to death.

AN EXTREME PENALTY FOR A PROPERTY CRIME

Then Joshua and all the Israelites took Achan, the silver, the robe, the bar of gold, his sons, daughters, cattle, donkeys, sheep, goats, tent, and everything he had, and they brought them to the valley of Achor. Then Joshua said to Achan, "Why have you brought trouble on us? The Lord will now bring trouble on you." And all the Israelites stoned Achan and his family and burned their bodies. They piled a great heap of stones over Achan, which remains to this day. That is why the place has been called the Valley of Trouble ever since. So the Lord was no longer angry (Joshua 7:24–26).

GILGAL

MEANING	"circle of stones" or "a wheel"
PRONUNCIATION	GILL-gal
SITE AND LOCATION	A place about two miles northeast of Jericho

Map 2, area C-5

When the Israelites under Joshua crossed the Jordan River into Canaan, they set up camp at Gilgal. Here they stayed for several years while they concentrated on taking the land from the Canaanites. Eventually they settled into cities and houses that provided permanent places to live. But here at Gilgal they had to live in tents as they had done while wandering in the wilderness.

Soon after settling in at Gilgal, Joshua led the people to memorialize this

The people crossed the Jordan on the tenth day of the first month. Then they camped at Gilgal, just east of Jericho. It was there at Gilgal that Joshua piled up the twelve stones taken from the Jordan River.

Then Joshua said to the Israelites, "In the future your children will ask, 'What do these stones mean?' Then you can tell them, 'This is where the Israelites crossed the Jordan on dry ground.' For the LORD your God dried up the river right before your eyes, and he kept it dry until you were all across, just as he did at the Red Sea when he dried it up until we had all crossed over. He did this so all the nations of the earth might know that the LORD's hand is powerful, and so you might fear the LORD your God forever" (Joshua 4:19–24).

historic occasion. They had crossed the Jordan River on dry land when God stopped the flow of the water (see "Jordan River," p. 193). From the stream bed they had selected twelve stones to represent the twelve tribes of Israel (see Joshua 3:14–4:7). Here at Gilgal they set up these stones as a monument honoring God's promise to give this land to His people (see sidebar, "Twelve Stones at Gilgal," above).

Gilgal became the base of operations for the Israelites for several generations while the people fanned out to settle the land. Also at Gilgal, Joshua circumcised all male Israelites to signify their covenant with the Lord. Apparently this ritual had not been practiced during their wilderness-wandering years (see Joshua 5:2–8). The first Passover observed in their new homeland also took place at Gilgal (see Joshua 5:10).

In later years, when the people of Israel asked for a king to rule over them, Gilgal was closely associated with the reign of Saul, their first king. Gilgal was the site of Saul's coronation (see 1 Samuel 11:15). At this place also, Saul made one of his colossal blunders that disqualified him as Israel's leader. He grew tired of waiting for the priest Samuel to arrive at Gilgal to

Ruins of Khirbet el Mafjir, a possible site of Gilgal.

perform a sacrifice for his troops, so he performed the ritual himself. Samuel reprimanded Saul for this act of disobedience and informed him that another person had been selected to replace him as king (see 1 Samuel 13:7–14).

The person who had been chosen as Saul's successor was David. Ironically, Gilgal was also associated with one of the saddest events that took place during David's reign as king. At Gilgal he was welcomed back from exile after he fled Jerusalem to escape his son Absalom's attempt to usurp the throne (see 2 Samuel 19:15–18). Absalom was killed in his battle with David's forces (see 2 Samuel 18:9–15)—an event that broke the king's heart (see 2 Samuel 18:31–33).

Whether and when Gilgal developed into a town is not clear. It was probably only a camping site in Joshua's time, but it may have grown into a town in later years. Some people identify it with the ruin known as Khirbet el Mafjir, located about two miles northeast of Jericho.

BETH-HORON

MEANING   "house of hollowness"

PRONUNCIATION   beth-HOE-run

SITE AND LOCATION   Twin towns—an upper and a lower—about eight miles northwest of Jerusalem   Map 4, area C-3

These twin towns were called Upper Beth-horon (see Joshua 16:5) and Lower Beth-horon (see Joshua 16:3) because of the great difference in elevation between them. The upper city sat about eight hundred feet higher than the lower city. Both were perched on opposite sides of a deep valley on the ancient road between Jerusalem and Joppa. Both towns were heavily fortified at various times in biblical history as military outposts for the defense of Jerusalem.

Joshua won a great victory over the Amorites near Beth-horon (see Joshua 10:9–10). In later years, King Solomon fortified both these towns (see 2 Chronicles 8:5). Two Arab villages stand on the site of Upper and Lower Beth-horon today.

EPHRAIM

MEANING "double fruit" or "double grainland"

PRONUNCIATION EE-freh-um

SITE AND LOCATION An unidentified village somewhere north of Jerusalem   Map 6, area C-5

This village is mentioned only once in the Bible. All we know about it is that it was a safe haven for Jesus during the closing days of His earthly ministry. After raising Lazarus from the dead, He withdrew here with His disciples when His enemies began to plot His death (see John 11:53–54).

How long did Jesus stay in Ephraim before emerging with His disciples to face His enemies? Apparently not very long, since John's Gospel tells us in the very next verse that "it was now almost time for the Jewish Passover celebration" (John 11:55). It was during that Passover celebration that Jesus was crucified, becoming the sacrificial Lamb of God to deliver us from our sins. Perhaps Jesus retreated to Ephraim to await the beginning of this Passover event in nearby Jerusalem.

The exact location of Ephraim is unknown. Some people believe the modern Palestinian town of Taybeh marks the site today.

Church at Taybeh, the last all-Christian town in the West Bank.

TIMNATH-SERAH

MEANING "extra portion," "portion of abundance," or "assigned portion"

PRONUNCIATION TIM-nath-SIR-uh

SITE AND LOCATION A city about ten miles northwest of Bethel

Map 5, area C-4

The tomb of Joshua in Kefel Hares.

Joshua received this city in the mountains as a reward for his faithful leadership of the tribes of Israel (see Joshua 19:49–50). No leader was ever more deserving of such an inheritance. He took over for Moses when he died, brought the people into Canaan, and then led them in their military campaigns to make the land their own. He left a legacy of courageous leadership for future generations (see sidebar, "Joshua the Leader: A Biblical Snapshot," below).

When Joshua died, he was buried at Timnath-serah (see Joshua 24:29–30). This town is identified today with the Arab village of Kefel Hares. Here, according to Muslim tradition, are the tombs of Joshua, Caleb, and Joshua's father, Nun (see Exodus 33:11). The Palestinian Authority controls this Muslim town, so Jews and Christians are allowed to visit these tombs only at prescribed times and with special permission.

JOSHUA THE LEADER: A BIBLICAL SNAPSHOT

- He received on-the-job training from Moses for his future leadership role (see Exodus 24:13; 33:11).
- Moses sent Joshua with others into Canaan on a fact-finding mission. Along with Caleb, he recommended that the Israelites overcome their fear, trust the Lord, and take the land. Because of his faith and courage, he and Caleb survived the wilderness-wandering years and were allowed to enter the promised land (see Numbers 14:26–30).
- After leading the Israelites to conquer Canaan, Joshua divided the land among the twelve tribes (see Joshua 23:1–5).
- At the end of his life, Joshua challenged the people to remain faithful to God (see Joshua 24:1–15), and he led them to renew their covenant with the Lord (see Joshua 24:25–28).

JORDAN RIVER

MEANING "descending river" or "a descender"

PRONUNCIATION JORE-dun

SITE AND LOCATION The major river of Israel that flows north to south across the entire length of the country before emptying into the Dead Sea

Map 5, area E

The Jordan River has a perception problem. You look at a map of Israel, and it shows the river running along the country's entire eastern border. Your natural assumption is that this is a large river, like the Missouri or the Ohio in the United States. But like so many of our assumptions, this one is wrong.

Israel's major river is more like a large creek. Its entire straight-line distance from its headwaters north of Lake Galilee to the Dead Sea is only about 120 miles. But it falls rapidly, descending about 1,500 feet to the lowest point on the earth's surface at the Dead Sea (see chapter 3, "Dead Sea," p. 40). This sharp fall has earned the Jordan its reputation as "the descender." It has so many twists and turns that it logs more than two hundred miles along its course through the Israeli countryside. Too swift and shallow to be a navigable waterway, it is only about twenty-five feet wide in most places.

With this accurate perception of the river in mind, we can understand the reaction of Naaman when the prophet Elisha directed him to wash in the Jordan to heal his leprosy (see sidebar, "Not in That River!" p. 194). Naaman was a high-ranking official in the army of Syria. He considered it a personal affront to be asked to take a bath in this muddy, shallow stream.

The Jordan River.

So Naaman went with his horses and chariots and waited at the door of Elisha's house. But Elisha sent a messenger out to him with this message: "Go and wash yourself seven times in the Jordan River. Then your skin will be restored, and you will be healed of your leprosy."

But Naaman became angry and stalked away. "I thought he would certainly come out to meet me!" he said. "I expected him to wave his hand over the leprosy and call on the name of the LORD his God and heal me! Aren't the rivers of Damascus, the Abana and the Pharpar, better than any of the rivers of Israel? Why shouldn't I wash in them and be healed?" So Naaman turned and went away in a rage (2 Kings 5:9–12).

But the officers under Naaman's command were wiser than their hot-headed commander. They told him, in effect, "What have you got to lose? Get in the water like the prophet says and see what happens." When Naaman did, he was miraculously healed of his leprosy (see 2 Kings 5:13–14). This battle-hardened military man learned that a muddy little river could work wonders in the hands of an all-powerful God.

Centuries after Naaman's bath in the Jordan River, another notable "washing" took place here. It happened to a young man from Galilee named Jesus, who heard that John the Baptist was baptizing people at a site on the Jordan River. At Jesus' request, John baptized Him here (see "Bethabara," p. 195). John protested that Jesus didn't need to be baptized because He was free of sin. But Jesus replied, "Let it be so for now. For in this way we shall do all that God requires" (Matthew 3:15 TEV).

By His baptism, Jesus identified with the message about the kingdom of God that John was preaching. He also set the example for all future believers to follow.

In Joshua's time, the Jordan River was a central part of the drama that allowed God's people to set foot in the promised land. When they arrived on the eastern border of Canaan, the river was at flood stage because of recent winter rains. But God miraculously stopped the flow of the water, and they were able to cross over safely into the land that God had promised to Abraham and his descendants (see Joshua 3:14–16). This crossing of the Jordan was similar to their miraculous escape across the Red Sea from the pursuing Egyptian army (see Exodus 14:15–28).

What happened to the Jordan River in Joshua's time could happen again. But environmentalists warn that it could be a permanent stoppage of the water's flow rather than a temporary phenomenon.

During the past fifty years, the nations of Israel and Jordan have drawn off 90 percent of the water from the river for irrigation purposes. This has reduced it to a trickle of its former self, particularly in the hot and dry summer months. Dams that nations north and east of Israel propose for the upper tributaries of the Jordan threaten to make the problem even worse.

THE JORDAN RIVER: A BIBLICAL SNAPSHOT

- Gideon chased the Midianite army across the Jordan (see Judges 8:4).
- David crossed the Jordan when he returned to Jerusalem after Absalom's rebellion (see 2 Samuel 19:15–18).
- Elisha succeeded Elijah after a series of miracles along the Jordan River (see 2 Kings 2:5–14).
- By a miracle, Elisha retrieved an ax head from the waters of the Jordan (see 2 Kings 6:1–7).

BETHABARA

MEANING "house of the ford"

PRONUNCIATION beth-AB-ah-ruh

SITE AND LOCATION A place near the Jordan River Map 6, area D-5

This site is mentioned only once in the Bible, but it is important for our understanding of the early ministry of Jesus. Bethabara is where John the Baptist was preaching east of the Jordan River or "beyond Jordan" (John 1:28 KJV) just before Jesus arrived to ask John to baptize Him. John protested that the sinless Jesus didn't need to be baptized. But when Jesus insisted, he baptized Him in the nearby Jordan River (see sidebar, "Jesus and John in the Jordan," p. 196).

The river near "Bethany beyond Jordan."

One interesting thing about the name "Bethabara" is that it would not even exist if not for the King James Version of the Bible. Most recent translations of the Bible render the name of this place as "Bethany" rather than "Bethabara." This is because modern translations follow a different Greek text of the Gospel of John than the one King James translators used. But this Bethany/Bethabara is a different place than the village near Jerusalem where Jesus often visited in the home of His friends Mary, Martha, and Lazarus (see chapter 7, "Bethany," p. 158).

Many scholars claim that the site of this Bethabara near the Jordan River has never been identified with certainty. But the nation of Jordan insists that it is on their side of the Jordan about six miles north of the Dead Sea. Jordanian officials are conducting extensive archaeological excavations in the area to develop it into a major tourism destination for Holy Land visitors.

No one knows exactly where Jesus' baptism in the Jordan River took place. The river in its lower reaches has changed course several times over the centuries, so any supposed site is a matter of speculation. After John baptized Jesus in the lower Jordan, he apparently also baptized along its upper reaches. Just before Herod Antipas arrested John, he was baptizing "at Aenon, near Salim, because there was plenty of water there" (John 3:23). Neither of these places has been precisely identified, although they were probably somewhere near Shechem (see p. 197).

JESUS AND JOHN IN THE JORDAN

Then Jesus went from Galilee to the Jordan River to be baptized by John. But John tried to talk him out of it. "I am the one who needs to be baptized by you," he said, "so why are you coming to me?"

But Jesus said, "It should be done, for we must carry out all that God requires." So John agreed to baptize him.

After his baptism, as Jesus came up out of the water, the heavens were opened and he saw the Spirit of God descending like a dove and settling on him. And a voice from heaven said, "This is my dearly loved Son, who brings me great joy" (Matthew 3:13–17).

A modern altar marking the place on the Jordanian side of the river where John the Baptist may have baptized Jesus.

SHECHEM

MEANING	"shoulder" or "ridge"

PRONUNCIATION	SHECK-uhm

SITE AND LOCATION	A city about thirty-five miles north of Jerusalem

Map 3, area C-4

In a list of Holy Land "firsts," this place must appear near the top. Here at Shechem, surrounded by a culture that worshipped false gods, Abraham built an altar devoted to the one true God. This was the first shrine for worship of the Lord erected in the land God had promised to Abraham and his descendants (see sidebar, "Abraham's Altar at Shechem," p. 198).

Shechem was probably nothing more than a camping spot when Abraham built an altar on the spot almost four thousand years ago. It was a good place to set up camp because plenty of water flowed from the numerous springs in the area. But over time, the site grew into a village, then a town, and finally a city.

Jacob's Well Church in the middle of modern Shechem.

Abraham's grandson Jacob also built an altar here, but by then Shechem was described as a town (see Genesis 33:18–20). Still later, Joshua gave his farewell address to the tribes of Israel at this place (see Joshua 24:1–15).

Shechem was probably one of the Canaanite cities Joshua captured, since it was allotted to the Levites and designated as a city of refuge for any Israelite who killed a person accidentally (see Joshua 20:7).

Several centuries beyond Joshua's time, Shechem had developed into a major city with a defensive wall. When the united kingdom of David and Solomon split into southern and northern factions, King Jeroboam I (ruled about 931–910 BC) turned Shechem into the capital city of the northern kingdom (see 1 Kings 12:25). Samaria eventually became the permanent political capital of the northern kingdom, but Shechem's religious importance continued. During the ministry of the prophet Hosea in the eighth century BC, it apparently was a worship center of some type. But it is not clear whether people worshipped the Lord or false gods here (see Hosea 6:9).

Shechem sat in a narrow valley between the twin peaks of Gerizim and Ebal in central Israel (see "Mount Gerizim and Mount Ebal," p. 202). Nearby was the village of Sychar (p. 200), where Jesus talked with the woman at the well (see John 4:1–30). Another famous landmark located here is the tomb of Joseph. His bones were eventually buried here on the property his father Jacob bought many years before Joseph's death in Egypt. How this burial came to be after about five hundred years is one of the most interesting stories in the Bible (see sidebar, "Following Joseph's Bones from Egypt to Shechem," p. 199).

Still another striking thing about Shechem is that it is home to a remnant of the ancient Samaritans, a people who occupied the

ABRAHAM'S ALTAR AT SHECHEM

So Abram departed as the LORD had instructed, and Lot went with him. Abram was seventy-five years old when he left Haran. He took his wife, Sarai, his nephew Lot, and all his wealth—his livestock and all the people he had taken into his household at Haran—and headed for the land of Canaan. When they arrived in Canaan, Abram traveled through the land as far as Shechem. There he set up camp beside the oak of Moreh. At that time, the area was inhabited by Canaanites. Then the LORD appeared to Abram and said, "I will give this land to your descendants." And Abram built an altar there and dedicated it to the LORD, who had appeared to him (Genesis 12:4–7).

Abraham by the Oak of Moreh.

surrounding territory for many centuries. The Samaritans were the offspring of marriages between Jews and Gentiles. This mixture of racial lines occurred after Assyria conquered the northern kingdom of Israel and repopulated the region with foreigners from many different pagan nations. Full-blooded Jews despised the Samaritans and refused to associate with them because of their "impure" racial heritage (see John 4:9).

At one time, more than one million Samaritans lived in Shechem and the region around Mount Gerizim. But their numbers dwindled dramatically when they were slaughtered after rebelling against the Romans in the sixth century AD. This catastrophe was followed in later years by their assimilation into Muslim ranks through forced mass conversion. Today, only a few hundred Samaritans remain, and most of them live on nearby Mount Gerizim—the site where their temple once stood (see John 4:20). Only a few stone remnants of this temple are visible today, but the Samaritans still conduct their worship rituals at this site.

Here they display an ancient copy of their scriptures, known as the Samaritan Pentateuch, which consist of the Old Testament books of Genesis, Exodus, Leviticus, Numbers, and Deuteronomy. Their version of the Pentateuch differs considerably from its Jewish/Christian counterpart, and it is the only section of the Bible they consider authoritative.

The ruins of ancient Shechem are identified with a mound known as Tel Balatah, a site not far from the modern Arab city of Nablus. This manufacturing and commercial center, with a population of more than 140,000 people, is one of the largest Palestinian cities in the West Bank.

FOLLOWING JOSEPH'S BONES FROM EGYPT TO SHECHEM

- Jacob, Joseph's father, buys property near Shechem (see Genesis 33:18–19).
- Joseph, who had become a high official in Egypt, asks to be buried someday back in Canaan (see Genesis 50:25–26).
- Moses and the Israelites take Joseph's bones with them when they leave Egypt (see Exodus 13:19).
- Finally, the Israelites bury Joseph's bones at Shechem on the plot of ground that his father, Jacob, had bought about five centuries before (see Joshua 24:32).
- The writer of the book of Hebrews commends Joseph for his faith to believe that God would lead the Israelites out of Egypt: "It was by faith that Joseph, when he was about to die, said confidently that the people of Israel would leave Egypt. He even commanded them to take his bones with them when they left" (Hebrews 11:22).

A soldier guards the supposed bones of Joseph in the early twentieth century.

SYCHAR

MEANING	**unknown**
PRONUNCIATION	**SIGH-car**
SITE AND LOCATION	**A village about two miles northeast of Shechem**
	Map 6, area C-4

A woman from this little town in the region of Samaria went out one day to draw water from the local well. Here she met a Jewish man named Jesus who surprised her by asking her to give Him a drink of water from the well. Jews normally had nothing to do with Samaritans. Then He surprised her even more when He offered her a different kind of water in return—living water that would fill the spiritual emptiness in her life (see sidebar, "Living Water Offered at Jacob's Well," p. 201).

Most scholars are convinced that the Sychar mentioned in this account from John's Gospel was on the site the Arab village of Askar now occupies. This identification is based on Askar's location—about a ten-minute walk from Jacob's Well, the site where Jesus' conversation with this woman took

The Church of Bir Yaqub.

place. Just a short distance away is Mount Gerizim, the place she mentioned as the site where her people, the Samaritans, worshipped (see John 4:20).

Jacob's Well is not mentioned in the Old Testament. But we do know that Jacob lived in this area. He bought some property near Shechem after returning to Canaan from his uncle Laban's home in Paddan-aram (see Genesis 33:16–20). The region around modern Askar and Shechem is noted for its numerous springs. But Jacob probably dug this well on his own land to ensure an undisputed water supply for his family and his large herds of cattle and sheep.

There is little doubt that the Jacob's Well tourists visit today is the same well where Jesus talked with this Samaritan woman. Throughout the centuries, numerous churches were built on the site to commemorate this important event in His ministry. Today the 135-foot-deep well is located within the complex of the Bir Yarqub Monastery, which the Eastern Orthodox Church owns.

LIVING WATER OFFERED AT JACOB'S WELL

Eventually he [Jesus] came to the Samaritan village of Sychar, near the field that Jacob gave to his son Joseph. Jacob's well was there; and Jesus, tired from the long walk, sat wearily beside the well about noontime. Soon a Samaritan woman came to draw water, and Jesus said to her, "Please give me a drink." He was alone at the time because his disciples had gone into the village to buy some food.

The woman was surprised, for Jews refuse to have anything to do with Samaritans. She said to Jesus, "You are a Jew, and I am a Samaritan woman. Why are you asking me for a drink?"

Jesus replied, "If you only knew the gift God has for you and who you are speaking to, you would ask me, and I would give you living water."

"But sir, you don't have a rope or a bucket," she said, "and this well is very deep. Where would you get this living water? And besides, do you think you're greater than our ancestor Jacob, who gave us this well? How can you offer better water than he and his sons and his animals enjoyed?"

Jesus replied, "Anyone who drinks this water will soon become thirsty again. But those who drink the water I give will never be thirsty again. It becomes a fresh, bubbling spring within them, giving them eternal life" (John 4:5–14).

Jacob's Well.

MOUNT GERIZIM AND MOUNT EBAL

MEANING Gerizim = unknown; Ebal = "bare"

PRONUNCIATION geh-RUH-zim; EE-buhl

SITE AND LOCATION Twin mountains near Shechem   Map 5, area D-2

These two mountains, only about half a mile apart at their bases, were prominent landmarks in the central section of Canaan. About three thousand feet above sea level, each towered over the surrounding terrain. When Moses looked across the Jordan River from Moab into the promised land, these two peaks caught his eye. He directed the Israelites to gather here after they entered the land to listen to the reading of the law. Blessings for keeping the law were to be pronounced to all the people from Mount Gerizim, while curses for disobeying the law were to be announced from Mount Ebal (see Deuteronomy 11:29–32).

Moses went on in chapters 27 and 28 of Deuteronomy to give more details about the ceremony to be conducted at this site. He also spelled out the specific blessings and curses that the people should expect for their obedience or disobedience of the law (see sidebar, "Blessings from Gerizim and Curses from Ebal," p. 203).

After Moses died, Joshua replaced him as the leader of the Israelites.

Mount Ebal, as viewed from Mount Gerizim.

One of the first things he did when he led the people to enter the land was to honor this request of Moses. He gathered the twelve tribes on the plain between these two mountains. He divided them into two groups, one facing Gerizim and the other facing Ebal. Then he read to all the people the blessings and curses that Moses had recorded in the book of Deuteronomy (see Joshua 8:33–35).

How could thousands of Israelites gathered in this valley hear and understand one reader? Many commentators speculate that these twin mountains with the short valley between them served as a natural amphitheater with perfect acoustics for the projection of Joshua's voice. But J. W. McGarvey, who visited the site in the 1880s, put this theory to the test and found that it didn't hold up.

McGarvey offered this explanation for the "miraculous hearing" between these two mountains: "Since Moses directed that Levites should be used in this ceremony (see Deuteronomy 27:14) it is probable that Joshua had them distributed throughout the crowd to take up the reading and repeat it after him sentence by sentence" (J. W. McGarvey, *Lands of the Bible*).

BLESSINGS FROM GERIZIM AND CURSES FROM EBAL

BLESSINGS:

"The LORD will conquer your enemies when they attack you. They will attack you from one direction, but they will scatter from you in seven!

"The LORD will guarantee a blessing on everything you do and will fill your storehouses with grain. The LORD your God will bless you in the land he is giving you.

"The LORD will give you prosperity in the land he swore to your ancestors to give you, blessing you with many children, numerous livestock, and abundant crops. The LORD will send rain at the proper time from his rich treasury in the heavens and will bless all the work you do" (Deuteronomy 28:7–8, 11–12).

CURSES:

"The LORD himself will send on you curses, confusion, and frustration in everything you do, until at last you are completely destroyed for doing evil and abandoning me. The LORD will afflict you with diseases until none of you are left in the land you are about to enter and occupy. The LORD will strike you with wasting diseases, fever, and inflammation, with scorching heat and drought, and with blight and mildew. These disasters will pursue you until you die. The skies above will be as unyielding as bronze, and the earth beneath will be as hard as iron. The LORD will change the rain that falls on your land into powder, and dust will pour down from the sky until you are destroyed" (Deuteronomy 28:20–24).

A Samaritan Passover
ceremony on Mount Gerizim.

MAHANAIM

MEANING "double camp" or "two armies"

PRONUNCIATION may-huh-NAY-im

SITE AND LOCATION An unidentified town in the territory east of the Jordan River near the Jabbok River — Map 2, area D-4

Jacob was returning to Canaan from his uncle Laban's home in Paddan-aram when he arrived at this place on the northern bank of the Jabbok River. Jacob had fled from Canaan about twenty years before to escape the wrath of his brother, Esau. Jacob's underhanded dealings had robbed Esau of his father's blessing and his inheritance rights as his father's oldest son. Now Jacob was facing the consequences of his shady actions. As soon as he arrived in Canaan, he feared, his brother would come looking for him with revenge on his mind.

But God had other plans. He sent angels to assure Jacob that He would be with him and protect him as he was reunited with his estranged brother. When Jacob saw these angels, he exclaimed, "This is God's camp!"

The Mahanaim region as seen from the northwest.

(Genesis 32:2). He named the place Mahanaim, meaning "two camps" or "double camp," apparently referring to his own camp as well as the camp of these protecting angels.

To Jacob's great relief, Mahanaim lived up to its name and its promise from the Lord. Esau's warm welcome assured him that all had been forgiven (see Genesis 33:1–4).

In the centuries after Jacob's naming of this camp site, it apparently developed into a city. This is the place from which King Saul's son Ishbosheth reigned for two years as king over parts of northern Israel, while David ruled in the south (see 2 Samuel 2:8–11). After two of Ishbosheth's own military commanders assassinated him, David became the undisputed king over all Israel (see 2 Samuel 4:5–7; 5:1–4).

Mahanaim also played an important role in the administration of King David. This is the city to which he fled from his capital city of Jerusalem after his son Absalom rebelled and tried to take the kingship by force. Here in friendly surroundings on the remote eastern side of the Jordan River, the king could hunker down while organizing his forces for a counterstrike against the rebel army.

What David failed to realize is that the ensuing battle would turn Mahanaim into heartbreak city. Here David waited by the city gate for news from the battlefront. When he learned that Abaslom had been killed, he reacted not as a victorious king but as a heartbroken father (see sidebar, "Good News/Bad News for King David," below). These words of David are some of the saddest in the Bible.

The site of Mahanaim has never been identified. But it was apparently near the place known as Peniel (see p. 206) on the Jabbok River.

GOOD NEWS/BAD NEWS FOR KING DAVID

Then the man from Ethiopia arrived and said, "I have good news for my lord the king. Today the LORD has rescued you from all those who rebelled against you."

"What about young Absalom?" the king demanded. "Is he all right?"

And the Ethiopian replied, "May all of your enemies, my lord the king, both now and in the future, share the fate of that young man!"

The king was overcome with emotion. He went up to the room over the gateway and burst into tears. And as he went, he cried, "O my son Absalom! My son, my son Absalom! If only I had died instead of you! O Absalom, my son, my son" (2 Samuel 18:31–33).

PENIEL

MEANING "face of God"

PRONUNCIATION pih-NIGH-uhl

SITE AND LOCATION An unidentified place east of the Jordan River near the Jabbok River
Map 6, area D-5

Jacob wrestling the angel at Peniel.

This is the only place in the Bible made famous by a wrestling match. This took place at a campsite close to Mahanaim (see p. 204) along the Jabbok River as Jacob was waiting for the arrival of his estranged brother, Esau.

During the night, a man—apparently an angel—came and wrestled with Jacob. Finally, when neither seemed to be gaining an advantage over the other, the angel struck Jacob's hip and knocked it out of joint. Then he changed his name from Jacob to Israel, meaning "prince of God" or "he who strives with God." From that point on, Israel was the formal name for the nation that sprang from the twelve sons of Jacob.

To commemorate this event, Jacob gave the name Peniel, meaning "face of God," to the site where this wrestling match took place. This name was a reminder to him that he had met God face-to-face and survived. Peniel demonstrated that the Lord specially favored the Israelites. He set them apart as His special people and expected them to serve as His channel of blessing to the other nations of the world (see Genesis 12:1–3).

In later centuries, Peniel developed into a city that served as an important defense outpost for the nation of Israel. King Jeroboam I, first king of the northern kingdom of Israel (ruled about 931–910 BC), fortified it to protect his nation from attack along its eastern border (see 1 Kings 12:25).

Several places along the Jabbok River have been proposed as possible sites of ancient Peniel. But its exact location has never been established. The modern name of the Jabbok is the Zerqa River. It runs for about sixty-five miles through deep ravines before emptying into the Jordan River about twenty-five miles north of the Dead Sea.

GILEAD

MEANING "mound of stones" or "heap of testimony"

PRONUNCIATION GILL-ee-ad

SITE AND LOCATION A mountainous region east of the Jordan River

Map 2, area D-4

While Gilead was a mountain territory, it also contained many fertile valleys where lush grasses grew. This is what impressed the tribes of Reuben and Gad when the Israelites explored this area under the leadership of Moses. The leaders of these tribes realized that these grasslands would be ideal for their herds of cattle. So they asked Moses to allow them to settle here rather than in Canaan on the western side of the Jordan River.

Moses agreed to their request. But he made them promise to support the other ten tribes militarily when they went to war with the Canaanites (see Numbers 32:1–5, 20–27). Eventually, half the tribe of Manasseh also settled in Gilead alongside Reuben and Gad (see Deuteronomy 3:12–13).

The region of Gilead was also noted for its spices and perfumes that it exported to other countries (see Genesis 37:25). Another of its valuable products was an ointment for the treatment of wounds known as the balm or medicine of Gilead. The prophet Jeremiah asked, "Is there no medicine in Gilead? Is there no physician there?" (Jeremiah 8:22). This rhetorical question implied that nothing—not even Gilead's famous medicine—could heal God's people unless they gave up their idolatry and turned back to the one true God.

The hills of Gilead in modern-day Jordan.

BETHEL

MEANING "house of God"

PRONUNCIATION BETH-uhl

SITE AND LOCATION A city about twelve miles north of Jerusalem
Map 5, area D-4

Bethel got its name because of Jacob's startling encounter with God on this site. He camped here while on his way out of the country because his brother, Esau, had threatened to kill him. Esau's anger was understandable. Jacob had fooled his father, Isaac, into blessing him rather than his oldest son, Esau (see Genesis 27:1–40). Earlier, Jacob had taken advantage of Esau's hunger and convinced him to trade his inheritance rights to Jacob for a bowl of stew (see Genesis 25:27–34). Jacob had to get out of Canaan—and fast.

That night at this campsite, Jacob had a dream in which angels were going up and down a stairway. At the top of the stairway in heaven was God, who renewed the promise He had made to Jacob's grandfather, Abraham (see sidebar, "God's Promise Renewed at Bethel," p. 209).

When Jacob woke up, he was visibly shaken by this awesome dream. He marked the place where he had been lying by setting up the stone he had used as a pillow as a makeshift altar. Then he named the place Bethel, meaning "house of God," to show that God had blessed him with His presence in this hallowed place. For many centuries after Jacob's dream on this spot, Bethel was considered a sacred site. For example, in the time of the judges, the ark of the covenant was kept here (see Judges 20:26–28).

But things took a turn for the worse when the united kingdom of David and Solomon split

An excavation of Canaanite houses at Bethel, 1954.

into two factions—south and north—after Solomon's death. King Jeroboam I of the northern kingdom (ruled about 931–910 BC) set up a calf idol at Bethel in the southern part of his territory. He also placed another calf idol at the city of Dan in the northern part of Israel. He told the people, "It is too much trouble for you to worship in Jerusalem. Look, Israel, these are the gods who brought you out of Egypt!" (1 Kings 12:28).

The prophets of the Old Testament were quick to denounce Jeroboam for encouraging his people to worship these false gods. Hosea used a play on words to show how far Bethel had fallen from its exalted position as a sacred site. Beth-el ("house of God") had degenerated into Beth-aven ("house of wickedness") (see Hosea 10:5).

On the site of Bethel today stands an Arab village known as Beitin. Not far away is a Jewish settlement named Beit El. Both these modern names preserve the meaning of Bethel's ancient name.

BETHEL: A BIBLICAL SNAPSHOT

- Bethel's original Canaanite name was Luz (see Genesis 28:19).
- When Abraham first arrived in Canaan, he set up an altar near Bethel (see Genesis 12:8).
- Bethel was on the regular circuit that Samuel traveled as judge of Israel (see 1 Samuel 7:15–17).
- Because of the calf idol at Bethel, the prophet Amos predicted that the city would be destroyed (see Amos 5:4–5).
- In his religious reformation, King Josiah of Judah (ruled about 640–609 BC) tore down the pagan calf idol and altar at Bethel (see 2 Kings 23:15).
- Some of the Jews who returned from the Babylonian exile settled in Bethel (see Nehemiah 11:31).

GOD'S PROMISE RENEWED AT BETHEL

"I am the LORD, the God of your grandfather Abraham, and the God of your father, Isaac. The ground you are lying on belongs to you. I am giving it to you and your descendants. Your descendants will be as numerous as the dust of the earth! They will spread out in all directions—to the west and the east, to the north and the south. And all the families of the earth will be blessed through you and your descendants.

"What's more, I am with you, and I will protect you wherever you go. One day I will bring you back to this land. I will not leave you until I have finished giving you everything I have promised you" (Genesis 28:13–15).

Jacob dreams of a ladder to heaven at Bethel.

KIRIATH-JEARIM

MEANING "city of forests"

PRONUNCIATION KIR-ih-ath JEE-uh-rim

SITE AND LOCATION A city about eight miles west of Jerusalem

Map 5, area C-4

This city's claim to fame is that the ark of the covenant was kept here for twenty years. Kiriath-jearim, it seems, won this honor by default because no city or town seemed to be willing to keep it for very long.

The first to give up the ark were the Philistines. They captured it from Israel, then sent it back after it caused sickness in their ranks (see 1 Samuel 6:1–12). The residents of the Israelite town of Beth-shemesh welcomed it at first. Then they pleaded with Kiriath-jearim to take it away after seventy men of

A statue of Mary, holding the baby Jesus and standing on the ark, rises above modern Kiriath-Jearim.

their town were killed when they looked into the ark (see 1 Samuel 6:13–21). It must have been with great reluctance—because of the ark's reputation for causing trouble—that "the men of Kiriath-jearim came to get the Ark of the LORD" (1 Samuel 7:1).

At Kiriath-jearim, the ark was lodged in the home of Abinadab. His son Eleazar was charged with its safekeeping. Finally, after twenty years, King David moved the ark to his new capital city, Jerusalem, where it was placed in the tabernacle where it belonged (see 2 Samuel 6:1–15).

Eleazar must have done a good job of looking after the ark. At least, no one was killed for treating it disrespectfully while it was in his care. What went through his mind when David took it away and he was relieved of this awesome responsibility? This is the question that occurred to Henry van Dyke when he visited the site of Kiriath-jearim in the early 1900s (see sidebar, "Was Eleazar Glad or Sad?" below).

WAS ELEAZAR GLAD OR SAD?

What strange vigils must have taken place in that little hilltop cottage where Eleazar watched over this precious, dangerous, gilded coffer. All the while King Saul was winning and losing his kingdom in a turmoil of blood and sorrow and madness, forgetful of Israel's covenant with the Most High. At last came King David, from his newly won stronghold of Jerusalem, seeking eagerly for this lost symbol of the people's faith. So the gray stone cottage on the hilltop gave up its sacred treasure, and David carried it away with music and dancing. But was Eleazar glad, I wonder, or sad, that his long vigil was ended?

—Henry van Dyke, *Out of Doors in the Holy Land*

SHILOH

MEANING   **unknown**

PRONUNCIATION   **SHY-low**

SITE AND LOCATION   **A city about twenty miles north of Jerusalem**

Map 3, area C-4

Shiloh was an important city to the Israelites during the period before the establishment of the united kingdom under David. Here is where the tabernacle was set up after Joshua and his forces defeated the Canaanites and claimed their land (see Joshua 18:1). Several tribes of Israel gathered at Shiloh to receive their share of the land (see Joshua 18:8–10). It was probably the main worship sanctuary for the Israelites from Joshua's time up through the period of the judges.

Shiloh also played an important role in the early life of the prophet Samuel. His mother, Hannah, had been unable to have children. So she traveled to the tabernacle at Shiloh to pray for a son. Here she met the high priest, Eli, who told her, "May the God of Israel grant the request you have asked of him" (1 Samuel 1:17).

Hannah eventually gave birth to a son, whom she named Samuel, meaning "name of God." She dedicated him to the Lord, as she had promised, and took him to live with Eli so Samuel could devote his life to service at the tabernacle (see sidebar, "The Boy Samuel at Shiloh," p. 213).

Shiloh apparently declined in importance during the ministry of Samuel. This happened when the ark of the covenant was removed to another place in Israel after its capture and returned by the Philistines (see 1 Samuel 6:1–12). When King David came to power over all Israel, he established his capital at Jerusalem, and this accelerated Shiloh's decline. Excavations at the site of Shiloh show that the city was destroyed about 1050 BC, perhaps by the Philistines.

All that remains of Shiloh today is a shapeless mass of rocks known as Khirbet Seilun. These ruins are a mute testimony to the days when it was Israel's central place of worship. The prophet Jeremiah used Shiloh's destruction as a word of warning from the Lord for the idol-worshipping Israelites of his time: "Go now to the place at Shiloh where I once put the Tabernacle that bore my name. See what I did there because of all the wickedness of my people, the Israelites" (Jeremiah 7:12).

Not far from the site of Old Testament Shiloh stands a modern Jewish synagogue, with interior furnishings that replicate the tabernacle from biblical times.

Inside the synagogue of modern Shiloh, built to look like the biblical tabernacle.

THE BOY SAMUEL AT SHILOH

When the child was weaned, Hannah took him to the Tabernacle in Shiloh. They brought along a three-year-old bull for the sacrifice and a basket of flour and some wine. After sacrificing the bull, they brought the boy to Eli. "Sir, do you remember me?" Hannah asked. "I am the woman who stood here several years ago praying to the Lord. I asked the Lord to give me this boy, and he has granted my request. Now I am giving him to the Lord, and he will belong to the Lord his whole life." And they worshiped the Lord there (1 Samuel 1:24–28).

Ruins of a Roman theater in Samaria.

CHAPTER 9

This section of the Holy Land takes in basically what is referred to in the New Testament as the region of Samaria—the territory between Galilee in the north and Judea in the south. This area took its name from the city of Samaria, capital city of the northern kingdom of Israel for a time. Many sites associated with the northern kingdom are located in this section of Israel.

The northern part of this territory extends into lower Galilee. Lower and upper Galilee make up the section of the Holy Land where Jesus spent most of His earthly ministry. Perhaps the most important site in Galilee is Nazareth, the town where Jesus grew up. When He was about thirty years old, He moved to nearby Capernaum on the northern shore of the Sea of Galilee. This became the headquarters of His Galilean ministry. The places He visited in Galilee, with the exception of Nain, are discussed in the next chapter.

DOTHAN

MEANING   "two wells"

PRONUNCIATION   DOE-thun

SITE AND LOCATION   A town about eleven miles north of Samaria

Map 2, area C-3

Dothan is a good example of the principle that God can turn tragedy into triumph. At this town, several of Jacob's sons sold their younger brother Joseph to a passing caravan of traders (see Genesis 37:26–28). These traveling merchants took Joseph to Egypt, where they sold him as a household slave. But God was with this young man, and he eventually became a high official in the Egyptian government (see Genesis 41:37–44).

Because of Joseph's influence and political pull, he was able to save his family from starvation by moving them to Egypt to escape a severe famine (see Genesis 46:28–34). Once they got settled, Joseph's brothers were afraid he would punish them because of the wrong they had committed against him. But Joseph assured them of his forgiveness because God had turned the tragedy of Dothan into a blessing for His people, the Israelites.

Several centuries after Joseph's time, Dothan was the scene of another example of God's provision and protection. Enemy soldiers were sent to arrest the prophet Elisha at this city. But God struck them with blindness, allowing the prophet to escape (see 2 Kings 6:12–18).

A well thought to be the one Joseph was left in, from a photograph taken in the early 1900s.

Today, a large twenty-five-acre mound known as Tel Dothan marks the site of the ancient city. Here archaeologists have unearthed the remains of twenty-one different levels of occupation going back for several thousand years. At the base of the mound is a spring, perhaps the water source that brought Joseph's brothers to this area to pasture their father's flocks (see Genesis 37:14–17). As Dothan's name implies, there may also have been wells nearby that served the same purpose.

BETH-SHAN

MEANING "place of security" or "house of ease"

PRONUNCIATION BETH-shan

SITE AND LOCATION A city about five miles southeast of Mount Gilboa
Map 2, area D-3

When the Israelites finally entered the promised land, many Canaanite cities fell to Joshua and his forces (see "Jericho" and "Ai" in chapter 8, pp. 184, 187). But they were not successful in capturing every city. Beth-shan was one stronghold that remained in Canaanite hands (see Joshua 17:11–12). Excavations at the site have shown that it was a well-fortified city for many centuries before Joshua's time.

Apparently the Philistines occupied the city or aligned with its Canaanite residents in the years after the Israelites entered the territory. Here is where the Philistines hung the body of King Saul on the city wall after overrunning

The uncovered streets of Beth-shan.

Saul's army on nearby Mount Gilboa (see sidebar, "A Gruesome Display at Beth-shan," below). This primitive "billboard" sent a sobering message to all Israel about the power and intentions of the Philistines. They were determined to take over Israelite territory by pushing eastward from their original settlements along the Mediterranean coast.

After David succeeded Saul as king, he defeated the Philistines (see 2 Samuel 8:1). His son and successor, Solomon, turned Beth-shan into one of his administrative cities that was responsible for collecting taxes and providing food from its surrounding territory for the royal court in Jerusalem (see 1 Kings 4:7–8, 12).

In later centuries, Beth-shan grew into a major Roman city known as Scythopolis. Archaeologists have uncovered the remains of this city, as well as several others that preceded it on this site. Known as Tel Beit Shean, it is one of the most impressive archaeological and tourism attractions in the Holy Land. Visible here are the remains of a Roman theater that would seat six thousand people, a paved street, and the huge stone columns that stood along the thoroughfare into the city.

The unique multimedia show staged at night during the busy tourist season awes modern visitors to ancient Beth-shan. They stroll through the streets of the excavated city while images from the past are projected onto its columns, walls, and temples. Realistic sound effects are added to the experience to make it seem like you are in the middle of a Roman city from two thousand years ago.

A GRUESOME DISPLAY AT BETH-SHAN

The next day, when the Philistines went out to strip the dead, they found the bodies of Saul and his three sons on Mount Gilboa. So they cut off Saul's head and stripped off his armor. Then they proclaimed the good news of Saul's death in their pagan temple and to the people throughout the land of Philistia. They placed his armor in the temple of the Ashtoreths, and they fastened his body to the wall of the city of Beth-shan (1 Samuel 31:8–10).

DOR

MEANING "habitation"

PRONUNCIATION dawr

SITE AND LOCATION A town on the Mediterranean Sea about eight miles north of Caesarea

Map 2, area B-3

What we know about this biblical city is about as little as its three-letter name. Here are the three facts about it that we know for sure: (1) Dor was a Canaanite town Joshua captured (see Joshua 12:7, 23 KJV); (2) it was part of the inheritance of the tribe of Manasseh (see Joshua 17:11 KJV); and (3) it was the seat of one of King Solomon's tax districts (see 1 Kings 4:7, 11 KJV). Some translations render the name of the city "Naphoth-dor" (Joshua 11:2).

Dor was an important port city on the Mediterranean Sea until Herod the Great built his more modern port at Caesarea just eight miles away (see "Caesarea," p. 220). This caused Dor to decline in importance. But to modern scholars, its seaside location gives it special status as an archaeological site. Excavations have been conducted here for several seasons, and it will probably eventually be developed into an Israeli archaeological park.

The coastline at Dor.

CAESAREA

MEANING   named for the Roman emperor Caesar Augustus

PRONUNCIATION   sess-uh-REE-uh

SITE AND LOCATION   A city on the coast of the Mediterranean Sea
Map 6, area B-4

Herod the Great was known for the building projects that he completed in the Holy Land (see chapter 3, "Herodium," p. 47). But the port city of Caesarea was probably his most impressive achievement.

On the site of an ancient Phoenician fortress known as Strato's Tower, he built a new city that he named for the Roman emperor Caesar Augustus. Caesarea served for about six centuries as the Roman government's administrative capital for the province of Palestine. Here is where several major events in the early years of the Christian church took place (see sidebar, "Caesarea: A Biblical Snapshot," p. 221).

The remains of the amphitheater at Caesarea Maritima.

Herod constructed a port for ships at Caesarea by creating a huge break-water wall to provide protection from the pounding surf and shifting sands. This was accomplished by towing huge wooden forms out to sea, then filling them with stones and concrete and sinking them into place on the sea floor. This is one of the first documented uses of concrete in the ancient world. Over time, this sea wall collapsed, but some of the huge concrete blocks that made up the wall still remain in the water. These are not visible from the shore, but they have been discovered through underwater archaeology.

Visitors to Caesarea are also impressed with the remains of a Roman theater that stand on the site. Archaeologists digging here found a stone tablet inscribed with the name of Pontius Pilate. Known as the Pilate Stone, it gives evidence of the existence of the Roman official who pronounced the death penalty against Jesus (see Luke 23:1). Visitors are shown a replica; the original stone is housed in a museum.

Another testimony to the skills of Herod's engineers is an aboveground aqueduct that brought water to the city from Mount Carmel about thirteen miles away. Then, as now, water was a precious commodity in Palestine. This ancient aqueduct may have provided water for a population center of as many as 100,000 people.

Today the site of this ancient Roman city has been turned into an Israeli national park. It is included on the itinerary of most Holy Land tours. It is often referred to as Caesarea Maritima ("Caesarea by the Sea") to distinguish it from the Caesarea (Caesarea Philippi) north of the Sea of Galilee.

CAESAREA: A BIBLICAL SNAPSHOT

- Philip the evangelist traveled to Caesarea on a preaching mission (see Acts 8:40). Philip may have lived at Caesarea, since the apostle Paul visited him here at the end of his second missionary journey (see Acts 21:8–9).
- Here a Roman military officer named Cornelius had a spiritual vision that caused him to ask the apostle Peter to visit him at Caesarea (see Acts 10:1–8).

The likeness of Herod Agrippa I on a coin.

- Cornelius and members of his household were converted at Caesarea and baptized by the apostle Peter (see Acts 10:44–48). This opened the doors for the reception of Gentiles into the church.
- A deadly disease struck Herod Agrippa I at Caesarea because he allowed the people to worship him as a god (see Acts 12:20–23).
- The apostle Paul was imprisoned for two years at Caesarea. Here he made his eloquent defense before Herod Agrippa II (see Acts 25:23–26:32).

NAZARETH

MEANING "watchtower"

PRONUNCIATION NAZ-ah-reth

SITE AND LOCATION A town about thirteen miles southwest of the southern tip of the Sea of Galilee Map 6, area C-3

Nazareth, Jesus' hometown, is a good example of the way He surprised people throughout His earthly ministry. Soon after John the Baptist baptized Him in southern Israel, He traveled northward into the area around the Sea of Galilee. Here He met Philip and called him to become one of His disciples. Philip, in turn, found his friend Nathanael and told Nathanael that he had met the Messiah, "the son of Joseph from Nazareth" (John 1:45).

Nathanael was shocked at the idea that an insignificant village such as Nazareth could be the Messiah's hometown. His eyes must have widened in surprise as he asked Philip, "Can anything good come from Nazareth?" (John 1:46). He probably thought the Messiah would come from one of the great centers of Jewish culture such as Jerusalem or Joppa.

Nathanael's skepticism is understandable. After all, Nazareth is not even mentioned in the Old Testament. No famous event from Israel's history had taken place there. This village was a quiet little settlement where only a few families lived. It sat in a basin of the hills that overlooked the Jezreel Valley (see p. 237). A major trade route did pass through this valley. But the traffic bypassed Nazareth—much like a sleepy little town of today that sits near an interstate highway without off or on ramps to provide access to the outside world.

Here in Nazareth is where Jesus grew up—from the time when He was a child (see Luke 2:39–40) until the age of about thirty, when He launched His public ministry (see Luke 3:23). He tried to explain His mission as the Messiah to His friends in the town (see Luke 4:14–21). But they were more skeptical about His claims than Nathanael had been about the place that Jesus called home. They refused to believe that one of their own could be the Messiah whom God had promised to send to redeem His people (see sidebar, "Just a Carpenter from Nazareth," p. 224).

According to Luke's Gospel, Jesus criticized the townspeople for their response to His claim to messiahship. Then He told them that Gentiles were more open to God's grace than the Jewish people. This infuriated them, and they tried to kill Jesus by throwing Him off a cliff. But He miraculously escaped and left the town (see Luke 4:23–30).

About thirty-one years before Jesus left Nazareth, this village—in spite of its lowly status—was the scene of one of the most important announcements in world history. Here an angel told the virgin Mary she would conceive by the action of the Holy Spirit and would give birth to the Messiah (see Luke 1:26–38).

As it turned out, Jesus was not born in Nazareth but in Bethlehem (see chapter 7, p. 154), another humble village located about sixty-five miles to the south, near Jerusalem. But He returned to Nazareth with His parents after they spent some time in Egypt to escape the death threat of Herod the Great, Roman ruler over Palestine (see Matthew 2:19–23).

After leaving Nazareth, Jesus moved to Capernaum (see chapter 10, p. 250) on the Sea of Galilee and made it the headquarters of His Galilean ministry (see Matthew 4:12–17). But during His earthly ministry, many people referred to Him as "Jesus of Nazareth" (Luke 4:34) or "Jesus the Nazarene" (Luke 18:37). Even the sign Pilate posted on His cross referred to Him as "Jesus of Nazareth" (John 19:19). Thus Nazareth was transformed into a famous place because of its association with the Savior of the world.

No Holy Land tour is complete without a visit to Nazareth. In recent years, what used to be an insignificant village has grown into one of the largest Arabic cities in Israel, with a population of about eighty thousand people. But Old Nazareth, with its holy sites preserved by churches, is still visible, and it welcomes thousands of visitors every year.

The number one attraction in Nazareth is the Basilica of the Annunciation, a Catholic church built over the reputed site of the angel Gabriel's announcement to Mary that she would give birth to the Messiah. This beautiful two-story church, with a spire that towers high over the city, is built over the ruins of several other churches that have stood here in the past. The interior of the building is decorated with murals that portray scenes in the life of Jesus during His growing-up years in Nazareth.

The Church of the Annunciation.

Nearby is another church that claims it marks the spot where this announcement took place. The Greek Orthodox Church of Saint Gabriel insists that Gabriel appeared to Mary at the village water source known as Mary's Spring. Water from this spring is still flowing

JUST A CARPENTER FROM NAZARETH

Jesus left that part of the country and returned with his disciples to Nazareth, his hometown. The next Sabbath he began teaching in the synagogue, and many who heard him were amazed. They asked, "Where did he get all this wisdom and the power to perform such miracles?" Then they scoffed, "He's just a carpenter, the son of Mary and the brother of James, Joseph, Judas, and Simon. And his sisters live right here among us." They were deeply offended and refused to believe in him.

Then Jesus told them, "A prophet is honored everywhere except in his own hometown and among his relatives and his own family." And because of their unbelief, he couldn't do any mighty miracles among them except to place his hands on a few sick people and heal them. And he was amazed at their unbelief (Mark 6:1–6).

today. It is channeled through the church building to an adjoining courtyard, where it collects in a pool known as Mary's Well.

Still another holy site in Nazareth is the Mount of Precipice, located near one of the entrances into the city. This is designated by tradition as the steep cliff from which the people of Nazareth tried to push Jesus to His death. From this high peak on a clear day, visitors get a breathtaking view of the surrounding territory, including the Mount Carmel mountain range to the west, the Jezreel Valley to the south, and the Sea of Galilee to the east.

Another place many pilgrims visit is Saint Joseph's Church, a Catholic Franciscan church built over the reputed site of Joseph's woodworking shop in Nazareth. Here the boy Jesus would have worked with His father, Joseph, making furniture and other items for their customers.

Modern Nazareth has added a new attraction to these classic Holy Land sites that have existed for centuries. It's called Nazareth Village. Here visitors can see costumed "residents" of the village from Jesus' time going about their daily activities—spinning thread, tending sheep, baking bread, drawing water, and harvesting wheat. These re-enactors show visitors what life in Nazareth would have been like when Jesus lived here almost two thousand years ago.

About three miles west of Nazareth during Jesus' time was a beautiful Roman city known as Sepphoris. This served as the capital of Herod Antipas, Roman ruler in this section of Palestine, until he built Tiberias (see chapter 10, p. 258) by the Sea of Galilee as his new capital. We have no record in the Gospels that Jesus ever visited Sepphoris. The site has been excavated and is included on many Holy Land tours.

NAIN

MEANING "delightful" or "pleasant"

PRONUNCIATION nane

SITE AND LOCATION A town about six miles southeast of Nazareth

Map 6, area C-3

Nain was less than a day's walk from Jesus' hometown of Nazareth, so He must have been very familiar with this village. He probably passed through Nain several times during His growing-up years and even later in life while teaching and healing in the region around the Sea of Galilee.

But only one visit of Jesus to Nain is recorded in the Gospels—and Luke's Gospel alone tells us about it. It was certainly a visit worth recording. Luke's account shows us a Jesus touched by the sad scene of a funeral procession coming out of the village. But Jesus did more than feel sorry for the person who had lost a loved one. He reached out and did something about it (see sidebar, "The Compassionate Christ in Action at Nain," p. 226).

One of the most interesting things about this miracle is how the people of the town reacted to it. They declared, "A mighty prophet has risen among us" (Luke 7:16). Perhaps they were comparing Jesus to the prophet Elisha, who had brought another widow's son back to life several centuries before. Elisha's miracle had taken place at Shunem (see p. 226), a town only about three miles north of Nain (see 2 Kings 4:8–37).

The Arab village of Nein or Kafr-Nin.

A comparison of these two miracles is also interesting. At Shunem, Elisha stretched himself out on the dead child's body. Then he walked around the room and stretched out on the body again before the boy finally came to life. But Jesus raised the son of the widow at Nain with a simple command. This left no doubt in the minds of the townspeople that they had seen the hand of God at work in Jesus' miracle (Luke 7:16).

An Arab village known as Nein or Kafr-Nin stands today on the site of the town where this miracle took place. A small church the Catholic Franciscan order built in the 1800s commemorates the event.

THE COMPASSIONATE CHRIST IN ACTION AT NAIN

Church of the Resurrection of the Widow's Son.

Soon afterward Jesus went with his disciples to the village of Nain, and a large crowd followed him. A funeral procession was coming out as he approached the village gate. The young man who had died was a widow's only son, and a large crowd from the village was with her. When the Lord saw her, his heart overflowed with compassion. "Don't cry!" he said. Then he walked over to the coffin and touched it, and the bearers stopped. "Young man," he said, "I tell you, get up." Then the dead boy sat up and began to talk! And Jesus gave him back to his mother (Luke 7:11–15).

SHUNEM

MEANING unknown

PRONUNCIATION SHOO-num

SITE AND LOCATION A city about twelve miles southwest of the southern tip of the Sea of Galilee

Map 6, area C-3

This city was the home of a kind woman who provided food and lodging for the prophet Elisha and his servant, Gehazi. In return for her kindness, the prophet promised her that she would give birth to a son. Later on, when this son died, she traveled all the way across the Jezreel Valley to Mount Carmel to ask for Elisha's help. He returned with her to Shunem, where he brought the boy back to life (see 2 Kings 4:8–37).

This town was also the home of a young woman named Abishag, who was brought to Jerusalem to serve as a nurse and companion for the aging and ill King David (see 1 Kings 1:1–4). She is referred to in the King James Version as a "Shunammite," or a person from Shunem.

A minor village in Bible times, Shunem never developed into much of a town in later centuries. An Arab village known as Sulem or Solam occupies the site today.

ENDOR

MEANING "fountain of habitation"

PRONUNCIATION IN-dawr

SITE AND LOCATION An unidentified village in the vicinity of Mount Gilboa
Map 2, area D-3

King Saul was looking a full-blown crisis in the face. Camped on Mount Gilboa, he knew his army was no match for the superior Philistine force stationed at the nearby city of Shunem. In previous situations like this, he had relied on the prophet Samuel for counsel. But Samuel was dead. So

Ruins in Tel Qudesh National Park mark a possible location for Endor.

the king decided to visit a witch or medium at the village of Endor just north of Mount Gilboa. Perhaps she could call up the spirit of Samuel for the prophet's advice (see 1 Samuel 28:3–7).

But Saul had banned all black-magic practitioners like her from Israel (see 1 Samuel 28:3). If she recognized him, she would refuse to call up the prophet. So Saul set out for Endor in the clothes of a common man rather than his royal robes. Here was the most powerful man in Israel trembling in fear before the enemy, trying to hide his true identity, seeking the services of a psychic whom he despised, and asking advice from a dead man! This was certainly one of the darkest moments in Saul's downward-spiraling career as the first king of Israel.

As it turned out, Saul was able to convince the woman to call up Samuel's spirit. But after Samuel told the king how the battle would go, he must have left the village with a heavy heart (see sidebar, "Shocking News for Saul at Endor," left). To the king's credit, he did not turn and run but led his men into battle the next day—with disastrous results (see "Mount Gilboa," p. 229).

The exact site of Endor has never been identified, although several possibilities have been suggested. One possibility is Tel Zafzefa, located a short distance from the abandoned Arab village of Indur, which preserves the ancient name.

Saul falls to the ground in fright as the spirit of Samuel gives him bad news.

MOUNT GILBOA

MEANING   perhaps "bubbling fountain"

PRONUNCIATION   gill-BOW-uh

SITE AND LOCATION   A mountain about three miles southeast of the city of Jezreel

Map 2, area C-3

Mount Gilboa is not a single mountain but a mountain range that serves as a natural boundary between the regions of Samaria and Galilee. This range is about eight miles long by four miles wide. Its highest peak rises to about 1,700 feet above sea level. Here on one of these high places, King Saul and his three sons lost their lives in a battle with the Philistines (see 1 Chronicles 10:1–6).

Severely wounded in the battle, Saul feared that he would be tortured if he fell into the hands of his Philistine enemies. So he committed suicide by falling on his own sword (see 1 Samuel 31:3–6). This was a tragic conclusion to the reign of the first king of Israel. He began with great promise but let his pride and his jealousy of David cloud his judgment until they brought him to this shameful end.

This sad event for which Gilboa is known contrasts sharply with the beauty of the mountains themselves. The Gilboa range is one of the most beautiful places in the Holy Land, offering breathtaking views of the surrounding valleys. Visitors come here to enjoy the cool, tranquil setting, with its hiking trails, forests, and picnic areas. In the spring, the beautiful blossoms of a purple wildflower known as the Gilboa Iris greet them.

One of the Gilboa peaks, Mount Shaul—a popular hang-gliding site—is named for the first king of Israel. A nearby major recreation site is known as Ketef Shaul or "Saul's Shoulder."

A war memorial on Jonathan Hill in the Gilboa Mountains.

OPHRAH

MEANING "fawn"

PRONUNCIATION AHF-rah

SITE AND LOCATION An unidentified city in the vicinity of Mount Gilboa
Map 3, area C-3

No one knows the exact site of this city, but what happened here is one of the most memorable events of the Bible. At Ophrah, God transformed a frightened farmer into one of the most courageous military leaders of all time.

This transformation happened during the period of the judges, when the Midianites terrorized Israel. These camel-riding raiders swooped into the territory of the tribe of Manasseh, stealing the Israelites' livestock and destroying their crops. Fear paralyzed God's people, and no one seemed to be willing to step forward as the leader for these perilous times.

A man named Gideon in the city of Ophrah was just as frightened as everyone else. He was threshing wheat in the bottom of a winepress to keep

Gideon's Cave in the Maayan Harod National Park.

the Midianites from detecting and destroying it. Imagine his surprise when an angel appeared and greeted him with these words: "Mighty hero, the LORD is with you!" (Judges 6:12). Gideon certainly didn't feel like a hero, and it seemed to him that God had forgotten His people. So he asked the angel, "If the LORD is with us, why has all this happened to us?" (Judges 6:13).

Through a series of miraculous signs, the angel convinced Gideon that God was still watching over His people and that Gideon was the right person to lead a military campaign against the Midianite raiders. Gideon gathered a huge army. But the Lord thinned it down from twenty-two thousand to ten thousand and then finally to just three hundred warriors. With this handful of men, and by relying on the Lord, Gideon overcame the Midianite horde and drove them from the land of Israel (see Judges 6:36–7:22).

The location of Gideon's hometown is a mystery that may never be solved. But Holy Land visitors are shown another site that is traditionally associated with his famous military campaign. On the northwestern slope of Mount Gilboa is a water source known as Harod Spring (see Judges 7:1). This is reputed to be the spring where the Israelite warriors quenched their thirst just before they routed the Midianites. At God's instructions, only the men who drank by scooping up water in their hands made the final cut as Gideon's recruits (see sidebar, "An Army of Three Hundred Hand-Drinkers," below).

This spring is part of a modern scenic attraction known as Harod Spring National Park. It flows from a cave named—you guessed it—Gideon's Cave.

AN ARMY OF THREE HUNDRED HAND-DRINKERS

The LORD told Gideon, "There are still too many! Bring them down to the spring, and I will test them to determine who will go with you and who will not." When Gideon took his warriors down to the water, the LORD told him, "Divide the men into two groups. In one group put all those who cup water in their hands and lap it up with their tongues like dogs. In the other group put all those who kneel down and drink with their mouths in the stream." Only 300 of the men drank from their hands. All the others got down on their knees and drank with their mouths in the stream.

The LORD told Gideon, "With these 300 men I will rescue you and give you victory over the Midianites. Send all the others home." So Gideon collected the provisions and rams' horns of the other warriors and sent them home. But he kept the 300 men with him (Judges 7:4–8).

Gideon and his 300 men blow their horns and wave their torches.

TIRZAH

MEANING   "delightful"

PRONUNCIATION   TUR-zuh

SITE AND LOCATION   A city about five miles northeast of Samaria

Map 2, area C-4

Tirzah's main claim to fame is that it served for about forty years as the capital city of the northern kingdom of Israel. Tirzah was Israel's second capital, preceded by Shechem (see chapter 8, p. 197) and then followed by Samaria (see p. 233). Tirzah must have been a beautiful city because King Solomon declared that his bride was as beautiful as "the lovely city of Tirzah" (Song of Solomon 6:4).

This city was also the site of one of the few suicides recorded in the Bible. This happened during the turbulent early years of the northern kingdom when a military commander named Omri (ruled about 885–874 BC) led a rebellion against King Zimri (ruled about 885 BC) at Tirzah. The city fell easily to Omri's forces. Realizing that he would be assassinated, Zimri "went into the citadel of the palace and burned it down over himself and died in the flames" (1 Kings 16:18).

After reigning at Tirzah for six years, King Omri built a brand-new

capital city at Samaria (see p. 233) just a few miles away (see 1 Kings 16:23–24). Excavations at Tirzah's ruins—known as Tel el-Farah—have uncovered buildings that were started but never finished. Archaeologists speculate that these were abandoned in mid-construction when Omri decided to move to Samaria's higher ground—a more defensible site.

Overlooking the ruins of Tirzah.

SAMARIA

MEANING   "lookout" or "watch station"

PRONUNCIATION   suh-MARE-ee-uh

SITE AND LOCATION   A city about midway between the Jordan River and the Mediterranean Sea

Map 6, area C-4

Omri, the builder of Samaria (ruled about 885–874 BC), is one of those minor biblical kings who could have used a public relations assistant. According to the Bible, his one noteworthy accomplishment was building this city to serve as the new capital city of the northern kingdom (see 1 Kings 16:21–28). At least he could have named the city after himself to make sure future generations remembered him. But no—that honor went to Shemer, the man from whom Omri bought the hill on which Samaria was built. If the king had hired a PR firm, we would probably be referring to this city today as "Omriville."

Omri deserves credit for putting an end to the "movable capital city" mentality. During the first fifty years of the northern kingdom's existence, the capital was located at Shechem (see chapter 8, p. 197), then Tirzah (see p. 232). But once Omri built Samaria, the capital remained here until the nation fell to the Assyrians about 150 years later.

Samaria sat atop a three-hundred-foot-high hill that gave it good protection on all sides from an enemy attack. The Syrians besieged the city until its residents ran out of food, but God destroyed the army with a mysterious plague (see 2 Kings 6:24–7:20). The mighty Assyrian army finally overran Samaria in 722 BC, but it took a three-year siege to bring the city to its knees (see 2 Kings 17:5–6). It seems that Omri did a good day's work when he selected the location for his new capital city.

Part of the Roman temple uncovered in Samaria.

The Assyrians did not destroy Samaria. Instead, they repopulated the city and other sections of the former northern kingdom with foreigners who worshipped pagan gods (see 2 Kings 17:24–25, 29–33). Over the centuries, intermarriage of the Jews with these Gentiles produced a half-breed race known as Samaritans. Pure-blooded Jews despised these people because of their mixed-blood ancestry.

Several centuries after Omri's time, Herod the Great built Samaria into a modern city and renamed it Sebaste in honor of the Roman emperor Caesar Augustus (*Sebaste* is the Greek term for *Augustus*). This is probably the "city of [the region of] Samaria" the evangelist Philip visited on a preaching mission after believers fled Jerusalem to escape persecution (see Acts 8:4–8).

In excavations at Samaria, remains of the Old Testament city as well as the Roman city of later centuries have been discovered. Modern visitors are shown the remains of a theater from Herod's time as well as a huge temple that he dedicated to Augustus. One of the most interesting Old Testament discoveries consists of pieces of ivory apparently used as inlays for furniture and as decorative wall panels. King Ahab (ruled about 874–853 BC) of the northern kingdom may have used these in the infamous "ivory palace" he built here after Omri's time (see 1 Kings 22:39; Amos 6:4).

Another find from Ahab's time is a large pool used for bathing, located not far from an ornate, two-story palace. Archaeologists speculate that this could have been the pool where King Ahab's blood was washed from his chariot after he was killed in a battle against the Syrians (see 1 Kings 22:37–38).

An Arab village known as Sebastiyeh now stands on part of the site of this ancient and historic city.

RAMOTH-GILEAD

MEANING "heights of Gilead"

PRONUNCIATION RAY-muth GILL-ee-ad

SITE AND LOCATION An unidentified city east of the Jordan River, perhaps near the Jabbok River   Map 2, area E-3

All of us have a bad day now and then—the kind when everything goes wrong and you get nothing done. But none of our disastrous days come close to what happened to King Ahab (ruled about 874–853 BC) of the northern kingdom of Israel.

The king set out one day to take back the city of Ramoth-gilead from the Syrians, also referred to as the Arameans. This city on the border of Israel and Syria had changed hands several times. The day ended with the city still in Syrian hands and the king mortally wounded by a stray arrow. This was definitely a day when the king should have stayed at home.

The king's death was not a random, accidental happening. At Ramoth-gilead, he suffered the Lord's punishment for all the evil acts he had committed during his reign as king of Israel. His greatest crime was encouraging idolatry in the land (see 1 Kings 16:29–33).

Ahab had also killed an innocent man named Naboth and taken his property and turned it into a vegetable garden near his palace. Because of this heinous act, the prophet Elijah told the king, "Dogs will lick your blood at the very place where they licked the blood of Naboth!" (1 Kings 21:19). The "random" arrow that took Ahab's life at Ramoth-gilead was a fulfillment of Elijah's prophecy of the divine punishment that the evil king deserved.

After Ahab's death, his son Joram succeeded him as king. Joram (ruled about 852–841 BC) continued Ahab's attempts to capture Ramoth-gilead, but he fared little better than his father. Wounded in a battle here, he was forced to retreat across the Jordan River to recover from his wounds at the city of Jezreel (see 2 Kings 8:28–29). Here a military commander named Jehu assassinated him. Ironically, Joram's body was dumped on the very plot of ground that his father had stolen from Naboth (see 2 Kings 9:21–26).

Ramoth-gilead was so named because it was located in Gilead, a territory of fertile pastureland on the eastern side of the Jordan River (see chapter 8, "Gilead," p. 207). This region was a part of Israel in Old Testament times, but it lies in the nation of Jordan today.

When in Israelite hands, Ramoth-gilead served as a city of refuge (see Deuteronomy 4:43)—a place to which a person could flee if he had accidentally killed someone. This kept him safe from retaliation by relatives of the person who had been killed while city officials investigated the homicide.

The site of ancient Ramoth-gilead is uncertain. Some scholars favor a mound known as Tel er-Ramith, located in northern Jordan near the Syrian border. Others identify the city with Reimun, a place near the Jabbok River.

JEZREEL

MEANING "God scatters" or "God sows"

PRONUNCIATION JEZ-real

SITE AND LOCATION A city about fifteen miles southwest of the southern tip of the Sea of Galilee   Map 2, area C-3

Ironically, the name of this city sounds a lot like Jezebel, the wicked wife of King Ahab (ruled about 874–853 BC) of the northern kingdom of Israel. So it is appropriate that this is the place where she finally got what she deserved (see sidebar, "Jezebel's Fall at Jezreel," p. 237). She was thrown over the city walls to her death. Then dogs ate her body, just as the prophet Elijah had predicted several years before (see 1 Kings 21:23).

Jezebel had plotted to have an innocent man killed so King Ahab could confiscate his property (see 1 Kings 21:1–16). The Lord had made it clear that this heinous act would not go unpunished (see 1 Kings 21:17–19). The instrument of His judgment was a man named Jehu, who took the throne after assassinating Ahab's son and successor, Joram (see 2 Kings 9:1–23).

Jezebel's death at the city of Jezreel was grisly enough. But Jehu didn't stop with her. He also executed all of Ahab's sons—possible threats to his kingship—and piled up their heads outside the city gate (see 2 Kings 10:6–8). These incidents at Jezreel are enough to give it a reputation as one of the

The view from Tel Jezreel, the site of the ancient city of Jezreel, across the plain of the same name.

bloodiest cities of the Old Testament.

During Ahab's reign over the northern kingdom, Samaria was his capital city (see 1 Kings 16:24, 29). So Jezreel, about thirty-three miles north of Samaria, must have been the site of his summer palace. The city's name was applied to a large nearby plain, the valley of Jezreel (see Joshua 17:16), also known as the Plain of Esdraelon.

JEZEBEL'S FALL AT JEZREEL

When Jezebel, the queen mother, heard that Jehu had come to Jezreel, she painted her eyelids and fixed her hair and sat at a window. When Jehu entered the gate of the palace, she shouted at him, "Have you come in peace, you murderer? You're just like Zimri, who murdered his master!"

Jehu looked up and saw her at the window and shouted, "Who is on my side?" And two or three eunuchs looked out at him. "Throw her down!" Jehu yelled. So they threw her out the window, and her blood spattered against the wall and on the horses. And Jehu trampled her body under his horses' hooves.

Then Jehu went into the palace and ate and drank. Afterward he said, "Someone go and bury this cursed woman, for she is the daughter of a king." But when they went out to bury her, they found only her skull, her feet, and her hands (2 Kings 9:30–35).

The dogs await Jezebel in Jezreel.

JEZREEL VALLEY / ESDRAELON VALLEY

MEANING	"God scatters" or "God sows"
PRONUNCIATION	JEZ-real / Ez-DREE-lun
SITE AND LOCATION	A valley about twenty miles southwest of the southern tip of the Sea of Galilee Map 7, area D-6

In a land noted for its mountains, hills, and deep ravines, this piece of real estate really stands out. Shaped like a triangular wedge about fifteen by fifteen by twenty miles in size, the Jezreel Valley is the largest section of flat land in the entire Holy Land. With a little creative stretching, we might even refer to it as "Israel's prairie."

References to this valley in the Bible can be confusing because it goes by so many different names. For example, the King James Version refers to it as the Plain of Tabor (see 1 Samuel 10:3) because Mount Tabor (see p. 239) is the only mountain that rises up from its otherwise flat landscape. The prophet Zechariah called this plain the valley of Megiddo because the city of Megiddo (see p. 241) overlooked it (see Zechariah 12:11).

To add to the confusion, the Valley of Jezreel is often referred to as the Plain of Esdraelon—the Greek equivalent of the Hebrew word *Jezreel*. But no matter what you call it, this valley has always served as the natural dividing line between the regions of Samaria and Galilee.

Throughout the centuries, dozens of battles have been fought in the Valley of Jezreel. Most of these conflicts were between major world powers that wanted to control the ancient international trade route that passed through the valley. But lesser battles have also taken place here or in the surrounding territory—for example, Gideon against the Midianites (see "Ophrah," p. 230), Saul against the Philistines (see "Mount Gilboa," p. 229), and Deborah and Barak against the Canaanites (see "Kishon River," p. 243).

At one time, the Valley of Jezreel was swampy and unproductive. But in recent years the Israeli government has drained the land and turned it into the most productive agricultural land in the country. Today it is considered the "breadbasket of Israel," producing as many as seven or eight crops of food and fiber a year to support the permanent residents of the Holy Land.

Crops of the Jezreel Valley under an early morning mist.

MOUNT TABOR

MEANING "height"

PRONUNCIATION TAY-buhr

SITE AND LOCATION A mountain about ten miles southwest of the southern tip of the Sea of Galilee   Map 2, area C-3

It's hard to miss Mount Tabor. It towers about 1,400 feet above the flat plains of the Jezreel Valley, standing out like a floating ball in a large swimming pool. The peak looks like an extinct volcano because of its distinctive cone shape, but no evidence of volcanic activity has been discovered at the site. Covered with trees, grass, and wildflowers, it is a colorful contrast to the drab landscape of much of the land of Israel. No wonder many tourists describe Mount Tabor as one of the most beautiful places in the entire Holy Land.

But its natural beauty is not the main thing for which Mount Tabor is noted. According to an early Christian tradition, this is the place where Jesus was transfigured before three of His disciples—Peter, James, and John (see sidebar, "Jesus Reveals His Glory," p. 240).

This appearance of Jesus in glorified form before these three disciples is one of the most puzzling events in His ministry. What did it mean?

He had told His disciples all along that He would eventually be glorified by the Father, received into heaven, and then return to earth one day in all His glory (see Matthew 25:31; Luke 24:26). So in His glorified appearance on Mount Tabor, Jesus must have been giving them a preview of His future glory. Perhaps He did this to prepare them for the ordeal that lay ahead—His suffering, crucifixion, and death.

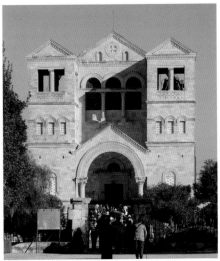

The Church of the Transfiguration on Mount Tabor.

Over the centuries, several churches, chapels, and shrines have been built on Mount Tabor to commemorate this place as the site of the Transfiguration. Two modern monasteries—one Catholic and one Greek Orthodox—stand on the ruins of several of these ancient buildings. Attached to the Catholic monastery is a church known as the Church of the Transfiguration, a stop included on many Holy Land tours.

Not everyone agrees that Tabor is the mountain where the Transfiguration took place. All three accounts of this event in the Gospels state that it happened on "a mountain" or "a high mountain," without mentioning a specific peak (see Matthew 17:1; Mark 9:2; Luke 9:28). Some scholars believe that Mount Hermon (see chapter 10, p. 266), north of the Sea of Galilee, is the likelier site.

JESUS REVEALS HIS GLORY

Six days later Jesus took Peter, James, and John, and led them up a high mountain to be alone. As the men watched, Jesus' appearance was transformed, and his clothes became dazzling white, far whiter than any earthly bleach could ever make them. Then Elijah and Moses appeared and began talking with Jesus.

Peter exclaimed, "Rabbi, it's wonderful for us to be here! Let's make three shelters as memorials—one for you, one for Moses, and one for Elijah." He said this because he didn't really know what else to say, for they were all terrified.

Then a cloud overshadowed them, and a voice from the cloud said, "This is my dearly loved Son. Listen to him." Suddenly, when they looked around, Moses and Elijah were gone, and they saw only Jesus with them (Mark 9:2–8).

The disciples fall to the ground in shock as Jesus is joined on Mount Tabor by Elijah and Moses.

MEGIDDO

MEANING "place of troops" or "rendezvous"

PRONUNCIATION muh-GID-doe

SITE AND LOCATION A city in the Carmel mountain range about midway between the Sea of Galilee and the Mediterranean Sea

Map 2, area C-3

Megiddo was one of the most important fortress cities in the land of Israel—and it's no mystery why. It was perched on a high hill overlooking the Jezreel Valley. A major trade route linking Egypt in the south to Syria in the north passed through this valley. Thus, the country that occupied Megiddo had a distinct commercial and military advantage over other nations in the ancient world. Many important battles have been fought for control of this city and the territory through which this ancient highway passed.

A city existed at this site at least 1,500 years before the Israelites entered the land of Canaan. Joshua defeated the king of Megiddo and allotted the city and its surrounding towns to the tribe of Manasseh (see Joshua 12:21; 17:11). In later centuries, Solomon strengthened the city's fortifications and turned it into the headquarters for his chariot corps (see 1 Kings 9:15; 10:26–29). About three hundred years after Solomon's time, King Josiah of Judah (ruled about 640–609 BC) was killed at Megiddo in a battle with the Egyptians (see 2 Kings 23:29).

Today, the site of ancient Megiddo is considered one of the most important archaeological locations in the Holy Land. Archaeologists have uncovered twenty different levels of occupation going back to about 4000 BC. The most important finding for Bible students consists of the remains of the city from Old Testament times. On display here is a scale model of the city showing its double gate system and its massive defensive wall with towers—all built on a one-hundred-foot-high hill for maximum protection against enemy attack.

On the excavated site itself, visitors may examine remains of the city gate and a large stone silo used to store grain in Bible times. But the highlight of the tour is a trip down 183 stone steps to a tunnel that leads outside the city wall to a hidden spring. This elaborate system gave residents of Megiddo access to a water supply in the event of a long siege against the city.

Megiddo's association with many decisive battles in ancient times may explain why the apostle John spoke of the battle of Armageddon in the book of Revelation (see Revelation 16:16). The word *Armageddon* means "mountain of Megiddo." Just south of the site of Megiddo are several high hills. Perhaps John used this ancient battleground as a symbol of the final battle between the forces of good and evil in the end times.

TAANACH

MEANING   unknown

PRONUNCIATION   TAY-uh-nack

SITE AND LOCATION   A city about five miles southwest of Megiddo
Map 2, area C-3

Taanach developed into an important royal city of the Canaanites long before the Israelites swept into their territory. Even though it was well defended with a massive wall, Taanach's Canaanite king is listed as one of many the Israelites defeated (see Joshua 12:7–8, 21). In later years, during the period of the judges, the Canaanites again became a threat to Israel. But Deborah and Barak, who were victorious over Sisera and his Canaanite army near Taanach, broke their power (see Judges 5:19).

Nearby Megiddo (see p. 241) and Taanach sat on opposite sides of an ancient trade route that ran from Egypt in the south to Mesopotamia in the north. Thus, control of these two cities was important for commercial and military reasons. King Solomon turned them both into administrative centers. His representatives at Taanach and Megiddo were responsible for collecting taxes and supplies throughout the surrounding territory to support the king's central government in Jerusalem.

The ruins of ancient Taanach are known today as Tel Taanek. At this site, remains of the city from its Canaanite origins more than 4,500 years ago have been discovered.

KISHON RIVER

MEANING "curving"

PRONUNCIATION KIGH-shun

SITE AND LOCATION A stream that originates near Nazareth and empties into the Mediterranean Sea near Mount Carmel   Map 2, area C-3

The Kishon is one of the few rivers in Israel that flows all the time. Unlike the wadis of the Holy Land, it never goes totally dry. But during the wet winter months, it does carry a larger volume of water and even overflows its banks in some places. This was one factor that enabled the Israelites to defeat the Canaanite army in the time of the judge Deborah and her military commander, Barak.

These two leaders realized the Israelite army would be no match for the iron chariots of the Canaanites. So they gathered their forces on higher ground near Mount Tabor (see p. 239) and waited for the right time to make their move. When the Kishon overflowed in a sudden rainstorm, they swooped

The Kishon River at Haifa.

down on the Canaanites in the valley along the riverbanks. The enemy chariots got stuck in the mud, making them an easy target for the Israelite warriors (see Judges 4:4–16).

In a hymn known as the Song of Deborah, this courageous leader gave credit to the Lord and the Kishon River for this decisive victory: "The stars fought from heaven. The stars in their orbits fought against Sisera," she sang. "The Kishon River swept them away—that ancient torrent, the Kishon. March on with courage, my soul!" (Judges 5:20–21).

Several centuries later, this river was also associated with the ministry of the prophet Elijah. Here is where he and his followers executed the prophets of the pagan god Baal after his famous victory over Baalism on Mount Carmel (see "Mount Carmel," below).

The Kishon in modern times has become a polluted waterway, especially in its lower reaches near the modern Israeli city of Haifa on the Mediterranean Sea. But the Israeli government is now waging an aggressive campaign to clean it up. Its master plan includes a series of parks and walking trails along the river.

MOUNT CARMEL

MEANING "fruit garden," "orchard," or "planted field"

PRONUNCIATION KAHR-muhl

SITE AND LOCATION A mountain range that extends from the Jezreel Valley to the Mediterranean Sea   Map 2, area B-3

The thirteen-mile ridge of low mountains just north of the Jezreel Valley is known as the Carmel range. But one specific peak of these mountains near the Mediterranean Sea is significant for Bible students. Here the prophet Elijah pitted the pagan god Baal against the one true God to show which was superior.

First, the prophets of Baal slaughtered a bull and placed it on a pile of wood. For an entire day, they implored their god to come down and set the wood on fire to complete the sacrifice. But nothing happened (see 1 Kings 18:20–29).

Then Elijah took over. He built an altar on which he heaped up wood with a sacrificial animal, just as the false prophets had done. But then he went one step further. He dug a trench around the altar and filled it with water, even dousing the wood as well. Then he drenched the altar two more times to ensure that it was thoroughly soaked. Finally, Elijah uttered a simple prayer to the Lord. What happened next was one of the most dramatic events in the Bible (see sidebar, "Fire from Heaven on Mount Carmel," below).

The place where this epic contest took place is believed to be a high point near the Mediterranean Sea known as Keren Carmel ("Horn of Carmel"), so named because this peak stands out like an animal's horn from the surrounding territory. Here a Catholic order known as the Carmelite monks have built a monastery and a little church to commemorate Elijah's victory at this site.

In the church courtyard stands a statue of Elijah with upraised sword. This symbolizes the mass execution of these false prophets at his command. This took place along the Kishon River (see p. 243) below Mount Carmel (see 1 Kings 18:40).

FIRE FROM HEAVEN ON MOUNT CARMEL

At the usual time for offering the evening sacrifice, Elijah the prophet walked up to the altar and prayed, "O Lord, God of Abraham, Isaac, and Jacob, prove today that you are God in Israel and that I am your servant. Prove that I have done all this at your command. O Lord, answer me! Answer me so these people will know that you, O Lord, are God and that you have brought them back to yourself."

Immediately the fire of the Lord flashed down from heaven and burned up the young bull, the wood, the stones, and the dust. It even licked up all the water in the trench! And when all the people saw it, they fell face down on the ground and cried out, "The Lord—he is God! Yes, the Lord is God!" (1 Kings 18:36–39).

Mount Carmel.

Skiers at Mount Hermon.

CHAPTER 10

This large section of the Holy Land covers basically the territory known as Galilee in the time of Jesus. Galilee was one of the three provinces into which the ruling Romans divided the land of Palestine for administrative purposes. The other two were Judea, in the south around Jerusalem, and Samaria, sandwiched between Judea and Galilee. Jesus grew up in Nazareth, a Galilean village (see chapter 9, "Nazareth," p. 222). Here in this territory around the Sea of Galilee, He spent most of His earthly ministry.

From the southern border of Galilee to Jerusalem was only about sixty-five miles. From our modern perspective, this doesn't seem like such a great distance. But they were worlds apart in New Testament times. Jerusalem was Palestine's religious center—the place where the temple stood and where the great religious traditionalists lived and taught. Imagine their shock when an unknown teacher from the backwater province of Galilee began to challenge their assumptions and even claim to be the Son of God. Not even His miracles could change their hardened opinion that "no prophet ever comes from Galilee!" (John 7:52).

Galilee in Jesus' time was noted for its forested hills, deep valleys, copious rainfall, numerous villages, and productive farms. Its mild climate was ideal for growing olives, grapes, figs, wheat, and barley. Many of Jesus' teachings used agricultural imagery from the farming practices of Galilee—for example, the parable of the sower (see Matthew 13:1–9) and the parable of the barren fig tree (see Luke 13:6–9).

Several centuries before Jesus began His public ministry, the prophet Isaiah predicted that the Messiah would bring light to "Galilee of the Gentiles" (Isaiah 9:1). This name was applied to Galilee because it was populated by many people of pagan Gentile background as well as Jews. This was Isaiah's way of saying that the Messiah would not be restricted to one nationality or ethnic group. He would be a Savior for all humankind.

SEA OF GALILEE

MEANING	"a circle"
PRONUNCIATION	GAL-ah-lee
SITE AND LOCATION	A lake in northern Israel fed by the Jordan River
	Map 7, area C-4

The Sea of Galilee is probably the most misunderstood body of water in the Bible. First off, it's not a sea but a freshwater lake. To make things even more confusing, it goes by three other names in the Bible: the sea of Chinnereth (from one of the ancient towns on its shore; see Numbers 34:11 KJV); the lake of Gennesaret (from a plain along its northern shore; see Luke 5:1 KJV); and the Sea of Tiberias (from a town on its western shore; see John 6:1).

But no matter what you call it, this lake will always be associated with the life and ministry of Jesus. On the Sea of Galilee and along its shores, He enlisted disciples, taught the people about the kingdom of God, and performed some of His most spectacular miracles (see sidebar, "Jesus and the Sea of Galilee: A Biblical Snapshot," p. 249).

21st-century fishermen on the Sea of Galilee.

Lake Galilee is small—only about thirteen miles long by seven miles wide at its widest point—in comparison to the great lakes of the world. But what it lacks in size, it makes up for in its several unique geographical features. It sits about seven hundred feet below the level of the Mediterranean Sea, just thirty miles to the west. And it is surrounded on three sides by high mountains, some as high as 1,500 feet.

The strikingly blue surface of Galilee is usually placid and peaceful. But cool winds sometimes rush down from the surrounding peaks and mix with the warmer air rising from the lake. This produces short but violent storms that strike without warning. This is probably what happened to Jesus and His disciples when they were crossing the lake in a fishing boat. Jesus was asleep on a cushion, unruffled by the crashing of the waves. When His frightened disciples woke Him up, He rescued them when He commanded the storm, "Silence! Be still!" (Mark 4:39). The Twelve were amazed. "Who is this man?" they asked. "Even the wind and waves obey him" (Mark 4:41).

Lake Galilee receives its water from the Jordan River (see chapter 8, p. 193), the main source of water for the nation of Israel. Many Holy Land visitors are surprised to discover that the lake and its beaches are a favorite recreation spot for the nation's citizens, especially on summer weekends. The area near the city of Tiberias (see p. 258) features such amenities as water slides, campgrounds, mineral springs, restaurants, and hotels.

JESUS AND THE SEA OF GALILEE: A BIBLICAL SNAPSHOT

Jesus walks on the Sea of Galilee.

- Jesus calls four fishermen on the lake as His disciples (see Matthew 4:18–22).
- Jesus calms a storm on Galilee (see Luke 8:22–25).
- Jesus walks on the surface of the lake (see John 6:16–21).
- Jesus teaches a crowd from a fishing boat (see Luke 5:1–3).
- At the beginning of His ministry, Jesus produces a miraculous catch of fish on Lake Galilee (see Luke 5:4–7).
- After His resurrection, Jesus creates another miraculous catch from the lake (see John 21:1–6).
- In the mouth of a fish from these waters, Jesus produces a coin for payment of the temple tax (see Matthew 17:24–27).

CAPERNAUM

MEANING	"village of Nahum"
PRONUNCIATION	kuh-PURR-nay-uhm
SITE AND LOCATION	A city on the northern shore of the Sea of Galilee
	Map 7, area C-4

Jesus grew up at Nazareth, a town not far from the Sea of Galilee (see chapter 9, "Nazareth," p. 222). But after His rejection at Nazareth, He moved to Capernaum and made it the center of His Galilean ministry. This village on the shore of the lake is the only place referred to in the Gospels as "his own town" (Matthew 9:1). He lived here for about two years—the longest time He spent at any one place during His public ministry.

Capernaum had no special features that set it apart from all the other villages in the region of Galilee. So why did Jesus decide to settle here? Perhaps because this was in the vicinity where at least five of His twelve disciples lived. Peter, Andrew, James, and John were fishermen on Lake Galilee near Capernaum (see Matthew 4:18–22), and Matthew was a tax collector in the town (see Luke 5:27–32).

Tourists at the Capernaum Synagogue.

Peter had a house at Capernaum. Here is where Jesus healed Peter's mother-in-law of a fever soon after He arrived in the village (see Matthew 8:14–15). This house may have been the place where Jesus lived while He ministered among the people of this area.

This healing at Capernaum was just the first of many Jesus performed here. Some of His most important teachings and healings took place in or near this little town (see sidebar, "Jesus at Capernaum: A Biblical Snapshot," right). But in spite of all these good works, the people were generally unresponsive to His message. He condemned the town for its unbelief—along with the nearby villages of Bethsaida (see p. 253) and Korazin (see p. 255).

The site of Capernaum is known today as Tel Hum. Here archaeologists have discovered the remains of a Jewish synagogue that was built during the AD 300s. This is obviously not the synagogue in which Jesus taught and healed. But underneath this building they discovered the ruins of another synagogue from the New Testament era. These could be the foundation stones of the synagogue from Jesus' time.

Another popular site at Tel Hum/Capernaum is the Octagon Church, built over the remains of another church from the AD 400s. This earlier church had been built over the reputed site of Peter's house, a place pilgrims have venerated as far back as the first Christian century. The modern church on the site was designed to protect the remains of the house. Visitors are allowed to view them from above through the church's glass floor.

About two miles southwest of Capernaum is a site known as Tabgha, the place where tradition claims Jesus miraculously

JESUS AT CAPERNAUM: A BIBLICAL SNAPSHOT

- Jesus taught with authority in Capernaum's synagogue (see Mark 1:21–22).
- Jesus healed a demon-possessed man in this same synagogue (see Mark 1:21–28).
- Here in the same synagogue, Jesus restored a man's deformed hand (see Luke 6:6–11).
- Near Capernaum, Jesus claimed to be the Bread of Life (see John 6:22–40).
- Jesus healed a Roman soldier's paralyzed servant at Capernaum (see Matthew 8:5–13).
- Here Jesus healed a lame man whose four friends carried him on a mat (see Mark 2:1–5).
- At Capernaum, Jesus used the example of a child to teach His disciples about service and humility (see Mark 9:33–37).

Jesus teaching at the synagogue.

multiplied a boy's lunch to feed a hungry crowd of more than five thousand people (see John 6:1–15). A church on the site known as the Church of the Multiplication commemorates this event. Just a few hundred feet away is the reputed site where Jesus met His disciples near Lake Galilee after His resurrection. Here He restored Peter to his leadership position among the disciples after Peter's earlier denial of Jesus (see John 21:1–17). The Catholic church on this site is known as the Church of the Primacy of Saint Peter.

While visiting Capernaum and Tabgha, most Holy Land pilgrims climb a nearby hillside where Jesus is reputed to have delivered His Sermon on the Mount to His followers. This place is known as the Mount of Beatitudes, named for the nine blessings or "Beatitudes" with which this famous sermon begins (see Matthew 5:1–12). A beautiful little chapel known as the Church of Beatitudes—a perfect place for prayer and meditation on these teachings of Jesus—marks this spot (see sidebar, "Jesus' Prescription for Worry from the Sermon on the Mount," below).

JESUS' PRESCRIPTION FOR WORRY FROM THE SERMON ON THE MOUNT

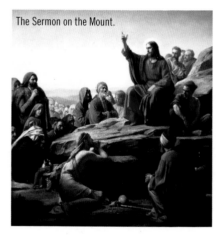

The Sermon on the Mount.

"So don't worry about these things, saying, 'What will we eat? What will we drink? What will we wear?' These things dominate the thoughts of unbelievers, but your heavenly Father already knows all your needs. Seek the Kingdom of God above all else, and live righteously, and he will give you everything you need.

"So don't worry about tomorrow, for tomorrow will bring its own worries. Today's trouble is enough for today" (Matthew 6:31–34).

BETHSAIDA

MEANING "house of fishing"

PRONUNCIATION beth-SAY-ih-duh

SITE AND LOCATION A village about one mile north of the Sea of Galilee
Map 7, area C-4

Some people believe there were two separate villages near Capernaum named Bethsaida during Jesus' Galilean ministry. But it seems unlikely that two towns of the same name would be so close together. So we will consider all mentions of Bethsaida in the Gospels as referring to the same town.

The first thing we notice about Bethsaida is that it was the hometown of three of Jesus' disciples—Peter, Andrew, and Philip (see John 1:44; 12:21). Peter and Andrew made their living as fishermen, and Bethsaida was not far from the northern shore of the Sea of Galilee. This tells us that Bethsaida, like nearby Capernaum, was probably a fishing village during Jesus' time.

Indeed, recent excavations at Bethsaida have confirmed this as fact. Discovered here was a house identified as a fisherman's residence because of the tools of the fishing trade that it contained—a fishhook, an anchor, stone net weights, and a needle used to repair fishing nets.

Ruins known as the "house of the fisherman" at Bethsaida.

Bethsaida was also the site of one of Jesus' healing miracles. Here He restored the sight of a blind man by rubbing saliva on his eyes. This is the only miracle in the Gospels that He performed in stages (see sidebar, "Jesus' Two-Stage Miracle at Bethsaida," below). We don't know why Jesus used this healing method in this particular case. But at least we can say that this shows He is no halfway Savior. He has the power to finish what He starts.

The tragedy of Bethsaida was its spiritual apathy—in spite of Jesus' healing and teaching among its residents. He condemned it, along with its sister towns of Korazin (see p. 255) and Capernaum (see p. 250), for its unbelief (see Luke 10:13–15).

JESUS' TWO-STAGE MIRACLE AT BETHSAIDA

When they arrived at Bethsaida, some people brought a blind man to Jesus, and they begged him to touch the man and heal him. Jesus took the blind man by the hand and led him out of the village. Then, spitting on the man's eyes, he laid his hands on him and asked, "Can you see anything now?"

The man looked around. "Yes," he said, "I see people, but I can't see them very clearly. They look like trees walking around."

Then Jesus placed his hands on the man's eyes again, and his eyes were opened. His sight was completely restored, and he could see everything clearly (Mark 8:22–25).

Jesus heals the blind man.

KORAZIN

MEANING "secret"

PRONUNCIATION koh-RAY-zin

SITE AND LOCATION A city two miles north of Capernaum not far from the northern shore of the Sea of Galilee   Map 7, area C-4

This city is mentioned only twice in the New Testament (see Matthew 11:21–22; Luke 10:10–13). These two passages are actually parallels that record the same event—Jesus' condemnation of Korazin (spelled "Chorazin" in the King James Version) because of its unbelief. Yet we have no record in the Gospels that Jesus ever visited this place. How could He condemn a city in which He had never taught?

The Gospel of John has a good answer to this question. John ended his account of the life and ministry of Jesus with this declaration: "Jesus also did many other things. If they were all written down, I suppose the whole world could not contain the books that would be written" (John 21:25).

This tells us that the Gospel writers did not record all of Jesus' actions and words. He must have visited Korazin several times, since it was near

The remains of the Korazin synagogue.

Capernaum, the center of His Galilean ministry. But for some reason unknown to us, nothing He said or did at Korazin made it into the New Testament.

Another interesting thing about Korazin is that it was one of three cities near the Sea of Galilee Jesus condemned because of their cool response to His message. The other two were Bethsaida (see Matthew 11:20–21) and Capernaum (see Matthew 11:23–24). These three cities, just a few miles apart, were like the points of a triangle on the northern shore of the Sea of Galilee (see Map 7, area C-4). Much of Jesus' Galilean ministry must have taken place in and around these three towns. This is why He had such strong words for their unbelief.

Archaeologists have uncovered the remains of Korazin at a site known as Khirbet Kerazeh, just north of Capernaum. Actually, the remains they found belong to a town built in the second century AD. This town was built on the site of the city from Jesus' time. They discovered a Jewish synagogue, several houses, an olive press, and a ritual bath. These are on display today in a tourist attraction known as Chorazin National Park.

MAGDALA

MEANING "tower"

PRONUNCIATION MAG-duh-luh

SITE AND LOCATION A village on the western shore of the Sea of Galilee

Map 7, area C-4

Only in the King James Version of the Bible is this village mentioned—and that only one time: "And he [Jesus]. . .came into the coasts of Magdala" (Matthew 15:39 KJV). Modern translations of the Bible render the name of this village "Magadan." This village is famous for one thing: it was either the birthplace or the home of Mary Magdalene, a follower of Jesus. Mary Magdalene means "Mary of Magdala." She is mentioned several times in all four Gospels.

About the only facts we know about this Mary are that Jesus healed her when He cast seven demons out of her (see Luke 8:2) and that she was present at His crucifixion (see Matthew 27:55–56). Jesus also appeared to Mary Magdalene when she visited His tomb on the day of His resurrection (see John 20:11–17). According to the Gospel of John, it was she who provided eyewitness testimony to the disciples that Jesus was alive (see John 20:18).

Magdala was a prosperous fishing village during the time of Jesus. Its Greek name, Tarichae, means "pickled fish." Here, fish taken from the Sea of Galilee were probably processed and preserved for shipment to all parts of Palestine.

Archaeology at Magdala is a work in progress. So far, a monastery from the fifth century AD has been discovered. Its stone floor contained a mosaic featuring a drawing of a fishing boat. But what tourists come to Magdala to see is the real thing—a vessel dubbed the "Jesus Boat" or the "Galilee Boat." This wooden vessel that once sailed the Sea of Galilee was pulled from the mud not far from the shore in 1986. Carbon-14 tests have dated it to the first century AD, the time when Jesus taught and healed along the shores of this body of water.

Following a particularly dry season, when the water was very low, two fishermen on Lake Galilee discovered the boat. Only a small portion of it was visible in the water. But the crew that pulled it out was astonished at its size—thirty feet long by eight feet wide by four feet deep—and that it had been preserved intact for almost two thousand years.

Experts speculate that this vessel could have been used as a ferry boat, a fishing boat, or even a warship the Romans used against first-century Jewish revolutionaries. But Christians prefer to associate it with the fishing industry on Lake Galilee during Jesus' time. Four of His disciples—Peter, Andrew, James, and John—were fishermen who made their living on this body of water until Jesus called them and promised to show them how to "fish for people" (see Matthew 4:19).

This boat is on display today in a museum not far from the site of ancient Magdala. Most tourists visit it during their trip to other sites near the Sea of Galilee.

The "Jesus Boat" in the Yigal Alon Museum.

TIBERIAS

MEANING   named for Tiberius Caesar, emperor of the Roman Empire

PRONUNCIATION   tie-BEER-ee-us

SITE AND LOCATION   A city on the western shore of the Sea of Galilee
Map 7, area C-4

Tiberias is an unusual city for two reasons: (1) the Gospels contain no record of Jesus visiting it, although it was only about eight miles from Capernaum, the headquarters of His Galilean ministry; and (2) Tiberias is the only city from Jesus' time located near the Sea of Galilee that still exists as an occupied city today.

Herod Antipas, a son of Herod the Great, built Tiberias in AD 20 to serve as his administrative capital for the province of Galilee. He named the city for the Roman emperor Tiberius Caesar. This was the Herod who executed John the Baptist (see chapter 3, "Machaerus," p. 49; see Mark 6:20–28). Herod Antipas heard about Jesus' miracles in Galilee and wanted to meet Him (see Luke 9:7–9). But Jesus didn't trust this Roman ruler and referred to him as a sly fox (see Luke 13:32). This is probably why Jesus never visited Herod's capital city.

Tiberias must have been an important city in New Testament times, since it gave its name to the body of water—the Sea of Galilee—along which it was built. Another name for this lake in Jesus' time was the Sea of Tiberias (see John 6:1). But in spite of its importance, the city is mentioned only once in the New Testament. After Jesus fed the five thousand, news about this miracle spread to all the villages around the Sea of Galilee. People from Tiberias crowded into several boats and paddled across the lake, looking for Jesus at the place where He had performed this miracle on its northwestern shore (see John 6:22–25).

Five miles south of Tiberias is a site known as Yardenit. Here, near the spot where the Jordan River exits the Sea of Galilee, thousands of Holy Land pilgrims are baptized every year in the same river that Jesus was baptized in as He began His public ministry. This site was developed for that purpose because the location of His baptism on the lower Jordan is along the border between Israel and the modern nation of Jordan. The lower Jordan has also slowed to a trickle in recent years because of the large volume of water being drawn off for the irrigation of Israeli farmland.

Two Christian sites of interest in Tiberias are the Church of Saint Peter and the Anchor Church. The original Church of Saint Peter was built about AD 1100. It was converted into a Muslim mosque at one time, then turned back into a church and finally rebuilt as a Christian house of worship in 1870 and improved in 1940.

The Anchor Church, located on a mountain overlooking Tiberias, is named for a huge rock that looks like an ancient anchor. Archaeologists speculate that it was part of a church that was built on this site in the sixth century AD.

A recently developed attraction at Tiberias is "The Galilee Experience," a short multimedia show that presents the four-thousand-year history of the region of Galilee. It is staged in a modern indoor theater on the shore of Lake Galilee.

Tiberias has been continually inhabited since Herod Antipas built it about two thousand years ago. Several older sections of the city have been abandoned over the years, but a newer and more modern settlement has always been established nearby. Today, modern Tiberias is a resort city of more than forty thousand people. Its mild climate, hot mineral springs, and beaches along the Sea of Galilee make it a favorite vacation spot for citizens of Israel as well as tourists from other nations.

Tiberias from the air.

CANA

MEANING "place of reeds"

PRONUNCIATION KANE-nuh

SITE AND LOCATION A village about thirteen miles west of the Sea of Galilee

Map 6, area C-3

Everyone knows that the bride is always the center of attention at a wedding. But it didn't turn out this way when Jesus and His disciples were invited to a wedding at Cana, a village not far from His hometown of Nazareth.

No sooner had they arrived on the scene than Jesus' mother, another invited guest, told Him about a problem that threatened to turn this happy occasion into a disaster. "They have no more wine," she told Him (see John 2:3). The host had miscalculated and failed to provide enough wine for the guests. And wedding celebrations in New Testament times sometimes went on for days.

The "Wedding Church" at Kafr Kanna.

At first, it seemed that Jesus wouldn't do anything to solve this problem. "Dear woman, that's not our problem," He told her. "My time has not yet come" (John 2:4). He had just launched His public ministry, and He must have thought this was not the right time or place to reveal His supernatural powers as the Messiah. But then He decided to act by performing a miracle to produce wine from common water (see John 2:6–10). This saved the host from embarrassment and prolonged the joyful celebration.

The Gospel of John cites this miracle at Cana as the first of seven "signs" Jesus performed to show His Messiahship and His unique mission as the Son of God. These signs increase in power and intensity throughout John's Gospel, concluding with Jesus' raising of His friend Lazarus from the dead (see sidebar, "The Seven Signs of Jesus' Messiahship in John's Gospel," below).

So Cana in Galilee is where Jesus began the process of revealing His glory (see John 2:11). This self-revelation ended with an exclamation point at Bethany (see chapter 7, p. 158) when He brought Lazarus back to life to show that He had power over death (see John 11:23–44). In a sense, the death and resurrection of Lazarus were a preview of Jesus' own death and glorious resurrection not many days away.

Cana was also the site of another miracle of Jesus. He was passing through this village on another occasion when a government official from nearby Capernaum approached Him. He begged Jesus to come to his city to heal his dying son. After verifying his faith, Jesus told the man to go back home and that his son would live. When this official reached his house, he discovered that his son had recovered at exactly the time when Jesus declared him healed (see John 4:46–53). This shows that Jesus could heal at a distance—that His power did not depend on His physical presence. Capernaum was about twelve miles from Cana.

According to a long Christian tradition, the modern Arab village of Kafr Kanna now occupies the site of ancient Cana. Located about five miles north of Nazareth, this village has a Catholic church known as the Wedding Church that is said to be built on the site where the water-into-wine miracle took place. This is a popular wedding site as well as a place where many married couples renew their wedding vows.

Near the Wedding Church is the Greek Orthodox Church of Saint George, which contains two large stone jars believed to be the ones filled with the water that Jesus turned into wine. A third church in Kafr Kanna is named for Saint Bartholomew, a disciple of Jesus. Bartholomew is another name for Nathanael, who lived at Cana (see John 21:2).

THE SEVEN SIGNS OF JESUS' MESSIAHSHIP IN JOHN'S GOSPEL

1. Turning water into wine (see John 2:1–11)
2. Healing a government official's son (see John 4:46–54)
3. Healing a paralyzed man (see John 5:1–9)
4. Feeding the five thousand (see John 6:5–14)
5. Walking on water (see John 6:16–21)
6. Healing a man born blind (see John 9:1–7)
7. Raising Lazarus from the dead (see John 11:38–44)

DECAPOLIS

MEANING	"ten cities" or "ten-city region"
PRONUNCIATION	dih-CAP-oh-liss
SITE AND LOCATION	A region east of the Sea of Galilee
	Map 6, area E-4

Jesus realized from the very beginning that He had limited time to perform His earthly ministry. As it turned out, He had only about three years to call and train His disciples, to teach and heal among the people, and to plant the principles that would guide the church after His ascension into heaven. This pressed-for-time situation probably explains why He directed His ministry mostly to the Jewish people (see Mark 7:27).

But He did make a few trips among the Gentiles to show that He was sent as a Savior for the entire world. One Gentile region that He visited at least twice was a territory known as the Decapolis.

This area contained ten cities (thus the name Decapolis, which means "ten cities") that were centers of Greek culture even before the Romans became the dominant force in the land. Under the Greeks, each of these cities was allowed a certain degree of autonomy and self-rule. When the Romans took over, they allowed this freedom to continue. This seemed to be the best way to encourage

The monastery at Kursi, possibly the site of the Gadarene miracle.

the spread of Roman values to the farthest reaches of their empire.

In this Gentile region, Jesus performed three of His most spectacular miracles. Perhaps it took such supernatural acts to get the attention of the pagan inhabitants of this area.

The first miracle in the Decapolis was the healing of a deaf man with a speech impediment. Jesus put His fingers into the man's ears, then spit on His fingers and touched the man's tongue. Instantly the man could hear and speak. This amazed the people, and news of His power spread throughout the territory (see Mark 7:31–37).

The second miracle in the Decapolis was the feeding of the four thousand (see Mark 8:1–10). In this miracle, Jesus did for a group of hungry Gentiles the same thing He had previously performed for a group of five thousand hungry Jews (see Mark 6:30–44). The details of these two separate miracles are very similar. Mark declared through this miraculous feeding that Jesus was a universal Savior. He did not play favorites; He was just as concerned about Gentiles as He was about the Jewish people.

According to some Christian traditions, the feeding of the four thousand took place near a site known today as Tel Hadar—the ruins of a city from Old Testament times. A monument has been erected on a section of the ruins to mark the reputed site. Tel Hadar is about three miles north of the northeastern shore of the Sea of Galilee.

The third and most spectacular miracle in the Decapolis was Jesus' healing of a demon-possessed man who lived among the tombs. Jesus ordered the demons to leave the man, and they did so, then entered a herd of pigs nearby. These animals rushed to their death down a hillside into the Sea of Galilee. This upset the residents of the area, and they asked Jesus to leave (see Mark 5:1–17).

The man Jesus healed was so grateful that he wanted to go with Him across Lake Galilee into Jewish territory. But Jesus told him to stay home and tell others what the Lord had done for him. According to Mark's Gospel, he traveled throughout the Decapolis doing exactly that, and "everyone was amazed at what he told them" (Mark 5:20). From that day forward, Jesus had a powerful witness in this pagan Gentile territory.

The specific place where this miracle took place is referred to in the Gospel records as the "region of the Gadarenes" (Matthew 8:28) or the "region of the Gerasenes" (Mark 5:1; Luke 8:26). This may have been the city known as Gadara, one of the cities of the Decapolis. Gadara was about six miles southeast of the Sea of Galilee.

But a Christian tradition dating back about 1,500 years has settled on another site as the place where this miracle took place. Known in ancient times as Gergesa, it sits on the eastern shore of the Sea of Galilee, almost directly across from Magdala (see p. 256) on the opposite shore. This tradition is based on the discovery at Gergesa of the ruins of a monastery and church from the sixth century AD. In the early years of the Christian movement, churches and shrines were often built on sites that were considered sacred because of their association with the life and ministry of Jesus.

Gergesa is known today by its Arabic name, Kursi. Here visitors view the remarkably intact remains of the huge monastery that may have been built here to commemorate Jesus' miracle. Covering an area of 170,000 square feet, it is the largest monastery complex ever discovered in the Holy Land.

Above the monastery on a rocky hillside, archaeologists also discovered the ruins of a small chapel that could be reached by a foot path. This may have been built to mark the site where the pigs rushed down into the lake after the demons Jesus cast out of the man entered them.

ZAREPHATH

MEANING "place of dyeing"

PRONUNCIATION ZAR-eh-fath

SITE AND LOCATION A city on the coast of the Mediterranean Sea about eight miles north of Tyre
Map 6, area C-1

Elijah is best known as the fiery follower of the Lord who executed the prophets of Baal after he defeated them in a contest on Mount Carmel (see chapter 9, "Mount Carmel," p. 244). But the city of Zarephath shows that he also had a softer side.

At Zarephath, Elijah worked a miracle for a starving woman and her son who gave him bread baked from the last bit of flour she owned. Because of her faith and kindness, the prophet made sure that she and her son would never go hungry.

This woman provided lodging for Elijah, just as a kind woman did for his successor, Elisha (see 2 Kings 4:8–10). Sometime after Elijah performed this miracle for her and her son, the boy died. Elijah brought him back to life (see 1 Kings 17:17–24). This miracle is similar to Elisha's raising of a woman's son at Shunem (see chapter 9, "Shunem," p. 226) and Jesus' raising of a widow's son at Nain (see chapter 9, "Nain," p. 225).

Zarephath was a Phoenician seaport city several centuries before Elijah's time. Archaeologists have uncovered more than twenty pottery kilns on the site, indicating that it was probably a center for manufacturing pottery at one time. The nearby modern village of Sarafand preserves the name of the ancient city.

WATERS OF MEROM

MEANING "elevated place"

PRONUNCIATION MEE-rahm

SITE AND LOCATION An unidentified lake or spring in northern Israel somewhere north of the Sea of Galilee   Map 7, area B-4

This water source is famous as the place where Joshua and the Israelites fought one of the last battles in their long campaign to claim the land of promise. Several Canaanite kings combined their forces to form a large army under the command of Jabin. But Joshua seized the initiative and attacked first, and "the LORD gave them victory over their enemies" (Joshua 11:8).

The exact location of the Waters of Merom is unknown, although some scholars think Lake Huleh in northern Israel is the likeliest site. It is a small body of water about three miles wide by five miles long that is fed by the Jordan River. Lake Huleh is shaped like a harp, much like its larger sister lake to the south, the Sea of Galilee.

Today the lake is part of the Hula Nature Reserve, a place the Israeli government has set aside for the protection of wildlife and aquatic plants. Its swampy terrain was drained at one time, but part of it has been restored to marshland in recent years. Lake Huleh is home to large flocks of waterfowl of several different species.

Lake Huleh.

MOUNT HERMON

MEANING "sacred mountain"

PRONUNCIATION HUR-mahn

SITE AND LOCATION A mountain about thirty-five miles northeast of the Sea of Galilee

Map 6, area E-1

In a land known for its mountains, this peak stands out above all the others. The highest point in Israel, Mount Hermon can be seen on a clear day from the Dead Sea—the nation's lowest point—about 120 miles away. And you should have no problem identifying this peak when you see it. It's the only mountain in the Holy Land with snow on its summit during the winter and spring months. The snow lingers even into the summer in some of its shaded ravines.

A panoramic view of the entire Holy Land from Mount Hermon was one of the high moments for pilgrims of the past who took the time to climb to the top. A traveler named Henry Baker Tristram did just that in the late

Mount Hermon is the place to go to ski in the Holy Land.

1800s and left us an eyewitness account of this experience (see sidebar, "A Spectacular View from Mount Hermon," below).

In Old Testament times, Mount Hermon was considered the northern limits of the land promised to the Israelites (see Deuteronomy 3:8; Joshua 11:16–17). Today, Israel occupies part of the territory on the slopes of Mount Hermon. But the mountain's highest peaks are within the borders of Syria and Lebanon.

During the summer months, the leftover snow on Mount Hermon condenses into water vapor. This causes a heavy dew to fall on the mountain, even while the surrounding area remains dry. The psalmist noticed this phenomenon, and he compared the dews of Hermon to the harmony that should exist among God's people: "How wonderful and pleasant it is when brothers live together in harmony! . . . Harmony is as refreshing as the dew from Mount Hermon that falls on the mountains of Zion" (Psalm 133:1, 3).

The snowfall and abundant rainfall on Mount Hermon are vital to Israel's water supply. This precipitation produces gushing springs at the base of the mountain. These eventually merge to form the headwaters of the Jordan River, the nation's major river and water source.

Mount Hermon may have been the "high mountain" where Jesus was transfigured before three of His disciples—Peter, James, and John (see Mark 9:2–8). Others believe the site of this event was Mount Tabor near the Sea of Galilee (see chapter 9, "Mount Tabor," p. 239).

A SPECTACULAR VIEW FROM MOUNT HERMON

Henry Baker Tristram and Ida Pfeiffer on their pilgrimage across the Holy Land.

We were at last on Hermon, whose snowy head had been a sort of pole-star for the last six months. We had looked at her from Sidon, from Tyre, from Carmel, from Gerizim, from the hills about Jerusalem, from the Dead Sea, from Mount Nebo. Now we were looking down on them all, as they stood out from the landscape that lay spread at our feet. We could scarcely realize that at one glance we were taking in the whole of the land through which for more than six months we had been incessantly wandering.

—Henry Baker Tristram, *The Land of Israel*

HAZOR

MEANING "an enclosure"

PRONUNCIATION HOT-zohr

SITE AND LOCATION A city about ten miles north of the Sea of Galilee
Map 2, area D-2

Hazor was an important fortress city of the Canaanites several centuries before the Israelites invaded their territory. Joshua overran the city, burned it, and killed all its inhabitants (see Joshua 11:10–13). These actions seem extreme to us today. But they show that Joshua was determined to break the power and influence of the Canaanites and their pagan religious system in this part of the land.

After Joshua's time, during the period of the judges, the Canaanites managed to rebuild and repopulate the city. They turned it into a command post from which they waged war against the Israelites. But again the Canaanites, under Jabin, king of Hazor, and his general, Sisera, were defeated—this time by Israelite forces under Deborah and Barak (see Judges 4:1–16).

In later centuries, the Israelites occupied the city. King Solomon built it into a heavily fortified military outpost to protect his kingdom from attack from the north. Hazor was one of three important military cities scattered throughout Solomon's kingdom. The other two were Megiddo (see chapter 9, p. 241) in central Israel and Gezer (see chapter 8, p. 183) in southern Israel near Jerusalem (see 1 Kings 9:15).

Hazor's location on the main north-south trade route through Israel explains its importance. The country that controlled this ancient highway that ran from Egypt into Babylon-Assyria had a significant economic and military advantage over the other nations of the ancient world.

Excavations at Hazor have revealed that the city had as many as twenty-five thousand inhabitants during Old Testament times. Remains of a massive city gate from Solomon's time show that he spared no expense in fortifying Hazor against enemy attack.

Visitors to this ancient city also marvel at its emergency water system, designed to give the city access to this precious commodity during a prolonged siege. A large shaft was dug down to the water table about 120 feet beneath the city. Residents of Hazor could walk down 123 stone steps to get water from a reservoir at the bottom of the shaft. Modern Holy Land visitors will tell you that the walk down is easy. But climbing back up gives them a new appreciation for the water carriers of the ancient world.

Old Testament Hazor, also known as modern Tel el-Qedah, is one of the largest and most important archaeological sites in the Holy Land. The Israeli government has set it aside as a national park.

The chambered gate from the time of King Solomon.

TYRE AND SIDON

MEANING   Tyre = "a stone" and Sidon = "a fishery"

PRONUNCIATION   tire/SIGH-dun

SITE AND LOCATION   Two cities on the coast of the Mediterranean Sea northwest of the Sea of Galilee   Map 6, area C-1

Jesus had to make a special effort to visit these two cities. They were at least a two-day journey from the area near the Sea of Galilee where He usually ministered. Like the territory known as the Decapolis (see p. 262), Tyre and Sidon were in Gentile territory. This region, in ancient Phoenicia, was the greatest distance He ever traveled from His headquarters at Capernaum during His Galilean ministry.

Somewhere in this pagan Gentile region, a desperate woman approached Jesus. Her daughter was possessed by a demon, and she begged Him to come to her house and heal her. At first Jesus ignored the request, but then He acted out of compassion when she persisted in her pleas (see sidebar, "Jesus Honors the Faith of a Gentile Woman," p. 271).

This event tells us that Jesus was concerned for all people, not just the Jews. While He ministered mostly among His Jewish countrymen—mostly because of the limitations of time and distance—God sent Him as Savior for

From the old (the Sea Castle) to the new (the city) in Sidon.

all the world. Jesus Himself made this clear in His Great Commission to His disciples before He ascended into heaven: "I have been given all authority in heaven and on earth. Therefore, go and make disciples of all the nations, baptizing them in the name of the Father and the Son and the Holy Spirit" (Matthew 28:18–19).

In the time of King Solomon, Tyre was a city-state ruled by King Hiram, who provided timber from his territory for the construction of the temple in Jerusalem (see 2 Kings 5:1–10). In New Testament times, Tyre's sister city, Sidon, farther north on the Mediterranean coast, was a stopping place for the apostle Paul on his way to Rome (see Acts 27:3).

JESUS HONORS THE FAITH OF A GENTILE WOMAN

Then Jesus said to the woman, "I was sent only to help God's lost sheep—the people of Israel."

But she came and worshiped him, pleading again, "Lord, help me!"

Jesus responded, "It isn't right to take food from the children and throw it to the dogs."

She replied, "That's true, Lord, but even dogs are allowed to eat the scraps that fall beneath their masters' table."

"Dear woman," Jesus said to her, "your faith is great. Your request is granted." And her daughter was instantly healed (Matthew 15:24–28).

DAN

MEANING	"a judge"
PRONUNCIATION	dan
SITE AND LOCATION	A city about thirty miles north of the Sea of Galilee

Map 2, area D-1

In most periods of biblical history, Dan was the northernmost city in Israel's territory. The phrase "from Dan to Beersheba" (see chapter 3, "Beersheba," p. 78) was an idiomatic way of referring to the entire country. For example, when David wanted to take a census of his kingdom, he ordered his aide Joab to "go now through all the tribes of Israel, from Dan even to Beersheba, and number ye. . .that I may know the number of the people" (2 Samuel 24:2 KJV).

Dan was an ancient city that dated back to the time when the

Canaanites inhabited it. Originally called Leshem or Laish, it was captured by members of the tribe of Dan—descendants of one of the twelve tribes of Israel—who named it after their famous ancestor (see Judges 18:27–29). The Danites who took over this city in northern Israel migrated here from their original territory near Joppa in central Israel. Perhaps they moved north because of oppression from Canaanites who remained in the land after Joshua's conquest (see Joshua 19:40–48).

In later years, Dan's far-north location made it an ideal city for a strategy that King Jeroboam I (ruled about 931–910 BC) of the northern kingdom of Israel adopted. After the united kingdom split into two factions following Solomon's death, Jeroboam placed a calf idol in a shrine at Dan near the northern border of his kingdom. He also set up another calf idol at Bethel (see chapter 8, p. 208) in the south. The king feared that the citizens of his country would remain loyal to the rival nation of Judah if they continued to worship at the temple in Jerusalem (see 1 Kings 12:26–30).

Excavations at Dan have uncovered a paved courtyard with a low stone platform. Some scholars believe this may have been the place where Jeroboam placed the calf idol, but other experts are skeptical about this suggestion. Another interesting discovery is a massive gateway into the ancient city that dates back to about 1750 BC. It has been dubbed "Abraham's Gate" because Abraham lived about this time and he rescued his nephew Lot from a raiding party near the city of Dan (see Genesis 14:14).

But the most intriguing find at Tel Dan, also known as Tel el-Qadi, is an inscription known as the Tel Dan Stele. This monument, engraved with Hebrew letters, was erected to celebrate the victory of an Aramean king over the city. It mentions the "House of David." Experts disagree on whether this refers to the famous king who succeeded Saul as king of Israel. If it does refer to the biblical David, this is the first mention of him ever discovered at any archaeological site in the Holy Land.

Excavation of the Canaanite Gate at Tel Dan.

ACCO

MEANING "hot sand" or "to hem in"

PRONUNCIATION ACK-coe

SITE AND LOCATION A city on the coast of the Mediterranean Sea about thirty miles west of the Sea of Galilee   Map 2, area C-2

This city is mentioned only one time in the Bible—and that in connection with a failure. After the conquest of Canaan, Joshua awarded Acco to the tribe of Asher. But this tribe failed to drive the Canaanites out of the city (see Judges 1:31). Asher's failure is understandable. Archaeologists have discovered that Acco stood on a high cliff surrounded by the Mediterranean Sea on three sides. On the fourth side was a marsh. This made the city easy to defend against enemy attack.

Before the Israelites invaded Canaan, Acco was an important port city. A river flowed into the sea at this site, giving it a natural landing place for ships that sailed the Mediterranean Sea. In New Testament times, the city was known as Ptolemais, named for the king of Egypt, Ptolemy, who captured it and rebuilt it about 100 BC. The apostle Paul visited Christian believers in Ptolemais at the end of his third missionary journey while his ship was anchored in the nearby harbor (see Acts 21:7).

In the Middle Ages, Acco/Ptolemais was known as Acre. This city became one of the last strongholds of the Crusaders, Christian militants who battled the Muslims for control of the Holy Land. A Catholic order known as the Knights of the Hospital of Saint John, or the "Hospitallers," built a combination fortress-monastery-

A church by the sea walls in Acre (Acco).

hospital on the site. Acre eventually fell to the Muslims, but remains of the massive Hospitaller complex are still visible today. Known as Knights' Hall, it takes in an area of about 15,000 square feet in a section of the old city that overlooks the sea.

Not far from Acco is the modern port city of Haifa, Israel's third largest city (behind Jerusalem and Tel Aviv-Joppa), with a population of more than 275,000 people. Haifa was just a small fishing village built on the slopes of Mount Carmel until the British occupation of Palestine in the early to mid-1900s. With the discovery of oil in the Middle East, the British built a pipeline from Haifa to Iraq in 1933 and developed a deep-water port for the shipment of oil to all parts of the world. This propelled Haifa into the modern age. Today, its refineries, steel mills, and manufacturing businesses have built the city into the industrial center of Israel.

Haifa is also known as the world headquarters of the Baha'i faith. This religious group sprang from Islam, but it claims to bring together the best teachings from several world religions. Its headquarters complex includes a shrine where two early leaders of the movement are buried, surrounded by beautiful gardens. This site is included on many Holy Land tours.

CAESAREA PHILIPPI

MEANING   "Caesar's city of Philippi"

PRONUNCIATION   sess-uh-REE-uh fill-uh-PIE

SITE AND LOCATION   A city about twenty-five miles north of the Sea of Galilee   Map 6, area D-1

This town was a quiet and secluded place, far from the crowds that usually followed Jesus when He was teaching and healing around Lake Galilee. He withdrew here for a little rest and relaxation and to ask His disciples an important question: "Who do people say I am?" (Mark 8:27). The disciples responded that several rumors about Jesus' identity were going around: "Some say John the Baptist, some say Elijah, and others say Jeremiah or one of the other prophets" (Matthew 16:14).

But Jesus wouldn't let them off the hook that easily. He wanted to know if they had grown in their own understanding of Him and His mission during the two to three years they had spent with Him. He asked them pointedly, "But who do *you* say I am?" (Matthew 16:15, italics added).

Peter spoke for all the other disciples when he answered,

The remnants of "Agrippa's City" in modern Banias.

"You are the Messiah, the Son of the living God" (Matthew 16:16). We can almost hear Jesus breathe a sigh of relief as He said to Himself, *Now we're getting somewhere. The time I've spent with these guys is finally beginning to pay off.*

Of course, we don't really know what Jesus thought when Peter made this great confession. But we do know Jesus was convinced that the church He had come to earth to establish with His own blood would be in good hands after He was gone. His disciples' declaration that He was the Messiah, God's Son, showed they recognized His divine mission and its importance. In time, they would put their lives on the line to continue the work that Jesus had started. Upon this apostolic confession, Jesus promised that He would build His church, "and all the powers of hell will not conquer it" (Matthew 16:18).

Peter's confession of Jesus as "the Son of the living God" has a special meaning because of the background of the city of Caesarea Philippi. In Old Testament times, it was a place where the Canaanites and the Phoenicians worshipped the pagan god Baal. When the Greeks occupied the territory, it had a shrine devoted to the nature god known as Pan. The city was named Panias then, in honor of this pagan deity. During the time of Jesus, the city may have contained a temple devoted to worship of the Roman emperor.

In contrast to these dead, impotent gods of the past, Peter declared that Jesus was the Son of the *living* God. He was alive and active on behalf of His people, as demonstrated by His revolutionary teachings and His compassionate healing of the sick and afflicted. Jesus was the *living* bread (see John 6:51) and the *living* water (see John 4:10) who brought abundant life to all people.

After the Greek period, this city came under the jurisdiction of the Roman ruler Herod Philip when his father, Herod the Great, died. Philip enlarged and rebuilt Panias and renamed it Caesarea in honor of the Roman emperor. In time, the name Philippi, a form of Philip, was added to its name to distinguish it from the coastal city of Caesarea to the south (see chapter 9, "Caesarea," p. 220).

Today, the site of Caesarea Philippi is also known by its Arabic name, Banias, a corruption of its ancient Greek name. Here visitors are shown a large spring that flows to the south, eventually joining other springs to form the headwaters of the Jordan River. Still visible in the rock face above the spring are hollowed-out spaces that contained statues of the pagan gods worshipped here in ancient times.

The region near Caesarea Philippi was one of the last places Jesus and His disciples visited before He began His final trip to Jerusalem to celebrate the Passover. Soon after arriving in the Holy City, His enemies arrested Him and executed Him on charges of blasphemy and sedition against the Roman government.

When Henry van Dyke visited Caesarea Philippi in the early 1900s, he was reminded of this long journey of Jesus to the death that awaited Him in Jerusalem. He reminded us of the major reason why this little corner of the world known as Israel will always be called the Holy Land (see sidebar, "We Call This the Holy Land," left).

Christ on the Mount of Olives.

INDEX

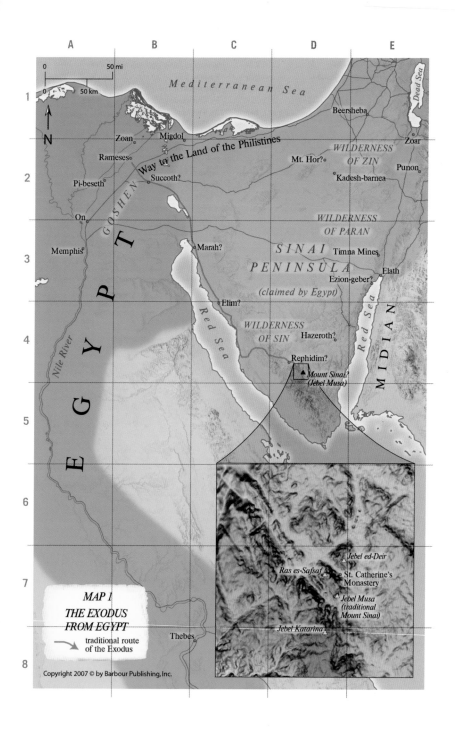

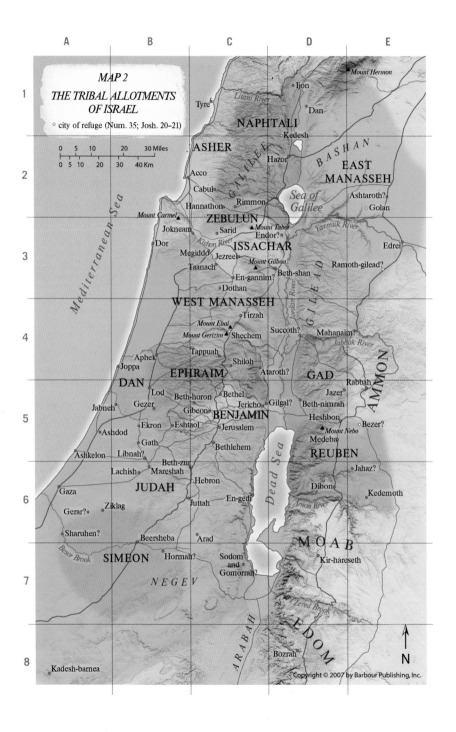

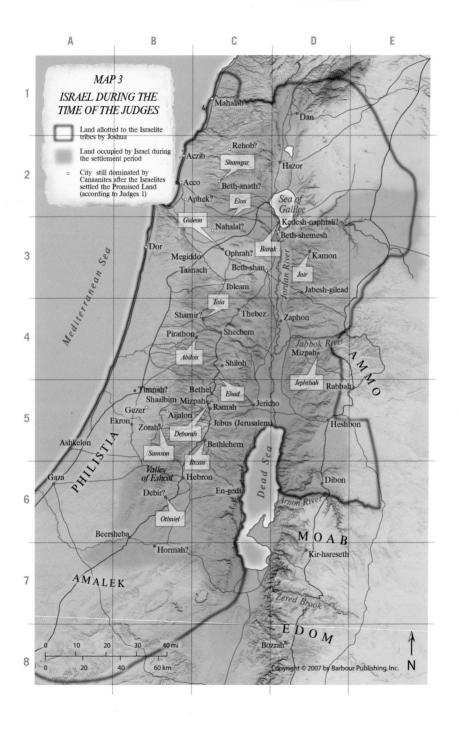

MAP 3

ISRAEL DURING THE
TIME OF THE JUDGES

Land allotted to the Israelite
tribes by Joshua

Land occupied by Israel during
the settlement period

○ City still dominated by
Canaanites after the Israelites
settled the Promised Land
(according to Judges 1)

Mediterranean Sea

Mahalab

Dan

Rehob?

Aczib

Shamgar

Hazor

Acco

Beth-anath?

Aphek?

Elon

Sea of
Galilee

Gideon

Nahalal?

Kedesh-naphtali?

Beth-shemesh

Dor

Megiddo

Ophrah?

Barak

Kamon

Taanach

Beth-shan

Jordan River

Jair

Ibleam

Jabesh-gilead

Tola

Shamir?

Thebez

Zaphon

Pirathon

Shechem

Jabbok River

Mizpah

Abdon

Shiloh

AMMO

Jephthah

Rabbah

Timnah?

Bethel

Shaalbim

Mizpah

Ehud

Gezer

Ramah

Jericho

Ekron

Aijalon

Jebus (Jerusalem)

Zorah

Deborah

Heshbon

Ashkelon

Samson

Bethlehem

Dead Sea

Gaza

Valley
of Eshcol

Ibzan

Hebron

Dibon

Debir?

En-gedi

Arnon River

Othniel

MOAB

Beersheba

Hormah?

Kir-hareseth

AMALEK

Zered Brook

EDOM

0   10   20   30   40 mi

0   20   40   60 km

Bozrah

Copyright © 2007 by Barbour Publishing, Inc.

N

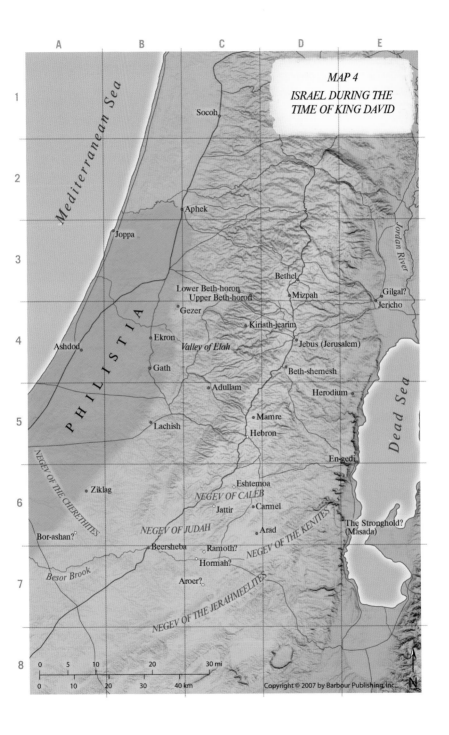

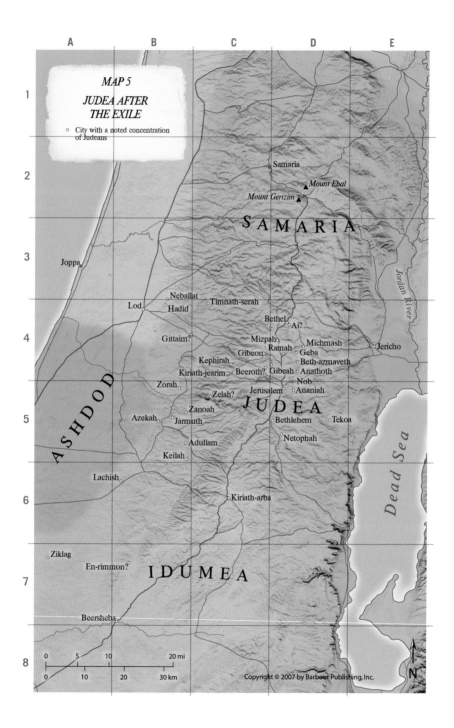

MAP 5

JUDEA AFTER
THE EXILE

○ City with a noted concentration
   of Judeans

Samaria

▲ Mount Ebal
Mount Gerizim ▲

S A M A R I A

Joppa

Jordan River

Neballat
Lod   Hadid   Timnath-serah

Bethel
Ai?

Gittaim?
Mizpah
Ramah   Michmash
Gibeon   Geba
Kephirah   Beth-azmaveth
Kiriath-jearim   Beeroth?   Gibeah   Anathoth
Zorah   Nob
Zelah?   Jerusalem   Ananiah

J U D E A

Azekah   Zanoah
Jarmuth   Bethlehem   Tekoa

Adullam   Netophah

Keilah

A S H D O D

Lachish

Kiriath-arba

Dead Sea

Ziklag
En-rimmon?   I D U M E A

Beersheba

0   5   10   20 mi
0   10   20   30 km

Copyright © 2007 by Barbour Publishing, Inc.

N

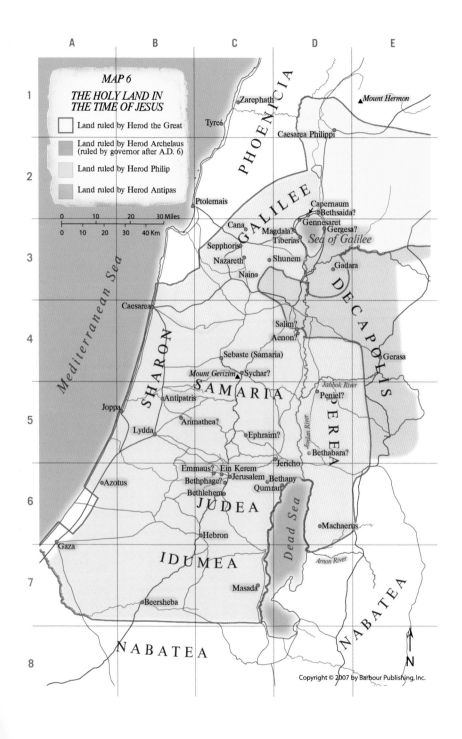

MAP 6
THE HOLY LAND IN THE TIME OF JESUS

- Land ruled by Herod the Great
- Land ruled by Herod Archelaus (ruled by governor after A.D. 6)
- Land ruled by Herod Philip
- Land ruled by Herod Antipas

0 10 20 30 Miles
0 10 20 30 40 Km

A **B** **C** **D** **E**

Zarephath
Tyre
PHOENICIA
Mount Hermon
Caesarea Philippi

Ptolemais
GALILEE
Capernaum
Bethsaida?
Cana
Magdala?
Gennesaret
Gergesa?
Tiberias
Sea of Galilee
Sepphoris
Nazareth
Shunem
Gadara
Nain
DECAPOLIS

Mediterranean Sea

Caesarea
SHARON
Salim?
Aenon?
Sebaste (Samaria)
Gerasa
Mount Gerizim
Sychar?
SAMARIA
Peniel?
PEREA
Antipatris
Joppa
Arimathea?
Lydda
Ephraim?
Jabbok River
Jordan River
Jericho
Bethabara?
Emmaus?
Ein Kerem
Bethphage?
Jerusalem
Bethany
Azotus
Bethlehem
Qumran
JUDEA
Dead Sea
Hebron
Machaerus
Gaza
IDUMEA
Arnon River
Masada
Beersheba
NABATEA
NABATEA

N

Copyright © 2007 by Barbour Publishing, Inc.

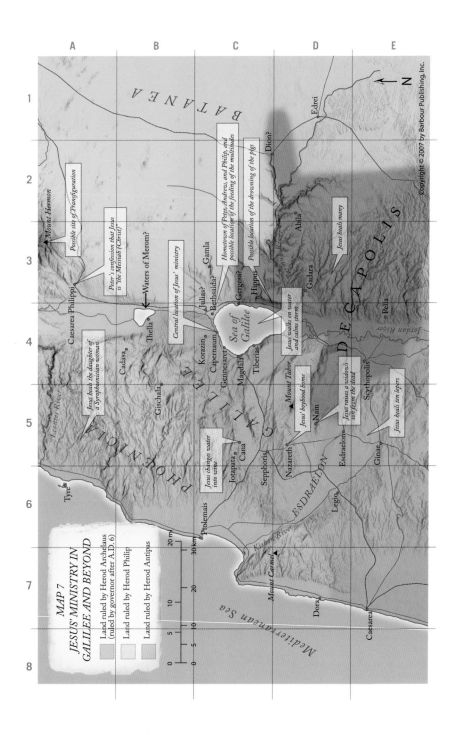

MAP 7
JESUS' MINISTRY IN
GALILEE AND BEYOND

Land ruled by Herod Archelaus
(ruled by governor after A.D. 6)

Land ruled by Herod Philip

Land ruled by Herod Antipas

Possible site of Transfiguration

Peter's confession that Jesus
is "the Messiah (Christ)"

Waters of Merom?

Central location of Jesus' ministry

Hometown of Peter, Andrew, and Philip, and
possible location of the feeding of the multitudes

Possible location of the drowning of the pigs

Jesus heals many

Jesus heals the daughter of
a Syrophoenician woman

Jesus walks on water
and calms storm

Jesus changes water
into wine

Jesus' boyhood home

Jesus raises a widow's
son from the dead

Jesus heals ten lepers

Mount Hermon

BATANEA

Edrei

Dion?

Abila

Gadara

Hippus

Pella

DECAPOLIS

Caesarea Philippi

Thella

Korazin

Capernaum

Gennesaret

Magdala

Tiberias

Sea of Galilee

Gamla

Julias?

Bethsaida?

Gergesa?

Cadasa

Gischala

GALILEE

PHOENICIA

Leontes River

Jordan River

Jabbok River

Tyre

Ptolemais

Jotapata

Cana

Sepphoris

Nazareth

Mount Tabor

Nain

Esdraelon

ESDRAELON

Legio

Ginae

Scythopolis

Kishon River

Mount Carmel

Dora

Caesarea

Mediterranean Sea

N

Copyright © 2007 by Barbour Publishing, Inc.

20 mi

30 km

20

10

30

20

10

5

0

0

5

10

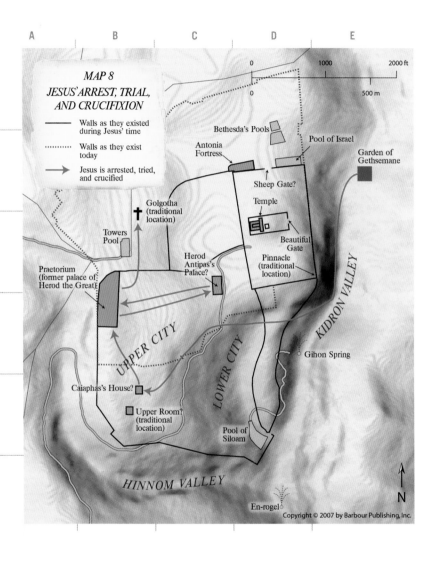

MAP 8
*JESUS' ARREST, TRIAL,
AND CRUCIFIXION*

—— Walls as they existed
during Jesus' time

········ Walls as they exist
today

——→ Jesus is arrested, tried,
and crucified

Bethesda's Pools

Pool of Israel

Antonia
Fortress

Garden of
Gethsemane

Sheep Gate?

Golgotha
(traditional
location)

Temple

Towers
Pool

Beautiful
Gate

Herod
Antipas's
Palace?

Pinnacle
(traditional
location)

Praetorium
(former palace of
Herod the Great)

KIDRON VALLEY

UPPER CITY

LOWER CITY

Gihon Spring

Caiaphas's House?

Upper Room?
(traditional
location)

Pool of
Siloam

HINNOM VALLEY

En-rogel

N

ART CREDITS

Adiel Io/WM 102
Adrianlw/WM 272
Adriatikus/WM 112
Almog/WM 173, 225, 230
AnnieCee/WM 276
Arkadi Voller/WM 273
Avishai Teicher/WM 101, 229
Berthold Werner/WM 110 (top), 111, 121, 141, 143 (bottom), 239, 250, 260
BiblePlaces.com 8, 24, 28, 29, 55, 56, 59, 66, 76, 83, 84, 105, 116, 124, 127, 138, 161, 163, 164, 169, 170, 174, 181, 195, 197, 202, 204, 208, 210, 214, 232, 246, 253
Bocachete/WM 31
Brooklyn Museum/WM 137, 251
Bukvoed/WM 220
Classic Numismatic Group, Inc./WM 221
Claudius Prößer/WM 120
Copper Kettle/WM 82
Daniel Baránek/WM 78
Daniel G. Bertrand/WM 146
Daniel Ventura/WM 212
Danny Herman/WM 133
David Bjorgen/WM 36, 207
David Shankbone/WM 98, 130, 223
Deror Avi/WM 118, 125, 144, 147
Djampa/WM 122
Dmitrij Rodionov/WM 23
EdoM/WM 99, 275
Edward Kaprov/WM 203
Effi Schweizer/WM 43
Eitan F/WM 123
Eman/WM 80
Eric Draper/WM 154
Gilabrand/WM 95
Goldstar/WM 262
Grausel/WM 54
Gus/WM 68
Hanay/WM 243
Hector Abouid/WM 37
Henrik Sendelbach/WM 35
Idobi/WM 238
Israeli Pikiwiki Project/WM 12, 16, 70, 72 (top), 183, 219, 227, 255
iStockphoto 26, 33, 41, 45, 47, 71, 86, 128, 152
J. Paul Getty Museum 30
Jack1956/WM 257
James Emery/WM 148 (top)
Jean Housen/WM 196
Joneikifi/WM 32
Kasper Nowak/WM 217
Leif Knutsen/WM 11
Library of Congress 17, 104, 155, 157 (top), 167, 201, 216

Maglanist/WM 193
Marion Doss/WM 158
Mark A. Wilson/WM 51, 94
Nborun/WM 150
Netanel H/WM 245
New York Public Library/WM 132
Or Hiltch/WM 265
Ori~/WM 61, 64, 226, 236
Pacman/WM 13
Ralf Lotys/WM 191
Reinhard Dietrich/WM 185
Sambach/WM 172
Shlomi Liss/WM 20
Shmuliko/WM 63
Shuki/WM 192, 233
Shy Halatzi/WM 38
Sustructu/WM 91
Svetlana Marakova/WM 148 (bottom)
Tamara/WM 97
The Yorck Project/WM 73
Thomas Bantle/WM 50 (top)
Tiamat/WM 200
Vorash/WM 179
Wayne McLean/WM 89
WikiMedia 14, 18, 27, 34, 44, 50 (bottom), 52, 60, 62, 64 (top), 67, 69, 72 (bottom), 74, 88, 90, 96, 106, 108, 110 (bottom), 114, 126, 131, 139, 140, 143 (top), 145, 151, 156, 157 (bottom), 159, 168, 171, 180, 188, 189, 198, 199, 206, 209, 213, 228, 231, 237, 240, 248, 249, 252, 254, 259, 266, 267, 269, 270
xta11/WM 42
Yair Talmor/WM 176
Yoav Dothan/WM 138
Yousef T. Omar/WM 46
????30/WM 160

(WM=WikiMedia)